Camping Montana

Camping Montana

A Comprehensive Guide to
Public Tent and RV Campgrounds

SECOND EDITION

Kenneth Graham

FALCON GUIDES

GUILFORD, CONNECTICUT

FALCONGUIDES®

An imprint of The Rowman & Littlefield Publishing Group, Inc.
4501 Forbes Blvd., Ste. 200
Lanham, MD 20706
www.rowman.com
Falcon and FalconGuides are registered trademarks and Make Adventure Your Story is a
trademark of The Rowman & Littlefield Publishing Group, Inc.

Distributed by NATIONAL BOOK NETWORK

Photos by author unless otherwise noted.

Maps by The Rowman & Littlefield Publishing Group, Inc.

British Library Cataloguing-in-Publication Information Available

Library of Congress Cataloging-in-Publication Data Available

ISBN 978-1-4930-3994-4 (paperback)
ISBN 978-1-4930-3995-1 (e-book)

♾™ The paper used in this publication meets the minimum requirements of American National
Standard for Information Sciences—Permanence of Paper for Printed Library Materials, ANSI/
NISO Z39.48-1992.

Printed in the United States of America

Contents

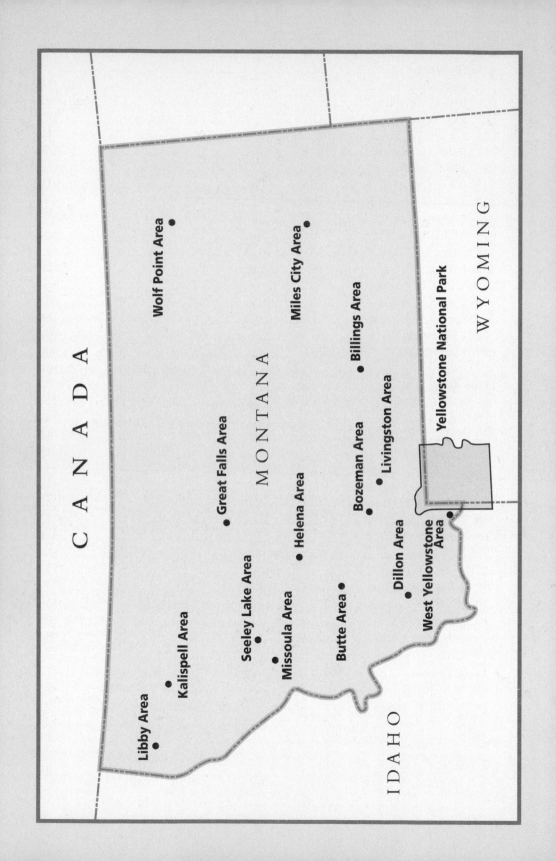

Acknowledgments

None of the Falcon publications that I have written could have been completed without the support and assistance that my wife, Sandy, so unselfishly supplied. Beyond that I wish to thank the multitude of campground hosts, campers, and official personnel who helped us throughout our travels.

There's a lot of mountain scenery to enjoy in Montana, such as this view south of Ennis.

About This Book

Of all the explorers who set foot in this land, Lewis and Clark are probably the best known. As you travel in their footsteps, take time to absorb some of the magic that exists here. Though civilization has put down its roots, the state of Montana maintains an identity all its own, an identity that echoes from a time before recorded history.

Unlike those who went before, with horses and oxen to feed, today's travelers use automobiles, synthetic tents, and "tin tepees." Therefore, campsites are no longer required to provide water and grass for livestock. Wildlife is now an attraction for watching and capturing via camera, instead of for eating. And rather than cooking dinner, campfires are mostly used to roast marshmallows and to take away the evening chill.

All the same, hazards still exist. A 30-foot pull trailer behind a full-sized pickup does not easily take a mountain road hairpin turn. I have attempted to provide information on access requirements along with what will be found upon arriving at a destination. This book lets you plan routes with a specific type of "wagon" in mind. This should eliminate hours of driving only to discover that the last few miles are accessible only by short-wheel-base, all-terrain vehicles.

For me, the appeal of camping is relaxing in the fresh mountain air, which holds an occasional wisp of campfire smoke, cowboy coffee, and marshmallows roasted to a golden brown. For anglers, lakes and streams offer not only plenty of trout but challenge and exploration as well.

Please keep in mind that much of Montana remains primitive by definition of modern camping practices. With extremely few exceptions, hookups are virtually nonexistent. Hard labor using ancient hand pumps will produce drinking water that has an unmistakable iron flavor. Self-contained units offer alternatives; however, finding sources of water for holding tanks will take some research. There are a lot of miles with no services available between towns. In fact, the only residents will be the wildlife common to the area. So plan your route in advance, check out the available resources in this book, and get ready for an adventure.

How to Use This Guide

For convenience the campgrounds are listed by their relation to an easily located city—at least on a map. This should make planning your trip simpler. Specific information on each campground includes the following:

Location: Distance and direction from the reference city, along with special features (lakes, streams, etc.), are reported here.

Facilities: Available services with respect to toilet types, drinking water, and other amenities are listed. Campgrounds are changing to accommodate the larger RVs of today's travelers, but not at the same pace. The increasing number of larger, longer RVs has easily outpaced the number of camping areas with adequate accessibility and parking space. There are still hand pumps for drinking water; however they tend to be more prevalent in areas not visited by the masses. In addition, firewood is becoming a difficult issue for those used to gathering it from the forest upon arrival. For the most part it will need to be purchased at or very near the campsite.

Sites: Numbers reported here represent the tables and fire rings in a designated camping area.

Fee: To allow for changing fees, dollar signs indicate values as follows:

$ $0–$10

$$ $10–$20

$$$ $20–$30

$$$$ $40 and above

Managing agency: Departments in control of specific sites are recorded here. A concessionaire may actually operate the campground; however, these companies are awarded a special permit by bid and can change. You'll find phone numbers and addresses in the appendix.

Activities: The activities listed here are choices available to campers in a given campground.

Finding the campground: "Windshield" directions are provided, beginning at the noted cities, but these may not be the shortest or most direct routes. On a map it could look like the campgrounds are closer to towns other than those listed. Mountains and other restrictive features determined my choices for more tranquil arrivals.

About the campground: The internet has provided a great deal of information for this book. We did manage to make a tour of Glacier National Park and Yellowstone, but several large fires have revisited the GNP since our stay. The information has been updated as much as possible, but it is difficult to tell what the final outcome will be for some of those areas, as the fires are still active as this is being written.

The quick reference charts listed at the beginning of each area give information about the campground services available, along with opening and closing dates.

High-elevation campgrounds do not open until later in the summer, sometimes the end of July. Keep in mind that these dates are not set in concrete, as weather affects everything involved. Following is the key to abbreviations used in the quick reference charts:

Toilets: C = Comfort Station, F = Flush, P = Pit, V = Vault

Sites: D = Dispersed

Fee: N = None

Recreation: B = Boating, F = Fishing, H = Hiking, R = Rockhounding, S = Swimming, W = Wildlife viewing

Missoula Area

Missoula by far offers the greatest number of campgrounds for the area included. Most are found in heavily forested mountain valleys with clear-running, ice-cold mountain streams adjacent. Access roads tend to be either very good or very rough, with no middle ground.

Recently the population has increased in the Missoula area, placing a good deal of pressure on the closer, or in some cases more scenic, campgrounds. Numerous roads dive off into any one of multiple canyons. The time it takes to travel to the more distant campgrounds could prove disenchanting, especially if the units are filled when you arrive. A call to the managing agency would be of great value, especially if your unit is one of the larger RVs.

	Group Sites	Tents	RV sites	Total sites	Hookups	Toilets	Showers	Drinking water	Dump station	Phone	Handicap Access	Recreation	Fee	Season	Stay limit (days)
1 Cabin City			24	24		V		*			*	H	$	Memorial Day to Labor Day	14
2 Cascade			12	12		V		*			*	HFB	$	5/15–10/15	14
3 Slowey			27	27		V		*				F	$	5/17–9/5	14
4 Trout Creek			12	12		V		*				HF	$	5/22–9/5	14
5 Quartz Flat			77	77		V		*			*	HF	$$	5/10–9/30	14
6 Lolo Creek		2	15	17		V		*				HFW	$	Memorial Day to Labor Day	14
7 Lee Creek			22	22		V		*				HFW	$	Memorial Day to Labor Day	14
8 Chief Looking Glass			25	25		V		*				FB	$	5/1–9/30	7
9 Charles Waters			26	26		V		*			*	HF	$$	Memorial Day to Labor Day	14
10 Gold Creek			4	4		V						HFW	N	Summer	14
11 Blodgett Canyon		1	5	6		V						HFW	N	Memorial Day to Labor Day	5
12 Black Bear			6	6		V					*	HF	N	6/1–9/15	16
13 Rock Creek Horse Camp			11	11		V					*	HFBW	$	Memorial Day to Labor Day	14
14 Lake Como			10	10	*	V		*			*	HF	$	Memorial Day to Labor Day	14
15 Three Frogs		4	16	20		V		*			*	HFW	$	6/1–9/15	16
16 Schumaker			16	16		V						HFB	N	7/15–9/15	14
17 Sam Billings Memorial			12	12		V						HF	N	5/1–12/1	14
18 Rombo			15	15		V		*				HF	$	5/1–12/1	14
19 Slate Creek			7	7		V						HFB	N	5/1–12/1	14
20 Painted Rocks State Park			25	25		V						HFB	N	All Year	14
21 Alta			15	15		V		*				HF	$	5/1–12/1	14
22 Spring Gulch			10	10		V		*			*	HF	$$	Memorial Day to Labor Day	14
23 Warm Springs			14	14		V		*				HFW	$	5/15–9/10	14
24 Crazy Creek			7	7		V		*				HF	$	5/1–12/1	14
25 Indian Trees			16	16		V		*				HW	$	Memorial Day to Labor Day	14
26 Jennings Camp			4	4		V						HFW	N	5/1–12/1	14
27 Martin Creek			7	7		V		*				HW	$	5/15–12/1	14
28 Beavertail Hill State Park			28	28		V		*				HF	$	5/1–10/31	14
29 Norton			13	13		V		*				F	$	May to Sept	14
30 Grizzly			9	9		V		*				HF	$	May to Sept	14
31 Dalles		2	8	10		V		*				HF	$	May to Sept	14
32 Harrys Flat			15	15		V		*				HF	$	May to Sept	14
33 Bitterroot Flat			15	15		V		*				HF	$	May to Sept	14

1 Cabin City

Location: 81 miles northwest of Missoula.
Facilities: Vault toilets, fire rings, tables, drinking water.
Sites: 24 for tents or RV/Trailer combinations up to 32 feet long.
Fee: $ per night, 14-day limit.
Managing agency: Lolo National Forest, Superior Ranger District, (406) 822-4233.
Activities: Hiking.
Finding the campground: Take I-90 northwest out of Missoula for 78 miles to Camel's Hump Road/exit 22. Take paved Camel's Hump Road for 2.5 miles to Forest Road 353. Turn left onto FR 353 and travel 0.25 mile to the campground.
About the campground: This hidden little spot settles into heavily forested mountain country along an all-but-forgotten stretch of highway. Historically when new roads like an interstate go through an area, towns and other features fade out of view. This campground qualifies as such and is open from Memorial Day through Labor Day.

2 Cascade

Location: 85 miles northwest of Missoula on the Clark Fork River.
Facilities: Vault toilets, fire rings, tables, drinking water.
Sites: 12 for tents or RV/Trailer combinations up to 32 feet long.
Fee: $ per night, 14-day limit.
Managing agency: Lolo National Forest, Plains/Thompson Falls Ranger District, (406) 826-3821.
Activities: Hiking, fishing, boating.
Finding the campground: Take I-90 northwest out of Missoula for 67 miles to St. Regis. At St. Regis take Montana State Highway 135 north for 18 miles.
About the campground: The Clark Fork River passes by on the opposite side of the highway, tempting angler and rafter alike. There is no boat launch available, but hand launching can be accomplished. Evening breezes whisper tales of past travelers in the pine trees, which offer a pleasant place to enjoy roasting marshmallows. The campground is open from May through October.

3 Slowey

Location: 60 miles northwest of Missoula on the Clark Fork River.
Facilities: Vault toilets, fire rings, tables, drinking water.
Sites: 27 for tents or RV/Trailer combinations up to 30 feet long.
Fee: $ per night, 14-day limit.
Managing agency: Lolo National Forest, Superior Ranger District, (406) 822-4233.
Activities: Fishing.

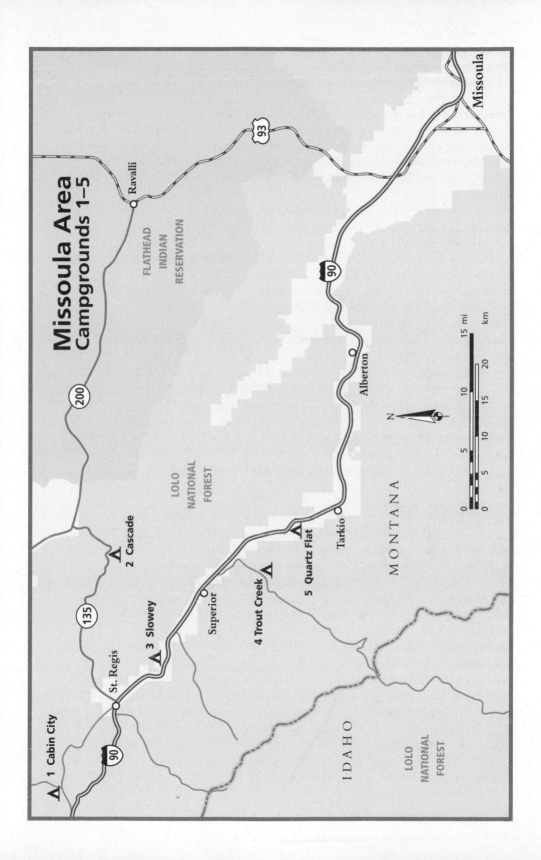

Finding the campground: Take I-90 northwest out of Missoula for 57 miles. Get off I-90 at Dry Creek Road/exit 43. Turn right and cross the Clark Fork River. Turn left onto the paved highway and travel 3 miles.

About the campground: Private land surrounds this island of pine trees squeezed between the river and the interstate. Fishing access is a primary attraction, though not the only one. Even with I-90 so close, not many make the trip down the side road, which is sort of like backtracking. Traffic noise and train horns are present and may not be acceptable to those with a desire to escape reminders of an overactive civilization. The campground is open from May 17 through September 5.

4 Trout Creek

Location: 63 miles northwest of Missoula on Trout Creek.
Facilities: Vault toilets, fire rings, tables, drinking water.
Sites: 12 for tents or RVs/Trailers up to 20 feet long.
Fee: $ per night, 14-day limit.
Managing agency: Lolo National Forest, Superior Ranger District, (406) 822-4233.
Activities: Hiking, fishing.
Finding the campground: Take I-90 northwest out of Missoula for 53 miles to Superior. Get off I-90 at Superior/exit 47 and turn left to access County Road 269 on the south side. Turn left onto paved CR 269 and travel 7 miles. CR 269 turns into Forest Road 250. Continue on gravel FR 250 for 3 miles.
About the campground: Noise from the interstate doesn't echo through this area, but there can still be plenty of traffic. The campground is open from May 22 through September 5.

5 Quartz Flat

Location: 42 miles northwest of Missoula on the Clark Fork River.
Facilities: Flush and vault toilets, fire rings, tables, drinking water.
Sites: 77 for tents or RV/Trailer combinations up to 50 feet long.
Fee: $$ per night, 14-day limit.
Managing agency: Lolo National Forest, Superior Ranger District, (406) 822-4233.
Activities: Hiking, fishing.
Finding the campground: Take I-90 northwest out of Missoula for 42 miles to the rest area. The campground is accessed from the rest area off-ramp from either direction.
About the campground: This unique campground is neatly divided by the interstate with paved roads and spurs. A one-lane tunnel allows travel from the north to the south without entering traffic on I-90. The Clark Fork River slides by on the north side, attracting more use than the south side. An active railroad also deters some campers on the south side; however, if you don't like a lot of company, the south side might be a good choice. If you are headed east on I-90 and prefer to settle in closer to the river, don't forget the tunnel. Firewood gathering is more of a memory in today's world, however some reviews report free firewood being available. If a campfire is a must it would be best to bring some firewood along. The campground is open from May 10 through September 30.

6 Lolo Creek

Location: 27 miles southwest of Missoula on Lolo Creek.
Facilities: Vault toilets, fire rings, tables, drinking water.
Sites: 2 for tents and 15 for RV/Trailer combinations up to 40 feet long.
Fee: $ per night, 14-day limit.
Managing agency: Lolo National Forest, Missoula Ranger District, (406) 329-3814.
Activities: Hiking, fishing, wildlife viewing.
Finding the campground: Take US Highway 93 south out of Missoula for 12 miles. At Lolo turn right onto US Highway 12 and travel 15 miles.
About the campground: Thick timber, paved parking units, and water spigots add to the appeal on this hillside. The campground is open from Memorial Day with a variable closing date when the weather is agreeable.

7 Lee Creek

Location: 38 miles southwest of Missoula on West Fork Lolo Creek.
Facilities: Vault toilets, fire rings, tables, drinking water.
Sites: 22 for tents or RV/Trailer combinations up to 40 feet long.
Fee: $ per night, 14-day limit.
Managing agency: Lolo National Forest, Missoula Ranger District, (406) 329-3814.
Activities: Hiking, fishing, wildlife viewing.
Finding the campground: Take US Highway 93 south out of Missoula for 12 miles. At Lolo turn right onto US Highway 12 and travel 26 miles.
About the campground: Lee Creek joins West Fork Lolo Creek nearby, thus lending its name to this camping area. Lodgepole pines share the hillside with seventeen of the camping units. The other five settle in with spruce trees mixed in along the creek. The campground is open from Memorial Day through Labor Day.

8 Chief Looking Glass

Location: 15 miles south of Missoula on the Bitterroot River.
Facilities: Vault toilets, fire rings, tables, drinking water.
Sites: 25 for tents or RV/Trailer combinations up to 48 feet long.
Fee: $ per night, 7-day limit.
Managing agency: Montana Fish, Wildlife & Parks, (406) 542-5500.
Activities: Fishing, boating.
Finding the campground: Take US Highway 93 south out of Missoula for 14 miles. At milepost 77 turn left onto the county road and travel 1 mile.

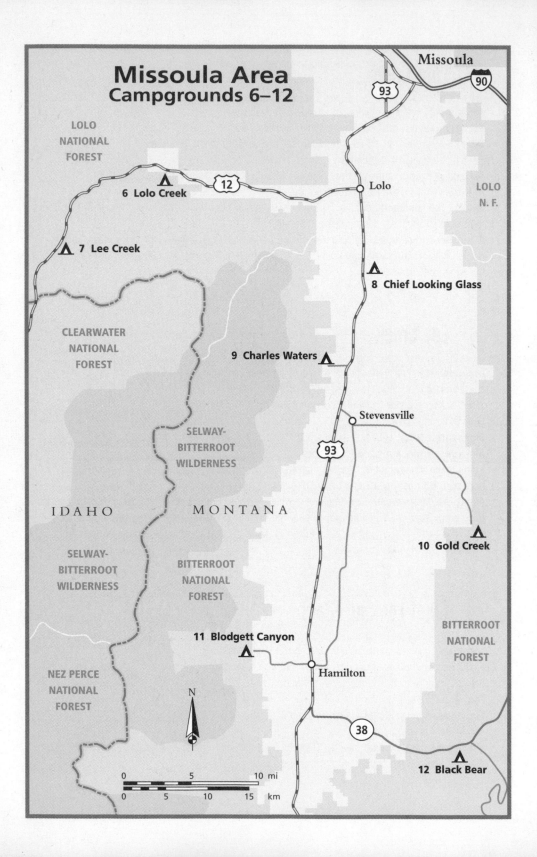

Missoula Area
Campgrounds 6–12

LOLO
NATIONAL
FOREST

Missoula

93

90

12

6 Lolo Creek

Lolo

LOLO
N. F.

7 Lee Creek

8 Chief Looking Glass

CLEARWATER
NATIONAL
FOREST

9 Charles Waters

Stevensville

93

SELWAY-
BITTERROOT
WILDERNESS

IDAHO   MONTANA

10 Gold Creek

SELWAY-
BITTERROOT
WILDERNESS

BITTERROOT
NATIONAL
FOREST

BITTERROOT
NATIONAL
FOREST

11 Blodgett Canyon

NEZ PERCE
NATIONAL
FOREST

N

Hamilton

38

12 Black Bear

| 0 | 5 | 10 mi |
| 0 | 5 | 10 | 15 km |

Flathead Indian women scraped out the inner bark of ponderosa pine trees. It was eaten raw as a sweet and chewy delicacy.

About the campground: The river attracts most campers to this location. Cottonwood trees are the dominant plants, with grass and cultured pasture on both sides of the river. Interpretive trails within the camping area enlighten visitors about the individual this area is named for. Although boating is listed as an activity, it will require a hand launch. Camping is allowed from May 1 through September 30.

9 Charles Waters

Location: 28 miles south of Missoula near Bass Creek.
Facilities: Vault toilets, fire rings, tables, drinking water.
Sites: 26 plus one double site for tents or RVs/Trailer combinations up to 70 feet long. (4 pull-throughs)
Fee: $$ per night, 14-day limit.
Managing agency: Bitterroot National Forest, Stevensville Ranger District, (406) 777-5461.
Activities: Hiking, fishing.
Finding the campground: Take US Highway 93 south out of Missoula for 25 miles. Turn right onto County Road 22 and travel 2 miles. Continue on Forest Road 1316 for 1 mile.
About the campground: Ponderosa pine takes over where the sagebrush quits. Keep an eye open for the local residents: deer, elk, an occasional bear, and many birds. The campground is open from Memorial Day through Labor Day.

10 Gold Creek

Location: 48 miles south of Missoula on Gold Creek.
Facilities: Vault toilet, fire rings, tables.
Sites: 4 for tents or RVs/Trailers up to 25 feet long.
Fee: None, 14-day limit.
Managing agency: Bitterroot National Forest, Stevensville Ranger District, (406) 777-5461.
Activities: Hiking, fishing, wildlife viewing.
Finding the campground: Take US Highway 93 south out of Missoula for 30 miles. Turn left onto Montana State Highway 372 and travel 5 miles, passing through Stevensville. Turn right onto County Road 27 and travel 5 miles. After about 2 miles the road surface will change to gravel; continue bearing left with CR 27 becoming County Road 29. Continue on unimproved dirt CR 29 for 8 miles.
About the campground: The rough access road does not deter campers. Hunters and local anglers tend to be most familiar with the area. For those brave enough to make the trip the "pot at the end of the rainbow" could be full or empty. The campground is open during summer months.

11 Blodgett Canyon

Location: 53 miles south of Missoula on Blodgett Creek.
Facilities: Vault toilets, fire rings, tables.
Sites: 1 tent and 5 for tents or RVs/Trailer combinations up to 45 feet long.
Fee: None, 5-day limit.
Managing agency: Bitterroot National Forest, Stevensville Ranger District, (406) 777-5461.
Activities: Hiking, fishing, wildlife viewing.
Finding the campground: Take US Highway 93 south out of Missoula for 48 miles. At Hamilton go west on Main Street for 1 mile. Turn right onto Ricketts Road and go 0.5 miles. Turn left on FR/736 and go 4 miles.
About the campground: Wilderness access brings plenty of company to this relatively easy to reach spot. Be sure to bring plenty of drinking water as the hand pump is no longer functioning. If you are looking for a place to stay for one day late in the morning it would be best to consider other options. On the other hand, if you want a mountain camping experience, you will likely find the five-day maximum stay too short. The campground is open from Memorial Day through Labor Day.

12 Black Bear

Location: 64 miles south of Missoula on Skalkaho Creek.
Facilities: Vault toilet, fire rings, tables, no garbage service.

Sites: 6 for tents or RVs/Trailer combinations up to 50 feet long.
Fee: None, 16-day limit.
Managing agency: Bitterroot National Forest, Darby/Sula Ranger District, (406) 821-3913.
Activities: Hiking, fishing.
Finding the campground: Take US Highway 93 south out of Missoula for 51 miles. Turn left onto Skalkaho Road/Montana State Highway 38 and travel 13 miles.
About the campground: Cedar and pine trees share the mountainsides that guide the ice-cold waters of Skalkaho Creek toward lower elevations. Things can get dusty as the paved road ends a short distance away from US 93. Skalkaho Falls awaits those who persevere through the dust and distance of about 7 miles. The campground is open from June 1 through September 15.

13 Rock Creek Horse Camp

Location: 65 miles south of Missoula on Lake Como.
Facilities: Vault toilet, fire rings, tables.
Sites: 1 for tent 10 for RV/Trailer combinations up to 40 feet long.
Fee: $ per night, 14-day limit.
Managing agency: Bitterroot National Forest, Darby/Sula Ranger District, (406) 821-3913.
Activities: Hiking, fishing, boating, wildlife viewing.
Finding the campground: Take US Highway 93 south out of Missoula for 61 miles. Turn right onto County Road 83 and travel 4 miles.
About the campground: Horses are welcome here, with a ramp available to assist disabled persons mount up. Anglers and boaters will likely find the 900 surface acres of water more tempting. The campground is open from Memorial Day through Labor Day.

14 Lake Como

Location: 66 miles south of Missoula.
Facilities: Vault toilet, fire rings, tables, drinking water (electric and water hookups available).
Sites: 10 paved pull-throughs for RVs/Trailer combinations up to 125 feet long.
Fee: $$ per night, 7-day limit.
Managing agency: Bitterroot National Forest, Darby/Sula Ranger District, (406) 821-3913.
Activities: Hiking, fishing.
Finding the campground: Take US Highway 93 south out of Missoula for 61 miles. Turn right onto County Road 83 and travel 5 miles.
About the campground: This is a very popular area and fills up fast, especially on weekends and holidays. Pine trees squeeze in between boulders in this mountain setting below the Lake Como dam. Boating and other related water sports are available at the lake; however, some travel is required. The campground is open from Memorial Day through Labor Day.

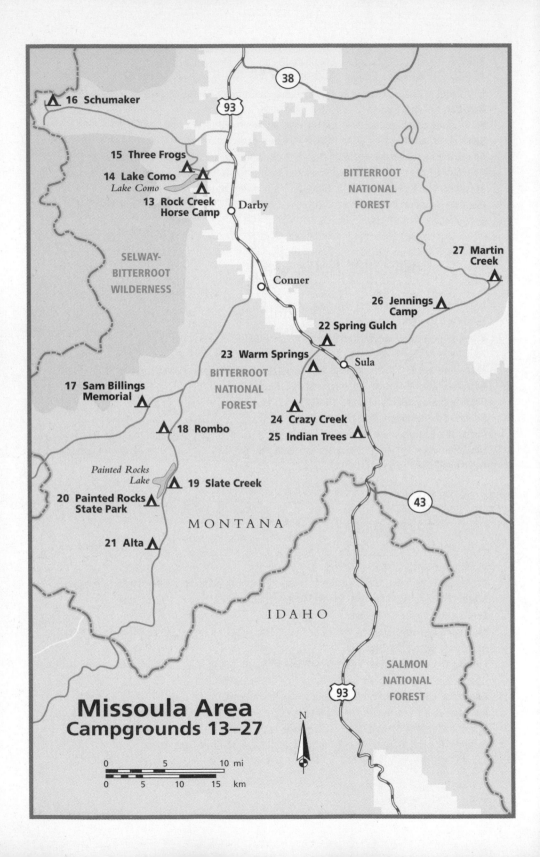

38

93

16 Schumaker

BITTERROOT
NATIONAL
FOREST

15 Three Frogs
14 Lake Como
Lake Como
13 Rock Creek
Horse Camp

Darby

27 Martin
Creek

SELWAY-
BITTERROOT
WILDERNESS

Conner

26 Jennings
Camp

22 Spring Gulch

23 Warm Springs

Sula

17 Sam Billings
Memorial

BITTERROOT
NATIONAL
FOREST

18 Rombo

24 Crazy Creek

25 Indian Trees

*Painted Rocks
Lake*

19 Slate Creek

43

20 Painted Rocks
State Park

M O N T A N A

21 Alta

I D A H O

93

SALMON
NATIONAL
FOREST

Missoula Area
Campgrounds 13–27

N

0   5   10 mi

0   5   10   15   km

15 Three Frogs (also known as Upper Como)

Location: 67 miles south of Missoula on Kramis Pond.
Facilities: Vault toilet, fire rings, tables, drinking water.
Sites: 4 for tents and 16 for tents or RVs/Trailer combinations up to 30 feet long.
Fee: $ per night, 16-day limit.
Managing agency: Bitterroot National Forest, Darby/Sula Ranger District, (406) 821-3913.
Activities: Hiking, fishing, wildlife viewing.
Finding the campground: Take US Highway 93 south out of Missoula for 61 miles. Turn right onto County Road 83 and travel 6 miles.
About the campground: The roads are gravel here, but that does not diminish the campground's popularity; it fills up quickly and typically stays full on weekends and holidays. Boaters will find nearby Lake Como more attractive, though some travel is required. This camping spot opens around June 1 and can stay open as late as September 15, weather permitting.

16 Schumaker

Location: 76 miles south of Missoula near Twin Lakes.
Facilities: Vault toilet, fire rings, tables.
Sites: 16 for tents or RVs/Trailer combinations up to 55 feet long.
Fee: None, 14-day limit.
Managing agency: Bitterroot National Forest, Darby/Sula Ranger District, (406) 821-3913.
Activities: Hiking, fishing, boating.
Finding the campground: Take US Highway 93 south out of Missoula for 58 miles. Turn right onto Lost Horse Road/Forest Road 429 and travel 16 miles. Turn right onto Forest Road 5505 and travel 2 miles. *Note:* Most of FR 429 is very rough; high-clearance vehicles are recommended. Please call to verify road conditions.
About the campground: The Selway-Bitterroot Wilderness almost surrounds this high mountain getaway. The campground overlooks Twin Lakes, beckoning to anglers and boaters alike. No motorized boats are allowed, however. Water levels drop with increasing demands for irrigation. The campground is open from July 15 through September 15.

17 Sam Billings Memorial

Location: 84 miles south of Missoula on Boulder Creek.
Facilities: Vault toilets, fire rings, tables.
Sites: 12 for tents or RVs/Trailer combinations up to 30 feet long.
Fee: None, 14-day limit.
Managing agency: Bitterroot National Forest, West Fork Ranger District, (406) 821-3269.

Activities: Hiking, fishing.

Finding the campground: Take US Highway 93 south out of Missoula for 69 miles. Turn right onto paved West Fork Road/Montana State Highway 473 and travel 13 miles. Turn right onto Forest Road 5631 and travel 2 miles.

About the campground: Mountains shadow the forest and campground alike. The Boulder Creek Trail starts near here, leading into the Selway-Bitterroot Wilderness. Be sure to bring warm clothing and plenty of drinking water. The campground is open from May 1 through December 1, when weather permits.

18 Rombo

Location: 87 miles south of Missoula on the West Fork Bitterroot River.

Facilities: Vault toilets, fire rings, tables, drinking water.

Sites: 15 for tents or RVs/Trailer combinations up to 40 feet long.

Fee: $ per night, 14-day limit. Reservations can be made at this site. Call (877) 444-6777.

Managing agency: Bitterroot National Forest, West Fork Ranger District, (406) 821–3269.

Activities: Hiking, fishing.

Finding the campground: Take US Highway 93 south out of Missoula for 69 miles. Turn right onto paved West Fork Road/Montana State Highway 473 and travel 18 miles.

About the campground: Pine trees and parking units overlook the river at spots appealing to anglers and scenic viewers alike. Pay attention to the signs and fences, as there is private property in the area. The campground is open from May 1 through December 1, when the weather allows. Camping is permitted in the off-season; however, no water is provided. If considering an off-season trip, call the Ranger District for road conditions or other hazards that may restrict access.

19 Slate Creek

Location: 91 miles south of Missoula on Painted Rocks Lake.

Facilities: Vault toilet, fire rings, tables.

Sites: 4 for tents or RVs up to 30 feet long.

Fee: None, 14-day limit.

Managing agency: Bitterroot National Forest, West Fork Ranger District, (406) 821–3269.

Activities: Hiking, fishing, boating.

Finding the campground: Take US Highway 93 south out of Missoula for 69 miles. Turn right onto paved West Fork Road/Montana State Highway 473 and travel 22 miles.

About the campground: A small stream runs through this campground on its way to the Painted Rocks Reservoir. Lodgepole pine and an assortment of brush fill the spaces between. This primitive camping spot can open as early as May 1 and stay open as late as December 1.

20 Painted Rocks State Park

Location: 92 miles south of Missoula on Painted Rocks Lake.
Facilities: Vault toilets, fire rings, tables, boat ramp.
Sites: 25 for tents or RVs up to 25 feet long.
Fee: None; Subject to resident or nonresident status; 14-day limit.
Managing agency: Painted Rocks State Park, call (406) 273-4253 at Travelers Rest State Park.
Activities: Hiking, fishing, boating.
Finding the campground: Take US Highway 93 south out of Missoula for 69 miles. Turn right onto paved West Fork Road/Montana State Highway 473 and travel 23 miles.
About the campground: Steep, rocky mountains stand guard over this reservoir. Pine trees peek over the top wherever they can, adding to the scenery. The reservoir tends to get very low as irrigation drains it, especially in the drought seasons. The campground is open all year long; however, winter camping takes some additional consideration and preparedness.

21 Alta

Location: 99 miles south of Missoula on the West Fork Bitterroot River.
Facilities: Vault toilets, fire rings, tables, drinking water.
Sites: 15 for tents or RVs/Trailers up to 30 feet long.
Fee: $ per night, 14-day limit. Reservations can be made at this site. Call (877) 444-6777.
Managing agency: Bitterroot National Forest, West Fork Ranger District, (406) 821-3269.
Activities: Hiking, fishing.
Finding the campground: Take US Highway 93 south out of Missoula for 69 miles. Turn right onto paved West Fork Road/Montana State Highway 473 and travel 30 miles.
About the campground: Ponderosa pine trees stand tall with plenty of history to tell. Some share the scars of past visitors. Native Americans stripped bark off selected trees to obtain a sort of chewing gum. In spite of the exploitation, the trees have survived long past the ordeal. The nearby river lures anglers and swimmers, though rafting can be difficult with the lower water levels common during late summer and drought seasons. The campground is open from May 1 through December 1.

22 Spring Gulch

Location: 80 miles south of Missoula on the East Fork Bitterroot River.
Facilities: Vault toilets, fire rings, tables, drinking water.
Sites: 10 for tents or RVs/Trailer combinations up to 50 feet long.
Fee: $$ per night, 14-day limit. Reservations can be made at this site. Call (877) 444-6777.
Managing agency: Bitterroot National Forest, Darby/Sula Ranger District, (406) 821-3913.

Activities: Hiking, fishing.

Finding the campground: Take US Highway 93 south out of Missoula for 80 miles.

About the campground: This campground has the handicapped in mind. Access to the water, toilets, and a paved trail along the riverbank are wheelchair friendly. Tall ponderosa pine trees peacefully watch over the manicured grass with some brush in selected areas adding to a secluded feeling. The campground is right off the highway, but the conveniences, including water spigots, help to offset any traffic annoyance. The campground is open from Memorial Day through Labor Day with a host, when available.

23 Warm Springs

Location: 81 miles south of Missoula on Warm Springs Creek.

Facilities: Vault toilets, fire rings, tables, drinking water.

Sites: 14 for tents or RVs/Trailers up to 26 feet long.

Fee: $ per night, 14-day limit.

Managing agency: Bitterroot National Forest, Darby/Sula Ranger District, (406) 821-3913.

Activities: Hiking, fishing, wildlife viewing.

Finding the campground: Take US Highway 93 south out of Missoula for 80 miles. Turn right onto County Road 100 and travel 1 mile.

About the campground: Douglas fir and pine trees settle in between camping units and help to soften the distant traffic noise. Parking units are a combination of pavement and gravel and for the most part are level. The water conveniently comes from spigots, though it is available only when the weather is warm enough to avoid freezing. Typically the campground is open from May 15 through September 10.

24 Crazy Creek

Location: 83 miles south of Missoula on Warm Springs Creek.

Facilities: Vault toilets, fire rings, tables, drinking water, no garbage service.

Sites: 7 for tents or RVs/Trailers up to 26 feet long.

Fee: $ per night, 14-day limit.

Managing agency: Bitterroot National Forest, Darby/Sula Ranger District, (406) 821-3913.

Activities: Hiking, fishing.

Finding the campground: Take US Highway 93 south out of Missoula for 80 miles. Turn right onto County Road 100 and travel 3 miles.

About the campground: Water comes from a hand pump here. The pine trees tend to have a dusty look from the gravel access road, though this area is far enough away that highway traffic is not noticeable. There is another camping area just above this one, but it is primarily for those with horses. The road can be rough, but if you plan to stay awhile, this could be a restful location. The campground is open from May 1 through December 1.

25 Indian Trees

Location: 90 miles south of Missoula.
Facilities: Vault toilets, fire rings, tables, drinking water.
Sites: 16 for tents or RVs/Trailer combinations up to 50 feet long.
Fee: $ per night, 14-day limit. Reservations can be made at this site. Call (877) 444-6777.
Managing agency: Bitterroot National Forest, Darby/Sula Ranger District, (406) 821–3913.
Activities: Hiking, wildlife viewing.
Finding the campground: Take US Highway 93 south out of Missoula for 89 miles. Turn right onto Forest Road 729 and travel 1 mile.
About the campground: Flathead Indians harvested the inner bark from living pine trees in this area. Some of the trees are still living and easily identified as the ones with a "gum tattoo". The bark, taken from pines with sap running, provided a sort of sweet chewing gum. Even after sugar made its way into the villages and camps of the area, this delicacy remained popular among the natives. Parking units are well separated among the rolling hillside, with open spaces between trees. The campground is open from Memorial Day through Labor Day.

26 Jennings Camp

Location: 94 miles south of Missoula on the East Fork Bitterroot River.
Facilities: Vault toilet, fire rings, tables.
Sites: 4 for tents or RVs/Trailers up to 20 feet long.
Fee: None, 14-day limit.
Managing agency: Bitterroot National Forest, Darby/Sula Ranger District, (406) 821–3913.
Activities: Hiking, fishing, wildlife viewing.
Finding the campground: Take US Highway 93 south out of Missoula for 84 miles. Turn left onto East Fork Road/County Road 472 and travel 10 miles.
About the campground: Wildlife provides the main attraction along this scenic portion of the river. Deer, elk, moose, and bighorn sheep beckon photographers and sightseers alike. Fires kept us from visiting the camping area. If the weather allows, the campground is open from May 1 through December 1.

27 Martin Creek

Location: 101 miles south of Missoula.
Facilities: Vault toilet, fire rings, tables, drinking water.
Sites: 7 for tents or RVs/Trailers up to 50 feet long.
Fee: $ per night, 14-day limit.
Managing agency: Bitterroot National Forest, Darby/Sula Ranger District, (406) 821–3913.

Activities: Hiking, wildlife viewing.

Finding the campground: Take US Highway 93 south out of Missoula for 84 miles. Turn left onto East Fork Road/County Road 472 and travel 17 miles to the Moose Creek/Martin Creek Junction. Turn left onto Martin Creek Road/FR 726 and travel 0.125 (1/8) mile.

About the campground: This campground moves farther up the mountain. Its exact condition is unknown. Lodgepole pine is well represented here with tall grass between units when the rain and sunshine combine in the right quantities. The campground is open from May 15 through December 1.

28 Beavertail Hill State Park

Location: 26 miles southeast of Missoula.

Facilities: Vault toilets, fire rings, tables, drinking water.

Sites: 28 for tents or RVs/Trailer combinations up to 45 feet long. Two Sioux-style tepees are available.

Fee: $ per night, dependent on resident/nonresident status; 14-day limit.

Managing agency: Beavertail Hill State Park, (406) 542–5500.

Activities: Hiking, fishing.

Finding the campground: Take I–90 east out of Missoula for 26 miles to Beavertail Hill/exit 130. Turn right and travel 0.25 mile.

About the campground: Cottonwood trees provide shade but little firewood on a consistent basis. The nearby Clark Fork River offers fishing, rafting, and swimming for those willing to make the hike. The two tepees are available for rent if you wish to revisit how past residents lived. The campground is open from May 1 through October 31.

29 Norton

Location: 33 miles southeast of Missoula on Rock Creek.

Facilities: Vault toilet, fire rings, tables, drinking water.

Sites: 13 for tents and RVs/Trailers up to 16 feet long.

Fee: $ per night, 14-day limit.

Managing agency: Lolo National Forest, Missoula Ranger District, (406) 329–3814.

Activities: Fishing.

Finding the campground: Take I–90 east out of Missoula for 22 miles to Rock Creek/exit 126. Turn right onto the gravel road and travel 11 miles.

About the campground: Moss-bearded fir trees make this campground seem somewhat mystical. Only the nearby residents and a busy road break the spell. The gravel road leading in to this spot gets real rough in a hurry. Access for trailers and motorhomes (RVs) can be a real challenge. It is not the best choice for a one night stay. The campground is open from May through September.

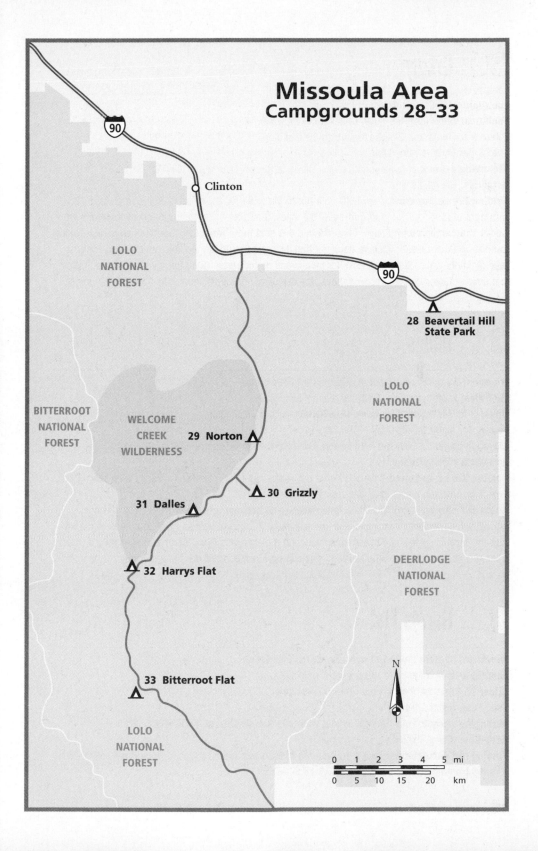

Missoula Area
Campgrounds 28–33

30 Grizzly

Location: 34 miles southeast of Missoula.
Facilities: Vault toilet, fire rings, tables, drinking water.
Sites: 9 for tents and RVs/Trailers up to 32 feet long.
Fee: $ per night, 14-day limit.
Managing agency: Lolo National Forest, Missoula Ranger District, (406) 329-3814.
Activities: Hiking, fishing.
Finding the campground: Take I-90 east out of Missoula for 22 miles to Rock Creek/exit 126. Turn right onto the gravel road and travel 12 miles. Turn left at the campground directional sign.
About the campground: Longer units will find this area more attractive, though anglers may not like the hike to Rock Creek. Sunshine does not find its way into this hidden little spot for very long, so take plenty of warm clothing. Access for trailers and motorhomes (RVs) can be challenging; if time is a limiting factor, consider other options. The campground is open from May through September.

31 Dalles

Location: 36 miles southeast of Missoula on Rock Creek.
Facilities: Vault toilets, fire rings, tables, drinking water.
Sites: 2 for tents and 8 for tents, RVs/Trailers up to 32 feet long.
Fee: $ per night, 14-day limit.
Managing agency: Lolo National Forest, Missoula Ranger District, (406) 329-3814.
Activities: Hiking, fishing.
Finding the campground: Take I-90 east out of Missoula for 22 miles to Rock Creek/exit 126. Turn right onto the gravel road and travel 14 miles.
About the campground: There is a little more space between units and trees here, but not enough to eliminate the mossy beards on the trees. The gravel access road continues to deteriorate the farther you travel. Access for trailers and motorhomes (RVs) can be challenging; if time is a limiting factor, consider other options. The campground is open from May through September.

32 Harrys Flat

Location: 40 miles southeast of Missoula on Rock Creek.
Facilities: Vault toilets, fire rings, tables, drinking water.
Sites: 15 for tents, RVs/Trailers up to 32 feet long.
Fee: $ per night, 14-day limit.
Managing agency: Lolo National Forest, Missoula Ranger District, (406) 329-3814.
Activities: Hiking, fishing.
Finding the campground: Take I-90 east out of Missoula for 22 miles to Rock Creek/exit 126. Turn right onto the gravel road and travel 18 miles.

About the campground: The dusty dirt road in the campground is actually smoother than the main access. Access for trailers and motorhomes (RVs) can be challenging; if time is a limiting factor, consider other options. There is considerable distance between camping spots, allowing for a sense of isolation. However, be prepared for lots of flying dirt on busy days. The campground is open from May through September .

33 Bitterroot Flat

Location: 46 miles southeast of Missoula on Rock Creek.

Facilities: Vault toilets, fire rings, tables, drinking water.

Sites: 15 for tents, RVs/Trailers up to 32 feet long.

Fee: $ per night, 14-day limit.

Managing agency: Lolo National Forest, Missoula Ranger District, (406) 329-3814.

Activities: Hiking, fishing.

Finding the campground: Take I-90 east out of Missoula for 22 miles to Rock Creek/exit 126. Turn right onto the gravel road and travel 24 miles.

About the campground: The farther you travel from the interstate, the less company you tend to notice. All the same, there is no small price to pay in the rough access road. This would be a nice spot to spend time if you do not mind the slow arrival. Access for trailers and motorhomes (RVs) can be challenging; if time is a limiting factor, consider other options. The campground is open from May through September.

Libby Area

Libby is the land of wide rivers and huge cedar trees. Rainfall tends to be more plentiful in this broad valley with thickly forested mountains defining the boundary. Easily accessible campgrounds such as those just off a paved road tend to fill up quickly on sunny weekends. The more difficult the access, the fewer the campers.

Wildlife is plentiful, and there seems to be no end of the shades of green produced from the variety of foliage.

	Group Sites	Tents	RV sites	Total sites	Hookups	Toilets	Showers	Drinking water	Dump station	Phone	Handicap Access	Recreation	Fee	Season	Stay limit (days)
1 Yaak River			44	44		V		*			*	HFW	$	5/20–9/30	16
2 Yaak Falls			7	7		V						HF	N	5/20–9/30	14
3 Whitetail			12	12		V		*				HFW	$	5/20–9/30	14
4 Pete Creek	4		8	12		V		*				HFW	$	5/20–9/30	14
5 Kilbrennan Lake			7	7		V						HF	N	Memorial Day to Labor Day	14
6 Dorr Skeels	5		2	7		V		*				FB	$	5/20–9/30	16
7 Bad Medicine			17	17		V		*				HFB	$	5/20–9/30	16
8 Bull River			26	26		V		*			*	HFB	$	Memorial Day to Labor Day	16
9 Spar Lake			13	13		V		*				HFB	$	5/20–9/30	16
10 North Shore			16	16		V		*				FB	$	Memorial Day to Labor Day	14
11 Willow Creek			6	6		V						H	N	5/15–9/30	14
12 Thompson Falls State Park			18	18		V		*				FB	$$	4/27–10/13	14
13 Gold Rush			7	7		V		*				HF	N	6/25–10/25	14
14 Howard Lake			10	10		V		*			*	HF	$	Memorial Day to Labor Day	14
15 Logan State Park			37	37		VF	*	*	*			HFB	$$	All Year	14
16 Fishtrap Lake			11	11		V		*				HFB	N	5/25–9/25	14
17 Copper King			5	5		V						HF	N	6/1–9/30	14
18 McGregor Lake	4		23	27		V		*			*	FB	$$	Memorial Day to Labor Day	14
19 McGillivray			33	33		F		*			*	HFB	$	mid-May to mid-Sept	14
20 Rocky Gorge			60	60		V		*			*	HFB	$	Memorial Day to Labor Day	14
21 Peck Gulch			22	22		V		*			*	HFB	$	Memorial Day to Labor Day	14
22 North Dickey Lake			25	25		V		*			*	HFB	$	5/20–10/15	14
23 Big Therriault Lake			10	10		V		*				HFB	$	6/29–9/8	14
24 Little Therriault Lake			6	6		V		*				HF	$	6/29–Labor Day	14
25 Rexford Bench			54	54		F		*			*	HFB	$$	5/15–10/1	14

1 Yaak River

Location: 25 miles northwest of Libby on the Yaak River.
Facilities: Vault toilets, fire rings, tables, drinking water.
Sites: 44 for tents or RVs up to 35 feet long.
Fee: $ per night, 16-day limit.
Managing agency: Kootenai National Forest, Three Rivers Ranger District, (406) 295–4693.
Activities: Hiking, fishing, wildlife viewing.
Finding the campground: Take US Highway 2 northwest out of Libby for 25 miles.

Yaak River Falls can be seen just above Yaak River Campground in northwestern Montana. PHOTO BY GREG HOOD.

About the campground: Cedar is noticeably present with the larch trees in both halves of this campground. The Yaak River splits camping units just before joining the Kootenai River, with some sites overlooking one of the two. Steep mountainsides surround the area with a continuing forest blanket well insulated with brush and tall grass. Some of the parking units are wide enough to unhook and park vehicles beside trailers. This popular campground is open from May 20 through September 30.

2 Yaak Falls

Location: 34 miles northwest of Libby on the Yaak River.
Facilities: Vault toilet, fire rings, tables.
Sites: 7 for tents, RVs/Trailers up to 24 feet long.
Fee: None, 14-day limit.
Managing agency: Kootenai National Forest, Three Rivers Ranger District, (406) 295–4693.
Activities: Hiking, fishing.
Finding the campground: Take US Highway 2 northwest out of Libby for 28 miles. Turn right onto paved Montana State Highway 508 and travel 6 miles.
About the campground: The waterfall can be heard from the campground, though it is a bit of a hike. Cedar trees mix with larch trees and a variety of brush wherever the soil allows. Hard, unmerciful rock otherwise stands out in stark contrast. The campground is open from May 20 through September 30.

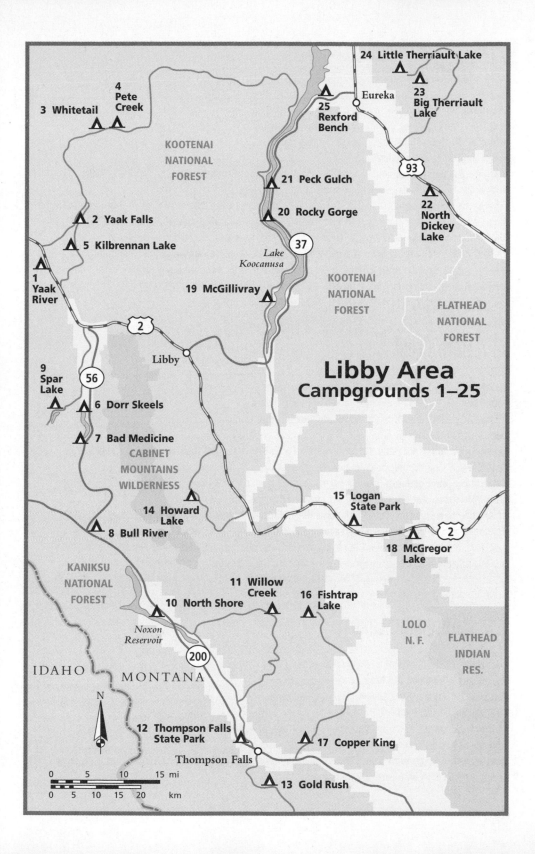

24 Little Therriault Lake

4 Pete Creek

3 Whitetail

Eureka

23 Big Therriault Lake

25 Rexford Bench

KOOTENAI
NATIONAL
FOREST

93

21 Peck Gulch

2 Yaak Falls

20 Rocky Gorge

5 Kilbrennan Lake

22 North Dickey Lake

37

Lake Koocanusa

1 Yaak River

19 McGillivray

KOOTENAI
NATIONAL
FOREST

FLATHEAD
NATIONAL
FOREST

2

Libby

Libby Area
Campgrounds 1–25

9 Spar Lake

56

6 Dorr Skeels

7 Bad Medicine

CABINET
MOUNTAINS
WILDERNESS

14 Howard Lake

15 Logan State Park

8 Bull River

18 McGregor Lake

2

KANIKSU
NATIONAL
FOREST

11 Willow Creek

16 Fishtrap Lake

10 North Shore

Noxon Reservoir

LOLO
N. F.

FLATHEAD
INDIAN
RES.

200

IDAHO   MONTANA

N

12 Thompson Falls State Park

17 Copper King

Thompson Falls

13 Gold Rush

0   5   10   15 mi

0   5   10 15 20   km

3 Whitetail

Location: 50 miles northwest of Libby on the Yaak River.
Facilities: Vault toilets, fire rings, tables, drinking water.
Sites: 12 for tents, RVs/Trailers up to 32 feet long.
Fee: $ per night, 14-day limit.
Managing agency: Kootenai National Forest, Three Rivers Ranger District, (406) 295–4693.
Activities: Hiking, fishing, wildlife viewing.
Finding the campground: Take US Highway 2 northwest out of Libby for 28 miles. Turn right onto paved Montana State Highway 508 and travel 22 miles. MT 508 becomes Forest Road 92.
About the campground: The cedar trees are replaced here with fir trees, but the larch are still present along with lots of tall grass and underbrush. Be watchful for the plentiful wildlife living in the area. Parking units are a combination of gravel, dirt, and grass that may require extra effort to level. The campground is open from May 20 through September 30.

4 Pete Creek

Location: 52 miles northwest of Libby on Pete Creek.
Facilities: Vault toilets, fire rings, tables, drinking water.
Sites: 4 for tents and 8 for RVs/Trailers up to 24 feet long.
Fee: $ per night, 14-day limit.
Managing agency: Kootenai National Forest, Three Rivers Ranger District, (406) 295–4693.
Activities: Hiking, fishing, wildlife viewing.
Finding the campground: Take US Highway 2 northwest out of Libby for 28 miles. Turn right onto paved Montana State Highway 508 and travel 24 miles. MT 508 becomes Forest Road 92.
About the campground: Pete Creek joins the Yaak River here with a host of witnesses. Fir, cedar, hemlock, spruce, and larch trees all preside over the merging of waters and hide campers as well. The mountains close in on this campground with dirt parking spots in a secluded and infrequently visited area. The campground is open from May 20 through September 30.

5 Kilbrennan Lake

Location: 30 northwest of Libby on Kilbrennan Lake.
Facilities: Vault toilet, fire rings, tables, boat ramp.
Sites: 7 for tents or RVs/Trailers up to 24 feet long.
Fee: None, 14-day limit.
Managing agency: Kootenai National Forest, Three Rivers Ranger District, (406) 295–4693.
Activities: Hiking, fishing.
Finding the campground: Take US Highway 2 northwest out of Libby for 20 miles. Turn right onto Forest Road 2394 and travel 10 miles.

About the campground: Fishing is the main attraction at this small and relatively popular mountain lake. For those who prefer not to wet a line the scenery and wildlife can offer a different sort of reward. Brook trout beckon anglers all year long, but the camping season runs from Memorial Day through Labor Day.

6 Dorr Skeels

Location: 31 miles southwest of Libby on Bull Lake.
Facilities: Vault toilet, fire rings, tables, drinking water, boat ramp.
Sites: 5 for tents, 2 for RVs/Trailers up to 32 feet long.
Fee: $ per night, 16-day limit.
Managing agency: Kootenai National Forest, Three Rivers Ranger District, (406) 295-4693.
Activities: Fishing, boating.
Finding the campground: Take US Highway 2 northwest out of Libby for 16 miles. Turn left onto Montana State Highway 56 and travel 14 miles. Turn right onto Forest Road 1117 and travel 1 mile.
About the campground: The mountains engulfing this popular waterskiing destination are filled with larch, cedar, and fir trees. The limited number of designated units could spell disappointment on a hot summer day. A weekday visit would be best when traveling through here. There is a security gate that is closed from 10 p.m. to 7 a.m. The campground is open from May 20 through September 30.

7 Bad Medicine

Location: 36 miles southwest of Libby on Bull Lake.
Facilities: Vault toilets, fire rings, tables, drinking water.
Sites: 17 for tents or RVs/Trailers up to 32 feet long.
Fee: $ per night, 16-day limit.
Managing agency: Kootenai National Forest, Three Rivers Ranger District, (406) 295-4693.
Activities: Hiking, fishing, boating.
Finding the campground: Take US Highway 2 northwest out of Libby for 16 miles. Turn left onto Montana State Highway 56 and travel 18 miles. Turn right onto Forest Road 398 and travel 1 mile. Turn right onto Forest Road 7170 and travel 1 mile.
About the campground: Bull Lake holds around 1,000 surface acres of water from Ross Creek, with some views in the campground's lower loop. Cedar and hemlock dominate this lower loop, at least in comparison with the upper one. Farther up Ross Creek, large cedars await the curious. So if the fish are not biting and the water is too cold to swim in, a trip upstream would be a worthwhile venture. There is a security gate that is closed from 10 p.m. to 7 a.m. The campground is open from May 20 through September 30.

8 Bull River

Location: 52 miles southwest of Libby on the Bull River.
Facilities: Vault toilets, fire rings, tables, drinking water.
Sites: 26 for tents or RVs/Trailer combinations up to 40 feet long.
Fee: $ per night, 16-day limit.
Managing agency: Kootenai National Forest, Cabinet Ranger District, (406) 827-3533.
Activities: Hiking, fishing, boating.
Finding the campground: Take US Highway 2 northwest out of Libby for 16 miles. Turn left onto Montana State Highway 56 and travel 35 miles. Turn left onto Montana State Highway 200 and travel about 1 mile.
About the campground: Douglas fir and cedar share this campground with a choice of three loops to stay in. The parking units allow longer units, though some maneuvering is required. Cabinet Gorge Reservoir impounds a little over 3,000 surface acres of the Clark Fork River. The campground is open from Memorial Day through Labor Day.

9 Spar Lake

Location: 33 miles southwest of Libby on Spar Lake.
Facilities: Vault toilet, fire rings, tables, drinking water, boat ramp.
Sites: 13 for tents or RVs up to 28 feet long.
Fee: $ per night, 16-day limit.
Managing agency: Kootenai National Forest, Three Rivers Ranger District, (406) 295-4693.
Activities: Hiking, fishing, boating.
Finding the campground: Take US Highway 2 northwest out of Libby for 17 miles. Turn left onto Lake Creek Road/Forest Road 384 and travel 16 miles.
About the campground: Mountains and fir trees march right up to the water's edge of this mountain lake. Nearby trails invite the adventurous to explore, while anglers will likely want to test their skill in the clear waters. The campground is open from May 20 through September 30.

10 North Shore

Location: 66 miles south of Libby on the Noxon Reservoir.
Facilities: Vault toilets, fire rings, tables, drinking water, boat ramp.
Sites: 16 for tents or RVs/Trailer combinations up to 40 feet long.
Fee: $ per night, 14-day limit.
Managing agency: Kootenai National Forest, Cabinet Ranger District, (406) 827-3533.
Activities: Fishing, boating.

Finding the campground: Take US Highway 2 northwest out of Libby for 16 miles. Turn left onto Montana State Highway 56 and travel 35 miles. Turn left onto Montana State Highway 200 and travel about 15 miles. Turn right at the campground directional sign and travel 0.5 mile.

About the campground: Campground roads and parking spurs, including three pull-throughs, are paved. The mountains are more distant here than they are at other nearby campgrounds, but they still provide a scenic backdrop. The Clark Fork River fills this reservoir, beckoning to swimmers, anglers, and boaters. There is a designated swimming area, but lifeguards are not present. The campground season runs from Memorial Day through Labor Day.

11 Willow Creek

Location: 88 miles south of Libby.
Facilities: Vault toilet, fire rings, tables.
Sites: 6 for tents or RVs/Trailer combinations up to 40 feet long.
Fee: None, 14-day limit.
Managing agency: Kootenai National Forest, Cabinet Ranger District, (406) 827-3533.
Activities: Hiking.
Finding the campground: Take US Highway 2 northwest out of Libby for 16 miles. Turn left onto Montana State Highway 56 and travel 35 miles. Turn left onto Montana State Highway 200 and travel 18 miles to Trout Creek. Take Forest Road 154 northeast out of Trout Creek for 19 miles.
Note: FR 154 is narrow, curvy and bumpy. High-clearance vehicles are recommended.
About the campground: Mature pine trees offer plenty of shade, though the designated camping units are limited. This is more of an access area for anglers and hunters. It is a long way to travel unless you are planning a prolonged stay. The campground is open from Memorial Day through Labor Day.

12 Thompson Falls State Park

Location: 90 miles south of Libby on the Clark Fork River.
Facilities: Vault toilets, fire rings, tables, drinking water, boat ramp.
Sites: 18 for tents, RVs/Trailers up to 30 feet long.
Fee: $$ per night, dependent upon resident/nonresident status; 14-day limit.
Managing agency: Thompson Falls State Park, (406) 752-5501 or (406) 751-4590.
Activities: Fishing, boating.
Finding the campground: Take US Highway 2 northwest out of Libby for 16 miles. Turn left onto Montana State Highway 56 and travel 35 miles. Turn left onto Montana State Highway 200 and travel 39 miles to Thompson Falls.
About the campground: Tall, well-spaced pine trees tower over grassy open areas with parking units scattered about. Nearby Thompson Falls provides all the amenities of a town without being too close. The campground is open from April 27 through October 12.

13 Gold Rush

Location: 99 miles south of Libby.
Facilities: Vault toilet, fire rings, tables, drinking water.
Sites: 7 for tents, RVs/Trailers up to 20 feet long.
Fee: None, 14-day limit.
Managing agency: Lolo National Forest, Plains/Thompson Falls Ranger District, (406) 826-3821.
Activities: Hiking, fishing.
Finding the campground: Take US Highway 2 northwest out of Libby for 16 miles. Turn left onto Montana State Highway 56 and travel 35 miles. Turn left onto Montana State Highway 200 and travel 39 miles to Thompson Falls. Take Forest Road 352 south out of Thompson Falls and travel 6 miles.
About the campground: A variety of evergreen trees blankets the mountain ridges with grassy, brush-filled stream banks at their feet. Be sure to have warm clothing as the temperature goes down with the sun. The better fishing will take some effort, but the hike can offer more rewards to the observant. The campground season typically runs from May 25 through September 25.

14 Howard Lake

Location: 40 miles south of Libby on Howard Lake.
Facilities: Vault toilets, fire rings, tables, drinking water.
Sites: 10 for tents, RVs/Trailers up to 20 feet long.
Fee: $ per night, 14-day limit.
Managing agency: Kootenai National Forest, Libby Ranger District, (406) 293-7773.
Activities: Hiking, fishing.
Finding the campground: Take US Highway 2 southeast out of Libby for 24 miles. Turn right onto dirt Forest Road 231 and travel 15 miles. Turn left at the campground directional sign and travel 1 mile.
About the campground: Howard Lake offers just over 400 surface acres of mountain water to play in. Motorized boats are not allowed, which keeps things quieter. The rough dirt access and dirt parking spots are the biggest deterrent. Cedar, spruce, and fir trees are well represented in the area. The campground is open from Memorial Day through Labor Day, when the weather allows.

15 Logan State Park

Location: 45 miles southeast of Libby on Middle Thompson Lake.
Facilities: Vault and flush toilets, dump station, showers, fire rings, tables, drinking water, boat ramp.
Sites: 37 for tents or RVs/Trailers up to 40 feet long.
Fee: $$, dependent upon resident/nonresident status; 14-day limit.

Managing agency: Logan State Park, from April 15–October 15, (406) 293-7190; from October 16–April 14, (406) 751-4590.

Activities: Hiking, fishing, boating.

Finding the campground: Take US Highway 2 southeast out of Libby for 45 miles.

About the campground: Douglas fir, ponderosa pine, and western larch march along the shoreline and then carpet the surrounding mountains. Water sports are popular here, but they are by no means the only activities available. This campground is open year-round, though the winter season makes things much more complicated.

16 Fishtrap Lake

Location: 125 miles south of Libby at Fishtrap Lake.

Facilities: Vault toilet, fire rings, tables, drinking water, boat ramp.

Sites: 17 for tents, RVs/Trailers up to 20 feet long.

Fee: None, 14-day limit.

Managing agency: Lolo National Forest, Plains/Thompson Falls Ranger District, (406) 826-3821.

Activities: Hiking, fishing, boating.

Finding the campground: Take US Highway 2 northwest out of Libby for 16 miles. Turn left onto Montana State Highway 56 and travel 35 miles. Turn left onto Montana State Highway 200 and travel 39 miles to Thompson Falls. Continue on MT 200 east out of Thompson Falls for 5 miles. Turn left onto Forest Road 56 and travel 13 miles. Take Forest Road 516 northwest for 15 miles. Take Forest Road 7953 west for 2 miles.

About the campground: Western larch trees provide some shade on this bench above the lake. There are some pull-through sites available, but most are the conventional back-in type. Fishing for trout is the main attraction. No motorized boats are allowed on the lake, which eliminates the engine noise and adds to the appeal of this campground for those who like a quieter, more solitude type of recreation. The campground is open from May 25 to September 25.

17 Copper King

Location: 99 miles south of Libby.

Facilities: Vault toilet, fire rings, tables.

Sites: 5 for tents or RVs up to 16 feet long; trailers are not recommended.

Fee: None, 14-day limit.

Managing agency: Lolo National Forest, Plains/Thompson Falls Ranger District, (406) 826-3821.

Activities: Hiking, fishing.

Finding the campground: Take US Highway 2 northwest out of Libby for 16 miles. Turn left onto Montana State Highway 56 and travel 35 miles. Turn left onto Montana State Highway 200 and travel 39 miles to Thompson Falls. Continue onto MT 200 east out of Thompson Falls for 5 miles. Turn left onto Forest Road 56 and travel 4 miles.

About the campground: Not far away, the Thompson River slides by with a variety of forest and open meadow available. Fishing can be good, but there are bugs that bite as well so be sure to have repellent. The campground is open from June 1 through September 30.

18 McGregor Lake

Location: 53 miles southeast of Libby on McGregor Lake.
Facilities: Vault toilets, fire rings, tables, drinking water.
Sites: 4 for tents and 23 for tents, RVs/Trailer combinations up to 32 feet long.
Fee: $$ per night, 14-day limit.
Managing agency: Kootenai National Forest, Libby Ranger District, (406) 293-7773.
Activities: Fishing, boating.
Finding the campground: Take US Highway 2 southeast out of Libby for 53 miles.
About the campground: Pine trees and around 1,600 surface acres of water beckon to anglers, boaters, and swimmers. The campground is open from Memorial Day through Labor Day, weather permitting.

19 McGillivray

Location: 25 miles northeast of Libby on Koocanusa Reservoir.
Facilities: Flush toilets, fire rings, tables, drinking water, boat ramp.
Sites: 33 for tents, RVs/Trailers up to 32 feet long.
Fee: $ per night, 14-day limit.
Managing agency: Kootenai National Forest, Libby Ranger District, (406) 293-7773.
Activities: Hiking, fishing, boating.
Finding the campground: Take Montana State Highway 37 northeast out of Libby for 15 miles. Turn left at the campground directional sign onto Forest Road 228 and travel 10 miles.
About the campground: The campground is set above the waterline of Koocanusa Reservoir, with open meadows guarded by Douglas fir trees and thick underbrush. Ospreys and bald eagles are resident anglers that compete with any visiting human anglers and can provide amusement along with excellent photo opportunities. Dates can vary from year to year, but the campground is typically open from mid-May to mid-September.

20 Rocky Gorge

Location: 36 miles northeast of Libby on Koocanusa Reservoir.
Facilities: Vault toilets, fire rings, tables, drinking water, boat ramp.
Sites: 60 for tents or RVs/Trailer combinations up to 32 feet long.
Fee: $ per night, 14-day limit.
Managing agency: Kootenai National Forest, Libby Ranger District, (406) 293-7773.

Activities: Hiking, fishing, boating.
Finding the campground: Take Montana State Highway 37 northeast out of Libby for 36 miles.
About the campground: The reservoir attracts the most attention, with pine-forested ridges along the shoreline. The campground is open from Memorial Day through Labor Day.

21 Peck Gulch

Location: 43 miles northeast of Libby on Koocanusa Reservoir.
Facilities: Vault toilets, fire rings, tables, drinking water, boat ramp.
Sites: 22 for tents or RVs/Trailer combinations up to 32 feet long.
Fee: $ per night, 14-day limit.
Managing agency: Kootenai National Forest, Libby Ranger District, (406) 293-7773.
Activities: Hiking, fishing, boating.
Finding the campground: Take Montana State Highway 37 northeast out of Libby for 43 miles.
About the campground: Forested mountains in the distance loom over the reservoir and present scenic views. Parking can be a little confusing, as it is gravel base and there are no designated spots. There are some tent pads available within the units, but they may take some searching. The campground is managed from Memorial Day through Labor Day.

22 North Dickey Lake

Location: 81 miles northeast of Libby on Dickey Lake.
Facilities: Vault toilets, fire rings, tables, drinking water.
Sites: 25 for tents or RVs/Trailer combinations up to 50 feet long.
Fee: $ per night, 14-day limit.
Managing agency: Kootenai National Forest, Rexford Ranger District, (406) 296-2536.
Activities: Hiking, fishing, boating.
Finding the campground: Take Montana State Highway 37 northeast out of Libby for 66 miles to Eureka. Take US Highway 93 southeast out of Eureka for 15 miles.
About the campground: Larch and lodgepole pine trees loom over parking units and short brush. The parking units tend to seem a bit close, but most campers are courteous. The gravel road does not make much dust, but what it does create can be bothersome. Dickey Lake holds around 800 surface acres of water for campers to enjoy from May 20 through October 15.

23 Big Therriault Lake

Location: 111 miles northeast of Libby on Big Therriault Lake.
Facilities: Vault toilets, fire rings, tables, drinking water.
Sites: 10 for tents or RVs/Trailer combinations up to 32 feet long.
Fee: $ per night, 14-day limit.

Managing agency: Kootenai National Forest,, Rexford Ranger District, (406) 296–2536.

Activities: Hiking, fishing, boating.

Finding the campground: Take Montana State Highway 37 northeast out of Libby for 66 miles to Eureka. Take US Highway 93 southeast out of Eureka for 7 miles. Turn left onto Grave Creek Road and travel about 14 miles. Take Forest Road 114 for 11 miles. Take Forest Road 319 for 13 miles.

About the campground: Douglas fir trees shade camping units and underbrush alike. This mountain lake will leave you wishing you could stay longer. Steep, forested mountainsides dive into the lake, presenting some unforgettable scenery. The campground is managed from June 29 through September 8 weather permitting.

24 Little Therriault Lake

Location: 111 miles northeast of Libby on Little Therriault Lake.

Facilities: Vault toilet, fire rings, tables, drinking water.

Sites: 6 for tents or RVs/Trailer combinations up to 32 feet long.

Fee: $ per night, 14-day limit.

Managing agency: Kootenai National Forest, Rexford Ranger District, (406) 296–2536.

Activities: Hiking, fishing.

Finding the campground: Take Montana State Highway 37 northeast out of Libby for 66 miles to Eureka. Take US Highway 93 southeast out of Eureka for 7 miles. Turn left onto Grave Creek Road and travel about 14 miles. Take Forest Road 114 for 11 miles. Take Forest Road 319 for 13 miles. Bear to the right at the Big Therriault Lake junction.

About the campground: Steep, forested mountains climb out of the clear water of this lake and move into the sky, terminating with snowcapped solid rock. Be sure to pack warm clothing, as this is mountain country in true form. The campground could open in May and close in September, but that is strictly subject to the climate of the particular year.

25 Rexford Bench

Location: 60 miles northeast of Libby on Koocanusa Reservoir.

Facilities: Flush toilets, fire rings, tables, drinking water.

Sites: 54 for tents or RVs/Trailer combinations up to 60 feet long.

Fee: $$ per night, 14-day limit.

Managing agency: Kootenai National Forest, Rexford Ranger District, (406) 296–2536.

Activities: Hiking, fishing, boating.

Finding the campground: Take Montana State Highway 37 northeast out of Libby for 60 miles. Turn left at the campground directional sign.

About the campground: Fifteen of the units can be reserved by calling (877) 444-6777. Koocanusa Reservoir impounds more than 40,000 surface acres of water, with the greatest appeal to water-sports enthusiasts. Pine trees with an assortment of brush settle in just above the lake. The campground is open from May 15 through October 1.

Seeley Lake Area

A whole series of lakes nestles into this extra-long valley. Snowcapped mountains stand guard on both sides, providing the observant traveler with changing panoramic views. The numerous lakes and a lack of wind make this a popular destination for those with water-related recreational equipment. At times, however, the noise level gets quite high.

Wildlife is plentiful; in fact, the local deer often browse in the campgrounds on their way for a drink of water or a resting place. Do keep in mind that they cross highways without warning and sometimes even seem intent on committing suicide. A slower rate of travel, especially just after sunrise and just before sunset, will reduce the number of fatalities.

	Group Sites	Tents	RV sites	Total sites	Hookups	Toilets	Showers	Drinking water	Dump station	Phone	Handicap Access	Recreation	Fee	Season	Stay limit (days)
1 Russell Gates Memorial			12	12		V		*			*	FB	$$	5/1–9/30	7
2 Salmon Lake		10	24	34		FV		*			*	FB	$$	5/1–9/30	14
State Park															
3 River Point			26	26		V		*			*	FB	$	5/28–9/3	14
4 Seeley Lake			29	29		FV		*			*	FB	$	5/22–9/5	14
5 Big Larch			48	48		V		*			*	HFB	$	5/15–9/15	14
6 Placid Lake State Park		9	40	49		FV		*			*	FB	$$	mid-May to mid-Sept	14
7 Lake Alva			39	39		V		*			*	HFB	$	5/15–9/30	14
8 Holland Lake	1		40	40		V		*				HFB	$$	mid-May to mid-Sept	16
9 Cedar Creek			D	D		P						HF	N	6/1–10/30	14
10 Soup Creek		9	9	18		P						HF	N	6/1–10/30	14
11 Point Pleasant	12	12	24			P						HF	N	6/1–10/30	14
12 Swan Lake	1		36	36		V		*			*	HFB	$$	5/15–9/30	16

1   Russell Gates Memorial

Location: 18 miles southeast of Seeley Lake on the Blackfoot River.
Facilities: Vault toilet, fire rings, tables, drinking water.
Sites: 12 for tents, RVs/Trailers up to 25 feet long.
Fee: $$ per night, 7-day limit.
Managing agency: Montana Fish, Wildlife & Parks, (406) 542-5500.
Activities: Fishing, boating.
Finding the campground: Take Montana State Highway 83 south out of Seeley Lake for 15 miles. Turn left onto Montana State Highway 200 and travel 3 miles.
About the campground: Camping in this popular mountain valley is restricted to designated sites. Anglers are most attracted to the clear waters of this mountain stream with an assortment of evergreen trees and open meadows. The bends and twists present numerous deep pools that no doubt prompt the desire to drop in a line. Do not plan on waterskiing here. The boating mentioned in the activities section refers to fishing or rafting. The campground services are available from May 1 through September 30, unless adverse weather dictates differently.

2   Salmon Lake State Park

Location: 5 miles south of Seeley Lake on Salmon Lake.
Facilities: Flush and vault toilets, fire rings, tables, drinking water.

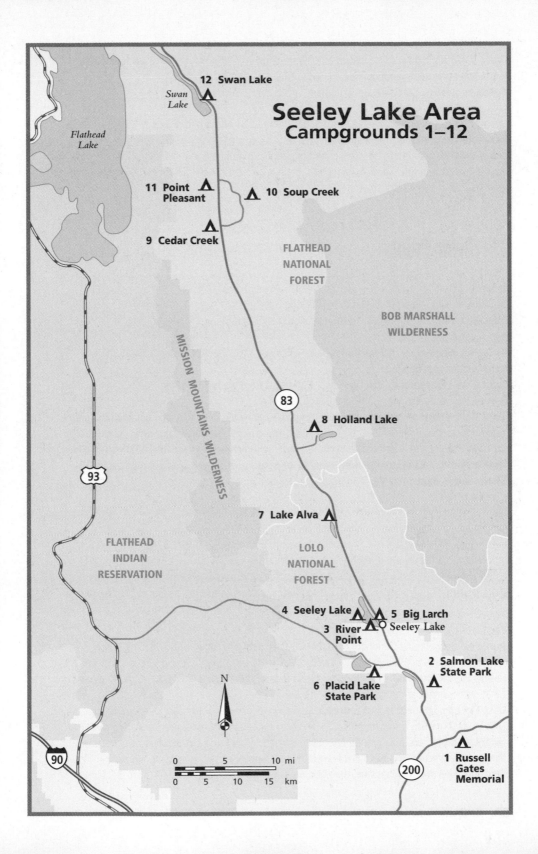

Sites: 10 for tents (hike-bike access) and 14 for tents, RVs and trailers up to 25 feet long.
Fee: $$ per day, dependent on resident/nonresident status; 14-day limit.
Managing agency: Salmon Lake State Park, (406) 677-6804.
Activities: Fishing, boating.
Finding the campground: Take Montana State Highway 83 south out of Seeley Lake for 5 miles.
About the campground: The Clearwater River settles into this portion of the valley to make a natural lake. Western larch, Douglas fir, and ponderosa pine share the shoreline and surrounding mountainsides with a few rock outcroppings sneaking a peek in the distance. The campground is open from May 1 through September 30.

3 River Point

Location: 2.5 miles northwest of Seeley Lake on Seeley Lake.
Facilities: Vault toilets, fire rings, tables, drinking water.
Sites: 26 for tents or RVs/Trailer combinations up to 60 feet long.
Fee: $ per night, 14-day limit.
Managing agency: Lolo National Forest, Seeley Lake Ranger District, (406) 677-2233.
Activities: Fishing, boating.
Finding the campground: Take Boy Scout Road past the Pyramid Mountain Lumber Company in Seeley Lake northwest out of Seeley Lake for 2.5 miles.
About the campground: This is a popular area with heavy use and daily law enforcement patrols. In addition to the camping units, there are eight picnic sites available along with a volleyball court and a group fire ring. As the directions show, the amenities of town are not far away either. Western larch seems to dominate the area, though pine and fir trees also are represented. The campground is open from May 28 through September 3.

4 Seeley Lake

Location: 3.5 miles northwest of Seeley Lake on Seeley Lake.
Facilities: Flush toilets, fire rings, tables, drinking water, boat ramp.
Sites: 29 for tents, RVs/Trailers up to 32 feet long.
Fee: $ per night, 14-day limit.
Managing agency: Lolo National Forest, Seeley Lake Ranger District, (406) 677-2233.
Activities: Fishing, boating.
Finding the campground: Take Boy Scout Road past the Pyramid Mountain Lumber Company in Seeley Lake northwest out of Seeley Lake for 3.5 miles.
About the campground: This pleasant campground doesn't seem to have the same amount of traffic as other nearby camping areas. There are daily law enforcement patrols. Without know-ing the directions, this area can be difficult to find. The gravel roads could also be a deterrent; however, if less active and more isolated camping is appealing, this would be the choice. Western larch, pine, and fir encompass the area. The campground is open from mid-May to September.

Local residents stop by for lunch at Seeley Lake.

5 Big Larch

Location: 1.5 miles north of Seeley Lake on Seeley Lake.
Facilities: Vault toilets, fire rings, tables, drinking water, boat ramp.
Sites: 48 for tents, RVs/Trailers up to 40 feet long.
Fee: $ per night, 14-day limit.
Managing agency: Lolo National Forest, Seeley Lake Ranger District, (406) 677-2233.
Activities: Hiking, fishing, boating.
Finding the campground: Take Montana State Highway 83 north out of Seeley Lake for 1 mile. Turn left at the campground directional sign and travel 0.5 mile.
About the campground: Three loops wander through the big western larch trees for which this campground must have been named. None of the camping units are at the shoreline, but a short hike will remedy this. Thick brush and timber do not allow long-range views of the scenery, but they do enhance the sense of seclusion—even with town only a short distance away. Plentiful deer provided some entertainment and excitement as they wandered slowly past our trailer, seemingly unafraid. Short, marked nature trails also provided interesting discoveries. Powerful motorboats and water-skiers bullied their way into the sound waves of the forest, increasing in intensity toward late afternoon. As the sun moved out of sight, so did the metal thunder. For those not desiring to hear mechanized recreation, this would be a good place to avoid on hot summer days. If the snow cover is not too deep, the campground opens on May 15 and closes on September 15. There are daily law enforcement patrols.

6 Placid Lake State Park

Location: 6 miles southwest of Seeley Lake.
Facilities: Flush and vault toilets, fire rings, tables, drinking water, boat ramp.
Sites: 9 tent and 40 for tents, RVs/Trailers up to 46 feet long.
Fee: $$ per night, 14-day limit.
Managing agency: Placid Lake State Park, (406) 677-6804.
Activities: Fishing, boating.
Finding the campground: Take Montana State Highway 83 south out of Seeley Lake for 3 miles. Turn left at the campground directional sign onto the paved road and travel 3 miles.
About the campground: These sites can be reserved and are all back in with lengths that vary from 25 to 46 feet in length. The most prevalent units are in the 30 foot range. There are also 17 units with electricity available. This beautiful area was logged off long ago, but one would not realize it from the abundant second-growth forest now in place. Douglas fir, spruce, pine, and western larch trees line the lakeshore and blanket the surrounding mountainsides. Massive tree stumps within the park and in the surrounding countryside testify to the past residents. The campground is open from mid-May to mid-September.

7 Lake Alva

Location: 12 miles north of Seeley Lake on Lake Alva.
Facilities: Vault toilets, fire rings, tables, drinking water, boat ramp.
Sites: 39 for tents, RVs/Trailers up to 22 feet long.
Fee: $ per night, 14-day limit.
Managing agency: Lolo National Forest, Seeley Lake Ranger District, (406) 677-2233.
Activities: Hiking, fishing, boating.
Finding the campground: Take Montana State Highway 83 north out of Seeley Lake for 12 miles.
About the campground: Spruce trees dominate the area with plenty of underbrush to help isolate units. Water sports attract the majority of campers, as there is no shortage of shoreline. A sandy beach invites swimmers as well. There are law enforcement patrols. The campground is open from May 15 through September 30, depending on weather.

8 Holland Lake

Location: 25 miles north of Seeley Lake on Holland Lake.
Facilities: Vault toilets, fire rings, tables, drinking water, boat ramp.
Sites: 40 for tents, RVs/Trailers up to 50 feet long.
Fee: $$ per night, 16-day limit.
Managing agency: Flathead National Forest; campground operated by Flathead Valley Campgrounds, Barta Enterprises, (406) 646-1012.
Activities: Hiking, fishing, boating.
Finding the campground: Take Montana State Highway 83 north out of Seeley Lake for about 22 miles. Turn right onto gravel Holland Lake Road/Forest Road 44 and travel 3 miles.
About the campground: Some sites can be reserved, call (877) 444-6777. An assortment of brush and thick evergreen forest snuggles up to these 400 surface acres of blue mountain water. The Swan Mountains loom over the top, presenting scenic views at numerous locations. Campers have a choice of two loops, some sites closer to the lakeshore than others. Dust can be noticeable on busy days, which seem frequent at this popular spot. The campground is open from mid-May to mid-September, weather permitting.

9 Cedar Creek

Location: 46 miles north of Seeley Lake on Cedar Creek.
Facilities: Pit toilet, fire rings.
Sites: Undesignated for dispersed camping for tents or RVs up to 16 feet long.
Fee: None, 14-day limit.

Managing agency: Department of Natural Resources & Conservation (406) 754-2301.

Activities: Hiking, fishing.

Finding the campground: Take Montana State Highway 83 north out of Seeley Lake for 45 miles. Turn left onto the gravel road at the campground directional sign and travel 1 mile.

About the campground: This is classified as a primitive camping area and as such will not appeal to most travelers. In the off chance that the day is getting long and other camping choices have been depleted it could offer a pleasant place to regroup. Cedar Creek joins the Swan River nearby. The wooded shoreline offers shade and the promise of some firewood, without a guarantee; if a campfire is important it would be best to bring some. There is private land in the area, so be careful of fences and signs. The campground is open from June 1 through October 30.

10 Soup Creek

Location: 56 miles north of Seeley Lake on Soup Creek.

Facilities: Pit toilet, fire rings, tables.

Sites: 9 for tents and 9 for tents, RVs/Trailers up to 12 feet long.

Fee: None, 14-day limit.

Managing agency: Department of Natural Resources & Conservation, (406) 754-2301.

Activities: Hiking, fishing.

Finding the campground: Take Montana State Highway 83 north out of Seeley Lake for 51 miles. Turn right onto the gravel road at the campground directional sign and travel 5 miles.

About the campground: This primitive campground is not for those who need hookups or other modern amenities. It does find appeal among those who like a more physical approach to camping with a touch of nostalgia.. The rough access road will be more difficult in adverse weather. The campground is open from June 1 through October 30.

11 Point Pleasant

Location: 50 miles north of Seeley Lake on the Swan River.

Facilities: Pit toilet, fire rings, tables.

Sites: 12 for tent and 12 for tents, RVs/Trailers up to 12 feet long.

Fee: None, 14-day limit.

Managing agency: Department of Natural Resources & Conservation, (406) 754-2301.

Activities: Hiking, fishing.

Finding the campground: Take Montana State Highway 83 north out of Seeley Lake for 50 miles. Turn left onto the improved dirt road and travel 0.5 mile.

About the campground: The clear, inviting waters of the Swan River run by just below the bench that this primitive camping area settles into. Fir and larch trees provide plenty of shade with brush between. Overall, this quiet spot would be a pleasant stay for those with self-contained units and a dislike for crowds and noisy toys. The campground is open from June 1 through October 30.

12 Swan Lake

Location: 57 miles north of Seeley Lake on Swan Lake.
Facilities: Vault toilets, fire rings, tables, drinking water.
Sites: 36 for tents, RVs/Trailers up to 50 feet long.
Fee: $$ per night, 16-day limit.
Managing agency: Flathead National Forest; campground operated by Flathead Valley Campgrounds, Barta Enterprises, (406) 646-1012
Activities: Hiking, fishing, boating.
Finding the campground: Take Montana State Highway 83 north out of Seeley Lake for 57 miles.
About the campground: Some sites can be reserved, call (877) 444-6777. Two loops offer a choice to campers; birch and fir trees provide shade and some isolation in one while the other is dominated by large open sites. The paved access and close proximity to the roughly 20-mile-long Swan Lake make this a popular spot. The campground is open from May 15 through September 30, dependent on weather.

Kalispell Area

Glacier National Park offers mountain majesty beyond imagination. Along with the glaciers, for which the park is named, all the other amenities of mountain life are abundantly present. Grizzly bears and a host of other wildlife reside here with little fear of humans.

Moving downstream into the valleys toward civilization, the contrast cannot be ignored. Man-made reservoirs still present scenic views, with wildlife adjusting to a coexistence of sorts. Modern conveniences tend to take the primitive aspect out of some spots, but the wilderness is only a short distance away.

	Group Sites	Tents	RV sites	Total sites	Hookups	Toilets	Showers	Drinking water	Dump station	Phone	Handicap Access	Recreation	Fee	Season	Stay limit (days)
1 Flathead Lake State Park: Wayfarers	9		21	30		VF		*	*	*	*	HFB	$$	5/1–9/30	14
2 Flathead Lake State Park: West Shore	7		24	31		V		*				HFB	$$	5/1–9/30	14
3 Lake Mary Ronan State Park			25	25		V		*				HFB	$$	5/31–9/30	14
4 Flathead Lake State Park: Big Arm			41	41		VF	*	*		*	*	HFBW	$$	5/1–9/30	14
5 Flathead Lake State Park: Yellow Bay	5			5		VF	*	*				HFBW	$$	5/1–9/30	14
6 Flathead Lake State Park: Finley Point	7		34	41	*	VF		*				FBW	$$	mid-May to Labor Day	14
7 Lost Johnny Camp			21	21		V			*			HFB	$$	mid-May to Sept 30	16
8 Lost Johnny Point			21	21		V		*				HFB	$	5/18–9/30	16
9 Lid Creek			23	23		V						HFB	$	5/18–9/30	16
10 Handkerchief Lake			9	9		V						HFB	$	6/1–9/30	14
11 Emery Bay			26	26		V		*				HFB	$$	5/18–9/30	16
12 Murray Bay			20	20		V		*				HFB	$$	5/18–9/18	16
13 Spotted Bear			13	13		V		*				HFW	$	5/25–9/20	14
14 Glacier National Park: Apgar			194	194		F		*			*	HFBW	$$$	5/9–10/20	14
15 Glacier National Park: Fish Creek	5		173	178		F		*			*	HW	$$$	6/20–9/2	14
16 Glacier National Park: Quartz Creek	7			7		V		*				HFW	$$$	6/29–10/28	14
17 Glacier National Park: Logging Creek			7	7		V		*				HFW	$	6/29–10/28	14
18 Glacier National Park: Bowman Lake			46	46		V		*				HFBW	$$	5/16–9/2	14
19 Glacier National Park: Kintla Lake			13	13		V		*				HFBW	$$	6/4–9/9	14
20 Glacier National Park: Sprague Creek	25			25		F		*			*	HFW	$$$	5/30–9/16	14
21 Glacier National Park: Avalanche			87	87		F		*			*	HFW	$$$	6/22–9/8	14
22 Devil Creek			14	14		V		*				HF	$	Mem. Day to Labor Day	16
23 Summit			17	17		V		*				H	$	Summer	14
24 Glacier National Park: Two Medicine			100	100		F		*			*	HFB	$$$	5/15–9/15	14
25 Glacier National Park: Cutbank			14	14		V		*				HW	$$	5/1–9/23	14

	Group Sites	Tents	RV sites	Total sites	Hookups	Toilets	Showers	Drinking water	Dump station	Phone	Handicap Access	Recreation	Fee	Season	Stay limit (days)
26 Glacier National Park: St. Mary Lake		7	141	148		F		*				HFB	$$$	6/1-9/3	14
27 Glacier National Park: Rising Sun			84	84		F		*			*	HFBW	$$$	6/8-9/9	14
28 Glacier National Park: Many Glacier			110	110		F		*			*	HFW	$$$	5/23-9/23	14
29 Whitefish Lake State Park		7	18	25		F	*	*				FB	$$	4/1-11/30	7
30 Tally Lake		1	40	41		V		*				HFB	$$	5/15-10/1	16

1 Flathead Lake State Park: Wayfarers

Location: 18 miles southeast of Kalispell on Flathead Lake.
Facilities: Vault and flush toilets, fire rings, tables, drinking water, dump station, public telephone.
Sites: 9 for tents and 21 for RVs/Trailer combinations up to 40 feet long.
Fee: $$ per night, dependent on resident/nonresident status; 7-day limit.
Managing agency: Wayfarers State Park, (406) 837-4196.
Activities: Hiking, fishing, boating.
Finding the campground: Take US Highway 93 south out of Kalispell for 8 miles. Turn left onto Montana State Highway 82 and travel 7 miles. Turn right onto Montana State Highway 35 and travel 3 miles.
About the campground: From May 1 through September 30, campers can enjoy a variety of experiences. A walk through the pine and fir trees to the cliffs allows scenic views and photo opportunities of Flathead Lake. A variety of wildflowers and colorful foliage add personalized touches at different times of the year.

2 Flathead Lake State Park: West Shore

Location: 20 miles south of Kalispell on Flathead Lake.
Facilities: Vault toilets, fire rings, tables, drinking water, boat ramp.
Sites: 7 for tents and 24 for RVs/Trailer combinations up to 40 feet long.
Fee: $$ per night, dependent on resident/nonresident status; 7-day limit.
Managing agency: West Shore State Park, (406) 844-3044.
Activities: Hiking, fishing, boating.
Finding the campground: Take US Highway 93 south out of Kalispell for 20 miles.
About the campground: The forest is both thick and thickly populated with fir, larch, and lodgepole pine trees. Rocky cliffs make swimming a bit of a task but offer excellent views of snow-capped mountains. The campground operates from May 1 through September 30, unless adverse weather dictates an adjustment.

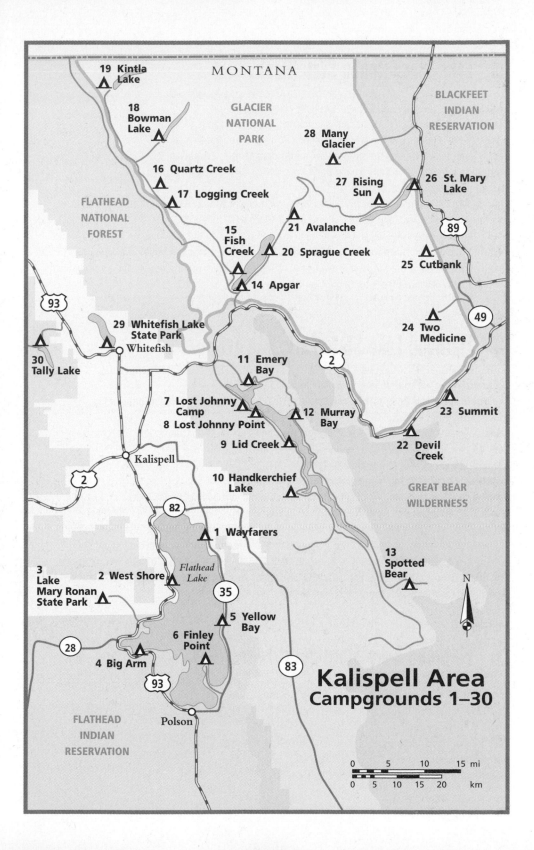

MONTANA

19 Kintla Lake

GLACIER NATIONAL PARK

18 Bowman Lake

BLACKFEET INDIAN RESERVATION

28 Many Glacier

16 Quartz Creek

FLATHEAD NATIONAL FOREST

17 Logging Creek

27 Rising Sun

26 St. Mary Lake

89

15 Fish Creek

21 Avalanche

20 Sprague Creek

25 Cutbank

14 Apgar

93

29 Whitefish Lake State Park

Whitefish

2

24 Two Medicine

49

30 Tally Lake

11 Emery Bay

7 Lost Johnny Camp

8 Lost Johnny Point

12 Murray Bay

23 Summit

9 Lid Creek

Kalispell

22 Devil Creek

2

10 Handkerchief Lake

GREAT BEAR WILDERNESS

82

1 Wayfarers

13 Spotted Bear

3 Lake Mary Ronan State Park

2 West Shore

Flathead Lake

35

N

5 Yellow Bay

6 Finley Point

28

4 Big Arm

83

Kalispell Area
Campgrounds 1–30

93

Polson

FLATHEAD INDIAN RESERVATION

0   5   10   15 mi

0   5   10   15   20 km

3 Lake Mary Ronan State Park

Location: 33 miles south of Kalispell on Lake Mary Ronan.
Facilities: Vault toilets, fire rings, tables, drinking water, boat ramp.
Sites: 25 for tents or RVs/Trailer combinations up to 50 feet long.
Fee: $$ per night, dependent on resident/nonresident status; 14-day limit.
Managing agency: Lake Mary Ronan State Park, (406) 849–5082.
Activities: Hiking, fishing, boating.
Finding the campground: Take US Highway 93 south out of Kalispell for about 26 miles to Dayton. Turn right onto Montana State Highway 352 and travel 7 miles.
About the campground: Douglas fir and larch trees march up to the shoreline on this clear-water lake. The park is out of the way, so it tends to get less attention than the better-known Flathead Lake just to the east. The longer maximum stay could be a very tempting option. The campground opens on May 31 and closes on September 30.

4 Flathead Lake State Park: Big Arm

Location: 38 miles south of Kalispell on Flathead Lake.
Facilities: Vault and flush toilets, showers, fire rings, tables, drinking water, boat ramp, public telephone.
Sites: 1 group, 41 for tents or RVs/Trailer combinations up to 40 feet long.
Fee: $$ per night, dependent on resident/nonresident status; 14-day limit.
Managing agency: Big Arm State Park, (406) 849–5256.
Activities: Hiking, fishing, boating, wildlife viewing.
Finding the campground: Take US Highway 93 south out of Kalispell for 38 miles.
About the campground: Ponderosa pine and juniper populate the camping area. The blue waters of Flathead Lake paint the background between trees, inviting anglers, boaters, swimmers, and sunbathers. Keep in mind that a Tribal Fishing License is required to fish at this location. The lengthy beach attracts numerous visitors each year. Bird-watchers will find the nature trail appealing. This is a popular takeoff point for Wildhorse Island, so it can get crowded. The campground is typically open from May 1 through September 30.

5 Flathead Lake State Park: Yellow Bay

Location: 32 miles southeast of Kalispell on Flathead Lake.
Facilities: Vault and flush toilet, showers, tables, grills, drinking water, boat ramp.
Sites: 5 for tents only.
Fee: $$ per night, dependent on resident/nonresident status; 7-day limit.
Managing agency: Yellow Bay State Park, (406) 982–3034.
Activities: Hiking, fishing, boating, wildlife viewing.

Finding the campground: Take US Highway 93 south out of Kalispell for 8 miles. Turn left onto Montana State Highway 82 and travel 7 miles. Turn right onto Montana State Highway 35 and travel 17 miles.

About the campground: No campfires are allowed here. The grills provided are for charcoal only. This peaceful hideaway is definitely more suited for tent campers. Pine trees define the sandy shoreline on one side with the blue waters of Flathead Lake on the other. Cherry trees explode with color and add to the view in the spring. The campground is open all year but water is only available from mid-May through Labor Day.

6 Flathead Lake State Park: Finley Point

Location: 42 miles southeast of Kalispell on Flathead Lake.

Facilities: Vault and flush toilets, fire rings, tables, drinking water, electric hookups, boat docks, boat ramp.

Sites: 7 for tents, 4 boat slips with electricity, 12 boat slips without electricity, and 18 for RVs/Trailer combinations up to 50 feet long.

Fee: $$ per night, dependent on resident/nonresident status; 7-day limit.

Managing agency: Finley Point State Park, (406) 837-3041.

Activities: Fishing, boating, wildlife viewing.

Finding the campground: Take US Highway 93 south out of Kalispell for 8 miles. Turn left onto Montana State Highway 82 and travel 7 miles. Turn right onto Montana State Highway 35 and travel 23 miles. Turn right onto the access road and travel 4 miles.

About the campground: Sites can be reserved online at montanastateparks.reserveamerica.com. Tall pines and the clear waters of Flathead Lake mix for scenic views and memories not to be forgotten. Firewood can be purchased; do not count on gathering much in the immediate camping area. The campground is open from mid-May through Labor Day.

7 Lost Johnny Camp

Location: 31 miles east of Kalispell at Hungry Horse Reservoir.

Facilities: Vault toilet, fire rings, tables, drinking water.

Sites: 21 for tents or RVs/Trailers up to 22 feet long.

Fee: $$ per night, 16-day limit.

Managing agency: Flathead Valley Campgrounds; Kalispell office, (406) 309-2018.

Activities: Hiking, fishing, boating.

Finding the campground: Take US Highway 2 northeast out of Kalispell for about 23 miles to Hungry Horse. Turn right onto paved Forest Road 895 out of Hungry Horse and follow the West Side Hungry Horse Reservoir Road across the dam, continuing for 6 miles.

About the campground: Short pine and fir trees are thick with lots of underbrush to provide a sense of privacy. Plenty of firewood appears to be present; however, it will take some time and effort to gather. The campground is open from mid-May through September 30, weather permitting.

8 Lost Johnny Point

Location: 32 miles east of Kalispell on Hungry Horse Reservoir.
Facilities: Vault toilets, fire rings, tables, drinking water, boat ramp.
Sites: 21 for tents or RVs/Trailers up to 22 feet long.
Fee: $ per night, 16-day limit.
Managing agency: Flathead Valley Campgrounds; Kalispell office, (406) 309-2018.
Activities: Hiking, fishing, boating.
Finding the campground: Take US Highway 2 northeast out of Kalispell for about 23 miles to Hungry Horse. Turn right onto paved Forest Road 895 southeast out of Hungry Horse and travel for 9 miles.
About the campground: This campground is more developed than Lost Johnny Camp. Consequently, more visitors frequent it during the open season from May 18 through September 30. The timber is not as thick, but the hillside is steeper. Camping units are well above the shoreline; however, once on the lake, there are more than 30 miles of water ranging from 1 to 4 miles in width to explore. For those who find the campgrounds in Glacier National Park full, this would be a pleasant option.

9 Lid Creek

Location: 38 miles east of Kalispell on Hungry Horse Reservoir.
Facilities: Vault toilets, fire rings, tables, boat ramp.
Sites: 23 for tents or RVs up to 16 feet long.
Fee: $ per night, 16-day limit.
Managing agency: Flathead Valley Campgrounds; Kalispell office, (406) 309-2018.
Activities: Hiking, fishing, boating.
Finding the campground: Take US Highway 2 northeast out of Kalispell for about 23 miles to Hungry Horse. Turn right onto paved Forest Road 895 southeast out of Hungry Horse and travel for 15 miles.
About the campground: This campground settles in near the end of the pavement. The well-developed campgrounds available before reaching this spot tend to make it a sleeper. The campground is open from mid-May 18 through September 30.

10 Handkerchief Lake

Location: 60 miles southeast of Kalispell on Handkerchief Lake.
Facilities: Vault toilet, tables.
Sites: 9 walk in tent sites.
Fee: $ per night, 14-day limit.
Managing agency: Flathead National Forest, Hungry Horse Ranger District, (406) 387-3800.

Activities: Hiking, fishing, boating.

Finding the campground: Take US Highway 2 northeast out of Kalispell for about 23 miles to Hungry Horse. Turn right onto paved Forest Road 895 southeast out of Hungry Horse and travel for 35 miles. FR 895 is gravel for the last 20 miles of this access. Turn right onto improved dirt Forest Road 897 and travel 2 more miles.

About the campground: With no boat ramp, the boating is limited on these 30 surface acres of water. Tall, thick pine and fir trees engulf the area, with plenty of brush in between. When weather allows, the campground is open from June 1 through September 30.

11 Emery Bay

Location: 30 miles east of Kalispell on Hungry Horse Reservoir.

Facilities: Vault toilets, fire rings, tables, drinking water.

Sites: 26 for tents or RVs/Trailer combinations up to 32 feet long.

Fee: $$ per night, 16-day limit.

Managing agency: Valley Campgrounds; Kalispell office, (406) 309-2018.

Activities: Hiking, fishing, boating.

Finding the campground: Take US Highway 2 northeast out of Kalispell for about 23 miles to Hungry Horse. Continue on US 2 through Hungry Horse for 0.5 mile. Turn right at the East Side Hungry Horse Reservoir sign and travel 6 miles. The road turns to gravel in about 1 mile.

About the campground: Campers and pine trees alike look over the bluff onto the blue waters of Hungry Horse Lake. Thick brush and young fir trees, along with tall grass, fill the areas in between sites. The campground is open from mid-May through September 30.

12 Murray Bay

Location: 45 miles east of Kalispell on Hungry Horse Reservoir.

Facilities: Vault toilets, fire rings, tables, drinking water, boat ramp.

Sites: 20 for tents or RVs up to 22 feet long.

Fee: $$ per night, 16-day limit.

Managing agency: Flathead Valley Campgrounds; Kalispell office, (406) 309-2018.

Activities: Hiking, fishing, boating.

Finding the campground: Take US Highway 2 northeast out of Kalispell for about 23 miles to Hungry Horse. Continue on US 2 through Hungry Horse for 0.5 mile. Turn right at the East Side Hungry Horse Reservoir sign and travel 22 miles. The road turns to gravel in about 1 mile and becomes Forest Road 38.

About the campground: This campground spreads out on a bluff along the east shore of Hungry Horse Lake. Fir and larch trees outlining roadways and parking units that can get very narrow await the traveler. Those with large RVs best not attempt navigating this spot. It can be done, but not without grief. The campground is open from mid-May through September 18.

13 Spotted Bear

Location: 78 miles southeast of Kalispell on the Spotted Bear River.
Facilities: Vault toilet, fire rings, tables, drinking water.
Sites: 13 for tents, RVs/Trailers up to 32 feet long.
Fee: $ per night, 14-day limit.
Managing agency: Flathead National Forest, Spotted Bear Ranger District, (406) 758-5376.
Activities: Hiking, fishing, wildlife viewing.
Finding the campground: Take US Highway 2 northeast out of Kalispell for about 23 miles to Hungry Horse. Continue on US 2 through Hungry Horse for 0.5 mile. Turn right at the East Side Hungry Horse Reservoir sign and travel 55 miles. The road turns into Forest Road 38 and deteriorates from gravel to very rough dirt.
About the campground: It is a long, rough road to this pleasant spot. Fir trees combine with larch to provide shade and scenic quality along the river. When weather allows, the opening date is May 25, but it could be as late as June 20. The campground can close as early as September 20. When the snow flies and things close up, the Spotted Bear Ranger District closes up as well.

14 Glacier National Park: Apgar

Location: 35 miles northeast of Kalispell on Lake McDonald.
Facilities: Flush toilets, fire rings, tables, drinking water, boat ramp.
Sites: 194 for tents or RVs/Trailer combinations up to 40 feet long).
Fee: $$ per night (not including $$$ park entrance fee); 14-day limit.
Managing agency: National Park Service, (406) 888-7800.
Activities: Hiking, fishing, boating, wildlife viewing.
Finding the campground: Take US Highway 2 northeast out of Kalispell for 33 miles to West Glacier. Turn left at the entrance and travel 2 miles.
About the campground: Majestic just does not fully describe the quality of scenery and awesome size presented in this international park. This campground settles in along the southern shoreline of Lake McDonald, with stores and other amenities very close by. Boat rentals are available along with horseback rides, restaurants, motels, and gift stores. Firewood cannot be gathered along roads or near developed campgrounds. Fires must be in fire grates at designated areas. Lofty, snowcapped mountains loom above the lake, with cedar and other assorted mountain trees blanketing the lower portions. The campground is open from May 9 through October 20, but only if winter does not hang on too tightly or return too soon. Camping without services is allowed outside these dates when road conditions allow.

15 Glacier National Park: Fish Creek

Location: 40 miles northeast of Kalispell.
Facilities: Flush toilets, fire rings, tables, drinking water.

Sites: 5 for tents only with no electricity, 173 for tents or RVs/Trailer combinations up to 35 feet long.

Fee: $$$ per night (not including park entrance fee $$$); 14-day limit.

Managing agency: National Park Service, (406) 888–7800.

Activities: Hiking, wildlife viewing.

Finding the campground: Take US Highway 2 northeast out of Kalispell for 33 miles to West Glacier. Turn left at the entrance and travel 2 miles to Apgar. Take paved Camas Road northwest for 5 miles.

About the campground: There are a few back-in sites, but most units are pull-through. Electricity is available in 168 of the units. Lake McDonald settles into the valley less than 1 mile away. Mature fir and other bushy evergreens snuggle up to the parking units in this fairyland setting. The campground is situated near the north shore of the southern part of the lake. Typically the season runs from June 20 through September 2.

16 Glacier National Park: Quartz Creek

Location: 65 miles northeast of Kalispell on Quartz Creek.

Facilities: Vault toilets, fire rings, tables.

Sites: 7 for tents or RVs up to 21 feet long.

Fee: $ per night (not including $$$ park entrance fee); 14-day limit.

Managing agency: National Park Service, (406) 888–7800.

Activities: Hiking, fishing, wildlife viewing.

Finding the campground: Take US Highway 2 northeast out of Kalispell for 33 miles to West Glacier. Turn left at the entrance and travel 2 miles to Apgar. Take paved Camas Road northwest for 11 miles. Continue on the gravel-becoming-paved Outside North Fork Road for 13 miles. Take the dirt Inside North Fork Road southeast out of Polebridge for 6 miles.

About the campground: This is defined as a primitive camping area with good reason. When your drinking water is gone and the camp stove is out of fuel it is a long trek to get them replenished. Tent campers and small camping units are best here. In fact, any units longer than 21 feet are prohibited. The campground is open from June 29 through October 28.

17 Glacier National Park: Logging Creek

Location: 67 miles northeast of Kalispell on Logging Creek.

Facilities: Vault toilet, fire rings, tables.

Sites: 7 for tents or RVs up to 21 feet long.

Fee: $ per night (not including $$$ park entrance fee); 14-day limit.

Managing agency: National Park Service, (406) 888–7800.

Activities: Hiking, fishing, wildlife viewing.

Finding the campground: Take US Highway 2 northeast out of Kalispell for 33 miles to West Glacier. Turn left at the entrance and travel 2 miles to Apgar. Take paved Camas Road northwest for 11 miles. Continue on the gravel-becoming-paved Outside North Fork Road for 13 miles. Take the dirt Inside North Fork Road southeast out of Polebridge for 8 miles.

About the campground: This is defined as a primitive camping area with good reason. When your drinking water is gone and the camp stove is out of fuel, it is a long trek to get them replenished. Tent campers and small camping units are best here. In fact, units longer than 21 feet are prohibited. The campground is open from June 29 through October 28.

18 Glacier National Park: Bowman Lake

Location: 65 miles northeast of Kalispell on Bowman Lake.
Facilities: Vault toilets, fire rings, tables, drinking water (seasonal), boat ramp.
Sites: 46 for tents or RVs up to 21 feet long.
Fee: $$ per night (not including $$$ park entrance fee); 14-day limit.
Managing agency: National Park Service, (406) 888–7800.
Activities: Hiking, fishing, boating, wildlife viewing.
Finding the campground: Take US Highway 2 northeast out of Kalispell for 33 miles to West Glacier. Turn left at the entrance and travel 2 miles to Apgar. Take paved Camas Road northwest for 11 miles. Continue on the gravel-becoming-paved Outside North Fork Road for 13 miles. Take the dirt Inside North Fork Road northeast out of Polebridge for 6 miles.
About the campground: This is not the place for those in a hurry or with time constraints. The road will test patience, endurance, and vehicle strength to the max. Units longer than 21 feet are prohibited as well. Glaciers hug the lofty mountainsides looming over the ice-cold waters of Bowman Lake. Conifers of all types cling to the shoreline in places and march as high as possible until rocks and ice take over. If the snow melts off and arrives in normal fashion, the campground has two seasons. The main season is from May 18 through September 9, with drinking water available. The primitive season runs from September 10 through October 31, with a lower fee and no drinking water.

19 Glacier National Park: Kintla Lake

Location: 74 miles north of Kalispell on Kintla Lake.
Facilities: Vault toilets, fire rings, tables, drinking water.
Sites: 13 for tents or RVs up to 21 feet long.
Fee: $$ per night (not including $$$ park entrance fee); 14-day limit.
Managing agency: National Park Service, (406) 888–7800.
Activities: Hiking, fishing, boating, wildlife viewing.
Finding the campground: Take US Highway 2 northeast out of Kalispell for 33 miles to West Glacier. Turn left at the entrance and travel 2 miles to Apgar. Take paved Camas Road northwest for 11 miles. Continue on the gravel-becoming-paved Outside North Fork Road for 13 miles. Take the dirt Inside North Fork Road northeast out of Polebridge for 15 miles.

About the campground: As with the sites listed above, units longer than 21 feet are prohibited; if your unit fits that description, this is not your place. Kintla Lake is very similar to the Bowman Lake area (campground 18) but with a different perspective. The fewer number of units tends to indicate that the longer travel distance is not worth the grief. The campground has three distinct seasons. The main summer season runs from June 4 through September 9, with a higher fee. The primitive seasons run from May 29 through June 3 and September 10 through October 31.

20 Glacier National Park: Sprague Creek

Location: 43 miles northeast of Kalispell on Lake McDonald.
Facilities: Flush toilets, fire rings, tables, drinking water.
Sites: 25 for tents.
Fee: $$ per night (not including $$$ park entrance fee); 14-day limit.
Managing agency: National Park Service, (406) 888-7800.
Activities: Hiking, fishing, wildlife viewing.
Finding the campground: Take US Highway 2 northeast out of Kalispell for 33 miles to West Glacier. Turn left at the entrance and travel 2 miles to Apgar. Take paved Going-to-the-Sun Road for 8 miles.
About the campground: Traffic noise does penetrate the camping area, but all is forgiven when silence arrives later in the evening. Mature cedar trees shelter this campground and blanket the surrounding area on the lake shoreline. In between trees and in open spaces, glacier-bearing mountains emerge triumphantly. Sprague Creek bubbles by on its way to Lake McDonald, adding to the overall experience. Towed units cannot enter here. Reservations are not accepted and the campground fills early, so if it's late in the afternoon don't plan on staying here. It is open from May 30 through September 16 when the winter lets go or holds back, depending upon the time of year.

21 Glacier National Park: Avalanche

Location: 51 miles northeast of Kalispell on Avalanche Creek.
Facilities: Flush toilets, fire rings, tables, drinking water.
Sites: 87 for tents or RVs/Trailer combinations up to 26 feet long.
Fee: $$ per night (not including $$$ park entrance fee); 14-day limit.
Managing agency: National Park Service, (406) 888-7800.
Activities: Hiking, fishing, wildlife viewing.
Finding the campground: Take US Highway 2 northeast out of Kalispell for 33 miles to West Glacier. Turn left at the entrance and travel 2 miles to Apgar. Take paved Going-to-the-Sun Road for 16 miles.
About the campground: Glaciers, clear water, cedar trees, and lots of wildlife beckon to the traveler. Avalanche Lake is a 2-mile hike one-way. Boat rides and other related activities are available at nearby Lake McDonald. The campground is open from June 22 through September 8.

22 Devil Creek

Location: 68 miles east of Kalispell near Devil Creek.
Facilities: Vault toilets, fire rings, tables, drinking water.
Sites: 14 for tents, RVs/Trailer combinations up to 44 feet long. (*Note:* All sites require backing in; if that is an issue, another campground is advised.)
Fee: $ per night, 16-day limit.
Managing agency: Flathead. Valley Campgrounds; Kalispell office, (406) 309-2018
Activities: Hiking, fishing.
Finding the campground: Take US Highway 2 northeast out of Kalispell then southeast for 68 miles.
About the campground: Lodgepole pine trees just off the main highway provide shade and some firewood. The gravel parking units are level, but some backing skills are needed for towed units. The railroad on the north side of the highway is obviously active, complete with regular train horn blasts. If trains and traffic do not bother you, this is a very pleasant place. This is a jumping off point for the Great Bear Wilderness. The campground is open from Memorial Day through Labor Day, weather permitting.

23 Summit

Location: 78 miles east of Kalispell.
Facilities: Vault toilet, fire rings, tables, drinking water.
Sites: 17 for tents or RVs up to 36 feet long. (*Note:* Units are available that are wide enough to allow unhooking a trailer and then parking the towing unit beside it.)
Fee: $ per night, 14-day limit.
Managing agency: Lewis and Clark National Forest, Rocky Mountain Ranger District, (406) 466-5341.
Activities: Hiking.
Finding the campground: Take US Highway 2 northeast out of Kalispell then southeast for 78 miles.
About the campground: This campground sits on the Continental Divide. Any rain dripping off the pine trees flows either west to the Pacific Ocean or east to the Atlantic, depending upon which side of the divide it drips on. Two loops present a choice for campers, and nearby historical sites beckon to the curious. The campground is open in the summer as the weather permits.

24 Glacier National Park: Two Medicine

Location: 104 miles northeast of Kalispell on Two Medicine Lake.
Facilities: Flush toilets, fire rings, tables, drinking water, boat ramp.

Sites: 100 for tents or RVs/Trailer combinations up to 35 feet long.

Fee: $$ per night (not including $$$ park entrance fee); 14-day limit.

Managing agency: National Park Service, (406) 888–7800.

Activities: Hiking, fishing, boating.

Finding the campground: Take US Highway 2 northeast out of Kalispell then southeast for 89 miles. Turn left onto Montana State Highway 49 at East Glacier and travel 3 miles. Turn left onto the park road and travel 12 miles.

About the campground: The majestic mountains overwhelm forest and lake alike with no shortage of ice. Ancient-looking spruce trees and water bluer than a summer sky meet the eye. The campground is open from mid-May through mid-September, weather permitting.

25 Glacier National Park: Cutbank

Location: 110 miles northeast of Kalispell.

Facilities: Vault toilet, fire rings, tables.

Sites: 14 for tents, RVs and/or vehicle-trailer combinations are not recommended.

Fee: $ per night (not including $$$ park entrance fee); 14-day limit.

Managing agency: National Park Service, (406) 888–7800.

Activities: Hiking, wildlife viewing.

Finding the campground: Take US Highway 2 northeast out of Kalispell then southeast for 89 miles. Turn left onto Montana State Highway 49 at East Glacier and travel 12 miles. Turn left onto US Highway 89 and travel 5 miles. Turn left onto dirt Cutbank Creek Road and travel 5 miles.

About the campground: This campground is considered a primitive camping area with no drinking water available, be sure to bring plenty. Backpackers are attracted to this location and its numerous nearby trails. The campground is situated on a bench with an open field and a lot of scenery. The campground is open from May 1 through September 23, weather permitting.

26 Glacier National Park: St. Mary Lake

Location: 121 miles northeast of Kalispell on St. Mary Lake.

Facilities: Flush toilets, fire rings, tables, drinking water.

Sites: 7 for tents, 140 for RVs/Trailer combinations that vary in length from 24 to 37 feet long, plus 1 for 40 feet long.

Fee: $$$ per night (not including $$$ park entrance fee); 14-day limit.

Managing agency: St. Mary Lake Campground, (406) 732-7708.

Activities: Hiking, fishing, boating.

Finding the campground: Take US Highway 2 northeast out of Kalispell then southeast for 89 miles. Turn left onto Montana State Highway 49 at East Glacier and travel 12 miles. Turn left onto US Highway 89 and travel 19 miles. Turn left onto Going-to-the-Sun Road at St. Mary and travel 1 mile.

About the campground: Water recreation, along with a store and a cafe, are within 1 mile. There is no wheelchair access. There is limited shade here, but the views are unhindered. The campground is open from June 1 through September 3.

27 Glacier National Park: Rising Sun

Location: 126 miles northeast of Kalispell on St. Mary Lake.
Facilities: Flush toilets, fire rings, tables, drinking water.
Sites: 84 for tents, RVs/Trailer combinations up to 25 feet long.
Fee: $$ per night (not including $$$ park entrance fee); 14-day limit.
Managing agency: National Park Service, (406) 888–7800.
Activities: Hiking, fishing, boating, wildlife viewing.
Finding the campground: Take US Highway 2 northeast out of Kalispell then southeast for 89 miles. Turn left onto Montana State Highway 49 at East Glacier and travel 12 miles. Turn left onto US Highway 89 and travel 19 miles. Turn left onto Going-to-the-Sun Road at St. Mary and travel 6 miles.
About the campground: Mountains crowd up against the lake here, with aged spruce trees and an assortment of brush separating pull-through units. A boat ramp and the lake water are within 1 mile of the camping area. Backcountry trails beckon to the adventurous and the curious alike. Keep in mind that vehicles longer than 21 feet must not travel on Going-to-the-Sun Road between Avalanche Campground and the Sun Point parking area near this campground. It is open from June 8 through September 9.

28 Glacier National Park: Many Glacier

Location: 140 miles northeast of Kalispell.
Facilities: Flush toilets, fire rings, tables, drinking water.
Sites: 110 for tents, RVs/Trailer combinations from 15 through 30 feet long. (*Note:* All of the units are narrow pull-throughs not suited for slide-outs; if they are required this is not the place to be.)
Fee: $$$ per night (not including $$$ park entrance fee); 14-day limit.
Managing agency: National Park Service, (406) 888–7800.
Activities: Hiking, fishing, wildlife viewing.
Finding the campground: Take US Highway 2 northeast out of Kalispell then southeast for 89 miles. Turn left onto Montana State Highway 49 at East Glacier and travel 12 miles. Turn left onto US Highway 89 and travel 29 miles. Turn left onto Many Glacier Road at Babb and travel 10 miles.
About the campground: In context with its name, many glaciers are in view with scenic lakes. This is a hiker's paradise, but keep in mind that it is bear country, too. The campground is open from May 23 through September 23.

29 Whitefish Lake State Park

Location: 16 miles north of Kalispell on Whitefish Lake.

Facilities: Flush toilets, showers, fire rings, tables, drinking water, boat ramp.

Sites: 7 for tents and 18 for RVs/Trailer combinations from 18 up to 40 feet long.

Fee: $$ per night, dependent on resident/nonresident status; 7-day limit.

Managing agency: Whitefish State Park; (406) 862-3991 (Apr 15–Oct 15); (406) 751-4590 (Oct 16–Apr 14).

Activities: Fishing, boating.

Finding the campground: Take US Highway 93 north out of Kalispell for 14 miles. Continue on US 93 for 1 mile west of Whitefish. Turn right at the access sign and travel 1 mile.

About the campground: Trains rumble by on a regular basis and, depending upon your point of view, can be either annoying or a pleasant change. Water-skiers and other water sports enthusiasts frequent the area. The scenic backdrops and the lack of wind combined with close access keep the park populated. Mature aspen mix with pine trees in this pleasant spot. Ferns and other assorted bushes fill the spaces in between, helping to provide some privacy. The campground is open from April 1 through November 30.

30 Tally Lake

Location: 33 miles northwest of Kalispell on Tally Lake.

Facilities: Vault toilets, fire rings, tables, drinking water, boat ramp.

Sites: 1 group, 40 for tents or RVs/Trailer combinations from 25 up to 60 feet long. (*Note:* The 60-foot parking areas are pull-throughs; all others are back-in.)

Fee: $$ per night, 16-day limit.

Managing agency: Flathead Valley Campgrounds; Kalispell office, (406) 309-2018.

Activities: Hiking, fishing, boating.

Finding the campground: Take US Highway 93 north out of Kalispell for 14 miles. Continue on US 93 for 4 miles west of Whitefish. Turn left at the sign onto Twin Bridges Road and travel 6 miles. Follow the campground directional signs.

About the campground: Drinking water is available near the entrance, and consequently will require some forethought. Larch and fir trees share the spot. Logan Creek passes through, presenting a choice for anglers, with nearly 1,300 surface acres of lake also available. The campground is open from mid-May through October 1.

Helena Area

Helena inhabits prairie, reservoir, recreation areas, high mountain seclusion, and every other type of landscape in between. Historic ghost towns and ancient log cabins defiantly battle the elements, some with more success than others. Native Americans have left evidence of their campsites, with tepee rings still visible. Abandoned mines have also bequeathed a legacy of relics and spoil piles here, though an active effort is being made to reclaim the land.

Gold can still be found in select spots, but be aware that the better locations are already claimed and prospecting is not welcomed. Gem quality crystals are plentiful and attract many to the area; specific spots are set aside for collecting.

Elk, deer, moose, and other wildlife frequently come into view. Exactly when and where is more a function of the time of year than of location. Keep in mind that the "wild" in wildlife means just that. The animals are not pets, nor do they want to be.

	Group Sites	Tents	RV sites	Total sites	Hookups	Toilets	Showers	Drinking water	Dump station	Phone	Handicap Access	Recreation	Fee	Season	Stay limit (days)
1 Park Lake			22	22		V		*			*	HFB	$	6/15-9/15	14
2 Moose Creek			9	9		V		*				H	$	6/15-9/15	14
3 Cromwell Dixon			7	7		V		*			*	H	$	6/1-9/15	14
4 Kading			14	14		V		*			*	HF	$	6/1-9/15	14
5 Aspen Grove	1		19	19		V		*				HF	$	5/29-10/15	14
6 Copper Creek			20	20		V		*			*	HF	$	5/22-9/30	14
7 Hooper Park			28	28		V		*			*	F	$	4/1-10/30	N
8 Big Nelson			4	4		V						HFB	N	6/15-9/15	14
9 Wood Lake			9	9		V		*				HFB	$	Summer	14
10 Benchmark			25	25		V		*				HFW	$	Summer	14
11 South Fork			7	7		V		*				HF	$	Summer	14
12 Home Gulch			15	15		V		*			*	HF	$	Summer	14
13 Mortimer Gulch			26	26		V		*				HFB	$	Summer	14
14 Hauser Lake/Black Sandy State Park	4		29	33		FV		*				FB	$$	All Year	7
15 Holter Lake			50	50		V		*				FB	$$	Memorial Day to Labor Day	7
16 Log Gulch	2		70	72		V		*				HFB	$$	All Year	7
17 Departure Point			6	6		V						HF	$	All year	7
18 Vigilante			12	12		V		*			*	HF	$	5/15-9/10	14
19 Court Sheriff	4		41	45		V		*			*	HFB	$$	All Year	14
20 Riverside			27	27		V		*			*	HFB	$$	All Year	14
21 Chinaman's Gulch			45	45		V		*			*	HHB	$$	All Year	14
22 Jo Bonner			28	28		V		*			*	HFB	$$	5/15-9/15	14
23 Hellgate			69	69		V		*			*	HFB	$$	5/15-9/15	14
24 White Earth			34	34		V		*			*	HFB	$$	5/1-9/30	14
25 Silos			77	77		V		*			*	HF	$	4/15-9/15	14
26 Indian Road			15	15		V		*			*	F	$	4/15-9/15	14
27 Toston Dam			7	7		V						HFB	N	All Year	14
28 Skidway			11	11		V		*				H	$	6/1-10/1	14

1　Park Lake

Location: 28 miles south of Helena on Park Lake.
Facilities: Vault toilets, fire rings, tables, drinking water.
Sites: 22 for tents or RVs/Trailer combinations up to 50 feet long.

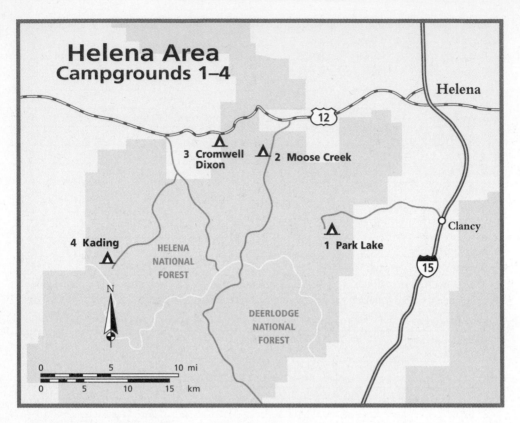

Fee: $ per night, 14-day limit.
Managing agency: Helena National Forest, Helena Ranger District, (406) 449-5490.
Activities: Hiking, fishing, boating.
Finding the campground: Take I-15 south out of Helena for 10 miles to Clancy/exit 182. Take gravel Lump Gulch Road west out of Clancy for 10 miles. Stay to the right on the Corral Gulch Road and travel 6 miles. Turn left onto gravel Forest Road 4009 and travel about 2 miles.
About the campground: About 5 surface acres of water settle into the pines, and there is a plentiful supply of boulders of all sizes. Boating is limited to nonmotorized vessels, with no boat ramp. If the weather allows it, the campground is open from June 15 through September 15.

2 Moose Creek

Location: 14 miles west of Helena.
Facilities: Vault toilets, fire rings, tables, drinking water.
Sites: 9 for tents or RVs/Trailer combinations up to 22 feet long.
Fee: $ per night, 14-day limit.
Managing agency: Helena National Forest, Helena Ranger District, (406) 449-5490.
Activities: Hiking.

Finding the campground: Take US Highway 12 west out of Helena for 10 miles. Turn left onto gravel Rimini Road and travel 4 miles.

About the campground: Tall lodgepole pine trees shade campers very well. The campground is open from June 15 through September 15.

3 Cromwell Dixon

Location: 15 miles west of Helena.

Facilities: Vault toilets, fire rings, tables, drinking water.

Sites: 7 for tents or RVs/Trailer combinations up to 30 feet long.

Fee: $ per night, 14-day limit.

Managing agency: Helena National Forest, Helena Ranger District, (406) 449-5490.

Activities: Hiking.

Finding the campground: Take US Highway 12 west out of Helena for 15 miles.

About the campground: This campground sits on MacDonald Pass, with grassy mountain meadows surrounding an island of pine trees hiding it. Traffic noise can be significant during the daylight hours, but it tends to drop off at night. Snow accumulation may alter the June 1 through September 15 season. Be sure to have warm clothing, as this elevation experiences dramatic temperature changes.

4 Kading

Location: 37 miles west of Helena on the Little Blackfoot River.

Facilities: Vault toilets, fire rings, tables, drinking water.

Sites: 14 for tents or RVs/Trailer combinations up to 24 feet long.

Fee: $, 14-day limit.

Managing agency: Helena National Forest, Helena Ranger District, (406) 449-5490.

Activities: Hiking, fishing.

Finding the campground: Take US Highway 12 west out of Helena for 24 miles. Turn left onto County Road 3 and travel 4 miles. Turn right onto gravel Forest Road 227 and travel 9 miles.

About the campground: Tall lodgepole pines engulf the area, including the campground. Brook trout invite anglers and ice-cold water tempts waders on a hot day. Parking units are well spaced for a sense of seclusion or privacy, depending on your point of view. The campground is open from June 1 through September 15.

5 Aspen Grove

Location: 44 miles northwest of Helena on the Blackfoot River.

Facilities: Vault toilets, fire rings, tables, drinking water.

Sites: 1 group, 19 for tents or RVs/Trailer combinations up to 35 feet long.

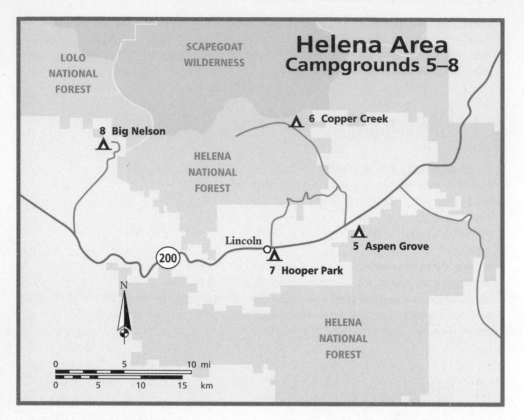

Fee: $ per night, 14-day limit.
Managing agency: Helena National Forest, Lincoln Ranger District, (406) 362-7000.
Activities: Hiking, fishing.
Finding the campground: Take I-15 north out of Helena for about 7 miles to Lincoln Road/exit 200. Turn left onto Montana State Highway 279 and travel 32 miles. Turn left onto Montana State Highway 200 and travel about 5 miles.
About the campground: Cottonwood trees shade campers and the Blackfoot River in this canyon setting. Rock cliffs and fir trees outline the nearby horizon. The campground tentatively opens on May 29 and closes on October 15.

6 Copper Creek

Location: 53 miles northwest of Helena on Copper Creek.
Facilities: Vault toilets, fire rings, tables, drinking water.
Sites: 20 for tents or RVs/Trailer combinations up to 40 feet long.
Fee: $ per night, 14-day limit.
Managing agency: Helena National Forest, Lincoln Ranger District, (406) 362-7000.

Activities: Hiking, fishing.

Finding the campground: Take I-15 north out of Helena for about 7 miles to Lincoln Road/exit 200. Turn left onto Montana State Highway 279 and travel 32 miles. Turn left onto Montana State Highway 200 and travel about 6 miles. Turn right onto gravel Copper Creek Road/Forest Road 330 and travel about 8 miles.

About the campground: Lodgepole pine trees dominate the area but share it with Douglas fir at various locations. Nearby Snowbank Lake is very scenic and offers an opportunity for anglers to test their skills. The campground loop includes a respectable amount of space between units. The road does deteriorate toward the end, and negotiating it can be a test of nerves. If the snowfall does not exceed normal levels, the campground is open from May 22 through September 30.

7 Hooper Park

Location: 49 miles northwest of Helena on the Blackfoot River.

Facilities: Vault toilets, drinking water.

Sites: 28 for tents or RVs/Trailer combinations up to 25 feet long.

Fee: $ per night, no stay limit.

Managing agency: City of Lincoln, (406) 362-4949.

Activities: Fishing.

Finding the campground: Take I-15 north out of Helena for about 7 miles to Lincoln Road/exit 200. Turn left onto Montana State Highway 279 and travel 32 miles. Turn left onto Montana State Highway 200 and travel about 10 miles to Lincoln.

About the campground: The Blackfoot River glides peacefully past this mountain town and entices anglers to try their luck. Units are available from April 1 through October 30.

8 Big Nelson

Location: 70 miles northwest of Helena on Coopers Lake.

Facilities: Vault toilet, fire rings, tables, boat launch.

Sites: 4 for tents or RVs up to 16 feet long.

Fee: None, 14-day limit.

Managing agency: Lolo National Forest, Seeley Lake Ranger District, (406) 677-2233.

Activities: Hiking, fishing, boating.

Finding the campground: Take I-15 north out of Helena for about 7 miles to Lincoln Road/exit 200. Turn left onto Montana State Highway 279 and travel 32 miles. Turn left onto Montana State Highway 200 and travel about 20 miles. Turn right onto gravel Forest Road 500 and travel 11 miles.

About the campground: Boating on Coopers Lake is the main attraction here. Hiking is limited because of the large amount of private land surrounding the campground. The area is open from June 15 through September 15, weather permitting.

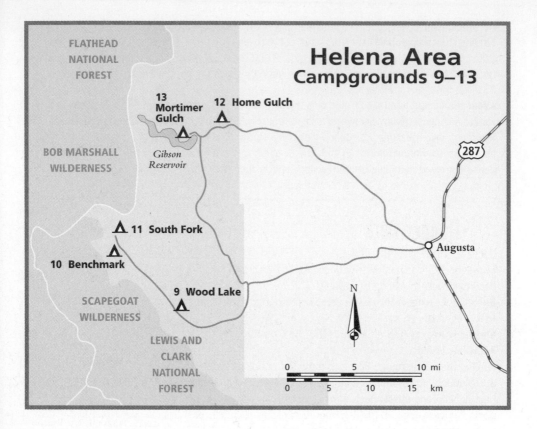

9 Wood Lake

Location: 99 miles northwest of Helena on Wood Lake.

Facilities: Vault toilet, fire rings, tables, drinking water.

Sites: 9 for tents or RVs/Trailer combinations up to 22 feet long.

Fee: $ per night, 14-day limit.

Managing agency: Lewis and Clark National Forest, Rocky Mountain Ranger District, (406) 466-5341.

Activities: Hiking, fishing, boating.

Finding the campground: Take I-15 north out of Helena for 36 miles to Wolf Creek/exit 228. Take US Highway 287 north for 39 miles to Augusta. Take gravel/dirt Benchmark Road/Forest Road 235 west out of Augusta for 24 miles.

About the campground: Wood Creek slows and settles into a small lake at this campground. Scenic views and wildlife make the journey even more special, especially after eating the dust for so long. Motorized boats are not permitted on the lake, making it especially attractive for canoeing. Like other campgrounds in the area, weather dictates when it will open and close.

10 Benchmark

Location: 105 miles northwest of Helena on Wood Creek.
Facilities: Vault toilets, fire rings, tables, drinking water.
Sites: 25 for tents or RVs/Trailer combinations up to 35 feet long.
Fee: $ per night, 14-day limit.
Managing agency: Lewis and Clark National Forest, Rocky Mountain Ranger District, (406) 466-5341.
Activities: Hiking, fishing, wildlife viewing.
Finding the campground: Take I-15 north out of Helena for 36 miles to Wolf Creek/exit 228. Take US Highway 287 north for 39 miles to Augusta. Take gravel/dirt Benchmark Road/Forest Road 235 west out of Augusta for 30 miles.
About the campground: Aspen trees are scattered among the pines here. There are three loops, two of which have feeding troughs for horses that pass through to the wilderness. Longer units can fit, but accommodating horse trailers is the primary function of the spacious parking areas. The camping season can vary depending upon the weather.

11 South Fork

Location: 106 miles northwest of Helena near the South Fork Sun River.
Facilities: Vault toilet, fire rings, tables, drinking water.
Sites: 7 for tents or RVs/Trailer combinations up to 22 feet long.
Fee: $ per night, 14-day limit.
Managing agency: Lewis and Clark National Forest, Rocky Mountain Ranger District, (406) 466-5341.
Activities: Hiking, fishing.
Finding the campground: Take I-15 north out of Helena for 36 miles to Wolf Creek/exit 228. Take US Highway 287 north for 39 miles to Augusta. Take gravel/dirt Benchmark Road/Forest Road 235 west out of Augusta for 31 miles.
About the campground: This wilderness access can have many visitors. Wildlife, conifers, and majestic mountains combine in an unforgettable panorama for photographs and memories. The weather dictates when this area is open or closed, and in this country, the calendar does not always identify the actual day summer starts.

12 Home Gulch

Location: 96 miles northwest of Helena on the North Fork Sun River.
Facilities: Vault toilet, fire rings, tables, drinking water.
Sites: 15 for tents or RVs/Trailer combinations up to 45 feet long.
Fee: $ per night, 14-day limit.

Managing agency: Lewis and Clark National Forest, Rocky Mountain Ranger District, (406) 466–5341.

Activities: Hiking, fishing.

Finding the campground: Take I–15 north out of Helena for 36 miles to Wolf Creek/exit 228. Take US Highway 287 north for 39 miles to Augusta. Turn left onto Manix Street and travel about 4 miles. Turn right at the directional sign for Gibson Reservoir onto dirt Gibson Reservoir Road and travel 15 miles. Continue on paved Forest Road 108 for 2 miles.

About the campground: Aspen and alder trees overlook the river and shade parking units between two towering cliffs at this spot. Not all the parking spots accommodate longer vehicles, so if your trailer fits, the spot is yours. The campground is open when the weather allows it.

13 Mortimer Gulch

Location: 101 miles northwest of Helena at Gibson Reservoir.

Facilities: Vault toilets, fire rings, tables, drinking water.

Sites: 26 for tents or RVs/Trailer combinations up to 45 feet long.

Fee: $ per night, 14-day limit.

Managing agency: Lewis and Clark National Forest, Rocky Mountain Ranger District, (406) 466–5341.

Activities: Hiking, fishing, boating.

Finding the campground: Take I–15 north out of Helena for 36 miles to Wolf Creek/exit 228. Take US Highway 287 north for 39 miles to Augusta. Turn left onto Manix Street and travel about 4 miles. Turn right at the directional sign for Gibson Reservoir onto dirt Gibson Reservoir Road and travel 15 miles. Continue on paved Forest Road 108 for 7 miles.

About the campground: Gibson Reservoir impounds enough water to create nearly 1,300 surface acres. The boat ramp, which is within 1 mile, requires a four-wheel drive. Two loops offer campers a choice between aspen in the lower units or fir trees in the upper units. After traveling over the dirt portion of the access, the level, paved parking is quite a treat. As with the other campgrounds in the area, weather dictates the season.

14 Hauser Lake/Black Sandy State Park

Location: 14 miles northeast of Helena on the Missouri River.

Facilities: Vault and flush toilets, fire rings, tables, drinking water, boat ramp.

Sites: 4 for tents and 29 for RVs/Trailer combinations up to 50 feet long.

Fee: $$ per night, 7-day limit.

Managing agency: Black Sandy State Park (direct line), (406) 458-3221.

Activities: Fishing, boating.

Finding the campground: Take I–15 north out of Helena for 7 miles to Lincoln Road/exit 200. Turn right onto paved Montana State Highway 453 and travel 4 miles. Turn left onto Hauser Dam Road and travel 3 miles.

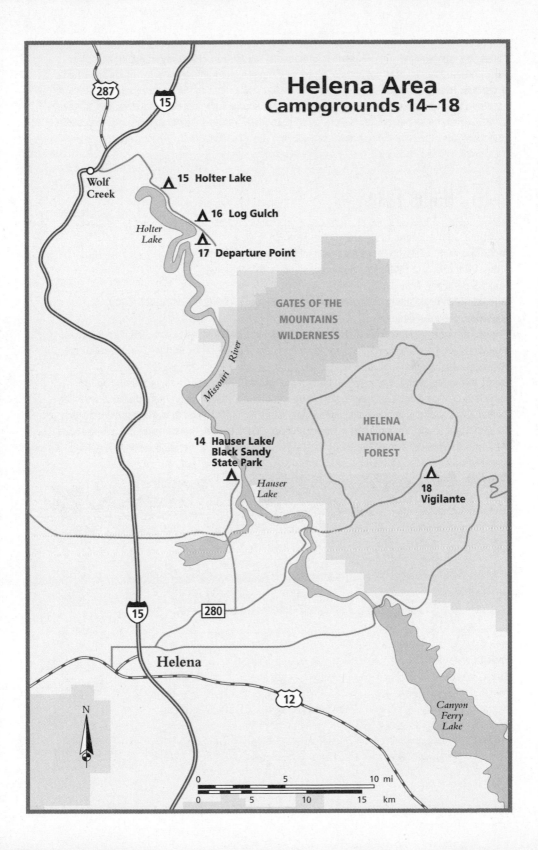

Helena Area
Campgrounds 14–18

287

15

Wolf Creek

△ 15 Holter Lake

△ 16 Log Gulch

Holter Lake

△ 17 Departure Point

Missouri River

GATES OF THE MOUNTAINS WILDERNESS

HELENA NATIONAL FOREST

14 Hauser Lake/ Black Sandy State Park

△

Hauser Lake

△ 18 Vigilante

15

280

Helena

12

Canyon Ferry Lake

N

0		5		10 mi
0	5		10	15 km

About the campground: The Hauser Dam impounds the Missouri River within rolling hills. Pine trees and an assortment of sagebrush, along with other related foliage, occupy roughly one half of the hillsides. Cottonwood trees along the shoreline are limited to the camping area. Units here are close together and quite often unavailable. Water sports are the main attraction, and, consequently, all of the associated noises are present. The types of noise generated are dictated by the time of year, as the campground never closes.

15 Holter Lake

Location: 40 miles north of Helena on the Missouri River.
Facilities: Vault toilets, fire rings, tables, drinking water, boat ramp.
Sites: 50 for tents or RV/Trailer combinations up to 40 feet long.
Fee: $$ per night, 7-day limit.
Managing agency: Bureau of Land Management, Butte Field Office, (406) 533-7600.
Activities: Fishing, boating.
Finding the campground: Take I-15 north out of Helena for 34 miles to exit 226. Turn left onto Missouri River Road and travel 3 miles. Just after crossing Wolf Creek Bridge, turn right onto the access road and travel 3 miles.
About the campground: Water sports bring many visitors to this spot. Rolling prairie spotted with clumps of pine trees and sagebrush close in on Holter Reservoir, granting precious little flat ground. Consequently, campers find little wiggle room. If boating or other water-related activities are important to you, the cramped quarters probably won't matter. The campground is open from Memorial Day through Labor Day.

More than one angler visits the water below Holter Lake.

16 Log Gulch

Location: 44 miles north of Helena on the Missouri River.
Facilities: Vault toilets, fire rings, tables, drinking water, boat ramp.
Sites: 2 tent, 70 for tents or RVs/Trailer combinations up to 50 feet long.
Fee: $$ per night, 7-day limit.
Managing agency: Bureau of Land Management, Butte Field Office, (406) 235-4480.
Activities: Hiking, fishing, boating.
Finding the campground: Take I-15 north out of Helena for 34 miles to exit 226. Turn left onto Missouri River Road and travel 3 miles. Just after crossing Wolf Creek Bridge, turn right onto the access road and travel 7 miles.
About the campground: This campground is a continuation of the main Holter Lake unit, with a little more gravel road to traverse. The lack of boat slips and large amount of dust tend to make this campground less appealing, at least for those heavily involved with boating. The campground is a bit farther away from the obvious private residences you will pass along the access, but be careful. If you are not sure about the ownership of the land you are on, it would be best to avoid it. Private land does not have to be posted for owners to enforce trespass laws. The campground is open all year long.

17 Departure Point

Location: 45 miles north of Helena on the Missouri River.
Facilities: Vault toilet, fire rings, tables.
Sites: 6 for tents or RVs/Trailer combinations up to 50 feet long.
Fee: $ per night, 7-day limit.
Managing agency: Bureau of Land Management, Butte Field Office, (406) 235-4480.
Activities: Hiking, fishing.
Finding the campground: Take I-15 north out of Helena for 34 miles to exit 226. Turn left onto Missouri River Road and travel 3 miles. Just after crossing Wolf Creek Bridge, turn right onto the access road and travel 8 miles.
About the campground: Camping seems a bit more the option here, even though water recreation still dominates. The dusty access and lack of firewood, however, do not make this campground the first choice for those who prefer lofty mountains and the smell of evergreens on a whispering wind. Nonetheless, a warm summer night could make for pleasant memories under a star-filled sky. The campground is open all year long; however, the services freeze up along with the cold temperatures of winter.

18 Vigilante

Location: 32 miles northeast of Helena on Trout Creek.
Facilities: Vault toilets, fire rings, tables, drinking water.

Sites: 12 for tents or RVs/Trailer combinations up to 40 feet long.
Fee: $ per night, 14-day limit.
Managing agency: Helena National Forest, Helena Ranger District, (406) 449–5490.
Activities: Hiking, fishing.
Finding the campground: Take Montana State Highway 280 northeast out of Helena for 20 miles. Continue northeast on County Road for 12 miles.
About the campground: Pine trees populate the campground but do not dominate it. Grass and an abundance of various types of brush occupy the spaces between. Firewood is scarce, so bring plenty for the campfire. The campground is open from May 15 through September 10.

19 Canyon Ferry Reservoir: Court Sheriff

Location: 18 miles northeast of Helena on Canyon Ferry Lake.
Facilities: Vault toilets, fire rings, tables, drinking water, boat ramp.
Sites: 4 for tent, 41 for RVs/Trailer combinations up to 55 feet long including 3 pull-throughs that can accommodate longer units.
Fee: $$ per night, 14-day limit.
Managing agency: Bureau of Reclamation, Project Office (406) 475–3291.
Activities: Hiking, fishing, boating.
Finding the campground: Take US Highway 287 east out of Helena for 9 miles. Turn left onto paved Montana State Highway 284 and travel 9 miles.
About the campground: A four-wheel-drive vehicle is recommended for the boat ramp here. This tends to lessen the impact on the area, but on a hot summer day, you would be hard-pressed to prove it. The campground is open all year long.

20 Canyon Ferry Reservoir: Riverside

Location: 19 miles northeast of Helena on the Missouri River.
Facilities: Vault toilets, fire rings, tables, drinking water, boat ramp.
Sites: 27 for tents or RVs/Trailer combinations up to 40 feet long.
Fee: $$ per night, 14-day limit.
Managing agency: Bureau of Reclamation, Project Office (406) 475–3921.
Activities: Hiking, fishing, boating.
Finding the campground: Take US Highway 287 east out of Helena for 9 miles. Turn left onto paved Montana State Highway 284 and travel 9 miles. Turn left onto gravel Forest Road 224 and travel 1 mile.
About the campground: There are not many trees at this site, but river access is excellent. Water sports are the main attraction, so this area can fill up on hot summer days. The campground is open all year long.

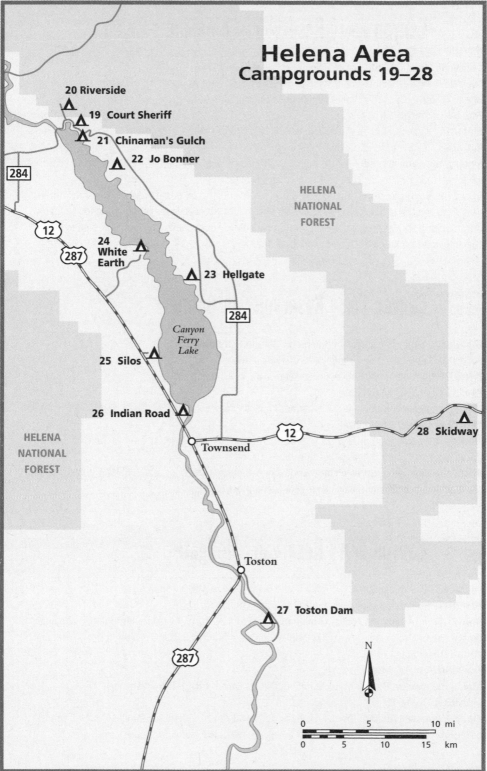

Helena Area
Campgrounds 19–28

20 Riverside

19 Court Sheriff

21 Chinaman's Gulch

22 Jo Bonner

284

12

287

24 White Earth

23 Hellgate

284

HELENA NATIONAL FOREST

Canyon Ferry Lake

25 Silos

26 Indian Road

Townsend

12

28 Skidway

HELENA NATIONAL FOREST

Toston

27 Toston Dam

287

N

| 0 | | 5 | | 10 mi |
| 0 | 5 | 10 | 15 | km |

21 Canyon Ferry Reservoir: Chinaman's Gulch

Location: 19 miles northeast of Helena on Canyon Ferry Lake.
Facilities: Vault toilets, fire rings, tables, drinking water, boat ramp.
Sites: 45 for tents or RVs/Trailer combinations up to 32 feet long.
Fee: $$ per night, 14-day limit.
Managing agency: Bureau of Reclamation, Project Office, (406) 475-3921.
Activities: Hiking, fishing, boating.
Finding the campground: Take US Highway 287 east out of Helena for 9 miles. Turn left onto paved Montana State Highway 284 and travel 10 miles.
About the campground: Elm trees and a few cottonwoods offer some shade to campers. Boulders make up the beach, which increases in size as the water recedes in late summer. Numerous ditches testify of previous activity, probably mining. Rockhounds may find some interesting specimens here. The campground is open all year long.

22 Canyon Ferry Reservoir: Jo Bonner

Location: 21 miles northeast of Helena on Canyon Ferry Lake.
Facilities: Vault toilet, fire rings, tables, drinking water.
Sites: 28 for tents or RVs/Trailer combinations up to 40 feet long.
Fee: $$ per night, 14-day limit.
Managing agency: Bureau of Reclamation, Project Office, (406) 475-3291.
Activities: Hiking, fishing, boating.
Finding the campground: Take US Highway 287 east out of Helena for 9 miles. Turn left onto paved Montana State Highway 284 and travel 12 miles.
About the campground: Huge cottonwood trees dominate this spot, which has no boat ramp. The campground is open from May 15 through September 15.

23 Canyon Ferry Reservoir: Hellgate

Location: 27 miles southeast of Helena on Canyon Ferry Lake.
Facilities: Vault toilets, fire rings, tables, drinking water, boat ramp.
Sites: 69 for tents or RVs/Trailer combinations up to 120 feet long. There are pull-through units that accommodate the longer combinations, but the majority are back-in units for combinations up to 50 feet long.
Fee: $$ per night, 14-day limit.
Managing agency: Bureau of Reclamation, Project Office, (406) 475-3291.
Activities: Hiking, fishing, boating.
Finding the campground: Take US Highway 287 east out of Helena for 9 miles. Turn left onto paved Montana State Highway 284 and travel 18 miles. The last 6 miles are gravel.

About the campground: Grass grows where it can, and there are a few trees here and there along this boulder-infested stretch of shoreline. The campground is open from May 15 through September 15.

24 Canyon Ferry Reservoir: White Earth

Location: 24 miles southeast of Helena on Canyon Ferry Lake.
Facilities: Vault toilets, fire rings, tables, drinking water, boat ramp.
Sites: 34 for tents or RVs/Trailer combinations up to 50 feet long.
Fee: $$ per night, 14-day limit.
Managing agency: Bureau of Reclamation, Project Office, (406) 475-3291.
Activities: Hiking, fishing, boating.
Finding the campground: Take US Highway 287 southeast out of Helena for 19 miles. Turn left at the campground sign and travel 5 miles.
About the campground: Canyon Ferry Dam holds the mighty Missouri River back in a large way. This campground is similar to those previously listed, but on the opposite shore of the reservoir. Its short distance from Helena in comparison to other campgrounds makes for a lot of visitors. White Earth is open all year long; however, services are available only from May through September.

25 Canyon Ferry Reservoir: Silos

Location: 26 miles southeast of Helena on Canyon Ferry Lake.
Facilities: Vault toilets, fire rings, tables, drinking water, boat ramp.
Sites: 77 for tents or RVs/Trailer combinations up to 60 feet long.
Fee: $ per night, 14-day limit.
Managing agency: Bureau of Reclamation, (406) 266-3100.
Activities: Hiking, fishing.
Finding the campground: Take US Highway 287 southeast out of Helena for 25 miles. Turn left at the campground sign and travel 1 mile.
About the campground: Water recreation attracts the majority of visitors here. Late summer after a year of little rainfall can result in a very large beach and not much to look forward to in terms of water sports. The campground is open all year long; however, services are available only from April 15 through September 15.

26 Canyon Ferry Reservoir: Indian Road

Location: 31 miles southeast of Helena on Canyon Ferry Lake.
Facilities: Vault toilets, fire rings, tables, boat ramp.

Sites: 15 for tents or RVs/Trailer combinations up to 40 feet long.
Fee: $, 14-day limit.
Managing agency: Canyon Ferry Visitor Center, (406) 475-3128.
Activities: Fishing.
Finding the campground: Take US Highway 287 southeast out of Helena for 31 miles.
About the campground: Firewood is scarce to nonexistent here. The campground settles along a flat portion of shoreline. It is open all year long; however, services are available only from April 15 through September 15.

27 Toston Dam

Location: 45 miles southeast of Helena on the Missouri River.
Facilities: Vault toilet, fire rings, tables, boat ramp.
Sites: 7 for tents or RVs/Trailer combinations up to 24 feet long.
Fee: None, 14-day limit.
Managing agency: Bureau of Land Management, Butte Field Office, (406) 494-5059.
Activities: Hiking, fishing, boating.
Finding the campground: Take US Highway 287 southeast out of Helena for 45 miles. Turn left at the access sign.
About the campground: Toston Dam holds back a portion of the Missouri River. The rolling prairie has some more prominent hills in this area, but no firewood is available. The campground is open all year long; however, the winters are usually brutal.

28 Skidway

Location: 57 miles southeast of Helena.
Facilities: Vault toilet, fire rings, tables, drinking water.
Sites: 11 for tents or RVs/Trailers up to 16 feet long.
Fee: $, 14-day limit.
Managing agency: Helena National Forest, Townsend Ranger District, (406) 266-3425.
Activities: Hiking.
Finding the campground: Take US Highway 287 southeast out of Helena for 32 miles. In Townsend turn left onto US Highway 12 and travel 23 miles. Turn right onto gravel Forest Road 4042 and travel 2 miles.
About the campground: Hazardous trees resulted in the closure of this campground for the 2018 season. Call ahead in late summer 2019 to see if it's reopened. Shade will be diminished and the scars from the tree removal will likely be visible for a few years, although stars should be more visible. Tall grass abounds in the less-traveled areas and provides feed for local deer. Firewood availability is in question, so it would be best to bring some. Note that it will take some preplanning and extra leveling work to make longer units fit in the uneven grassy parking spots. The campground is open from June 1 through October 1.

Butte Area

History permeates Butte and its environs, which has no shortage of relics. Gold first brought miners into this rich location, but copper soon topped the list. There is still gold and some copper here, along with other metals, but the real treasure is the mountain terrain hiding the majority of the campgrounds.

Wildlife is plentiful so keep the camera handy. A bull moose wandered through the Philipsburg Bay campground at Georgetown Lake during our visit. He very much looked the part of a property owner checking up on tenants.

The majority of campgrounds in this area are off the main roads. Consequently, only the local residents tend to frequent them. This can be both good and bad, but suffice it to say the better ones are full by Friday night.

	Group Sites	Tents	RV sites	Total sites	Hookups	Toilets	Showers	Drinking water	Dump station	Phone	Handicap Access	Recreation	Fee	Season	Stay limit (days)
1 Delmoe Lake			22	22		V		*				HFBS	$	Memorial Day to Labor Day	16
2 Toll Mountain			5	5		V						H	N	Memorial Day to Labor Day	16
3 Pigeon Creek	6			6		V		*				HF	N	5/25-9/15	14
4 Lewis and Clark Caverns State Park			43	43		VF	*	*				HFW	$$	All Year	14
5 Lowland			11	11		V		*			*	HW	$	5/25-9/15	16
6 Mormon Gulch			16	16		P						H	N	5/25-12/1	14
7 Ladysmith	6			6		P						H	N	Memorial Day to Labor Day	14
8 Whitehouse			5	5		P		*				HFW	N	Memorial Day to Labor Day	16
9 Basin Canyon			2	2		P						H	N	5/25-9/15	14
10 Racetrack			13	13		V		*			*	HF	$	Memorial Day to Labor Day	14
11 Orofino			10	10		P						H	N	5/25-9/15	14
12 Lost Creek State Park			25	25		V		*				HFW	$	5/11-11/30	14
13 Warm Springs	6			6		V		*				HF	N	5/25-9/25	14
14 Spring Hill			13	13		V		*				HW	$$	5/25-9/5	16
15 Cable Mountain			11	11		V		*				HF	$$	5/29-9/15	14
16 Lodgepole			31	31		V		*				HF	$$	5/22-9/30	16
17 Philipsburg Bay			66	66		V		*			*	HFWBS	$$	5/15-9/30	16
18 Piney			48	48		V		*			*	HFWBS	$$	5/22-9/15	16
19 Stony			10	10		V		*			*	HFW	N	5/25-9/30	14
20 Flint Creek			16	16		V						HF	N	5/22-9/30	14
21 East Fork			7	7		V		*				HF	N	5/1-9/30	14
22 Spillway			13	13		V		*			*	HFB	N	5/1-11/1	16
23 Copper Creek			7	7		V		*				HF	N	6/15-9/30	14
24 Beaver Dam			15	15		V		*				H	$	6/17-9/30	16

1 Delmoe Lake

Location: 15 miles east of Butte on Lake Delmoe.

Facilities: Vault toilets, fire rings, tables, drinking water, picnic area, boat ramp.

Sites: 25 for tents or RVs/Trailer combinations up to 50 feet long.

Fee: $ per night, 16-day limit.

Managing agency: Deerlodge National Forest, Butte Ranger District, (406) 494-2147.

Activities: Hiking, fishing, boating, swimming.

Finding the campground: Take I-90 east out of Butte for 5 miles to Home-stake/exit 233. Turn left onto improved dirt Forest Road 222 north and travel 9 miles. Turn left at the Delmoe Lake Recreational Area sign and travel 1 mile.

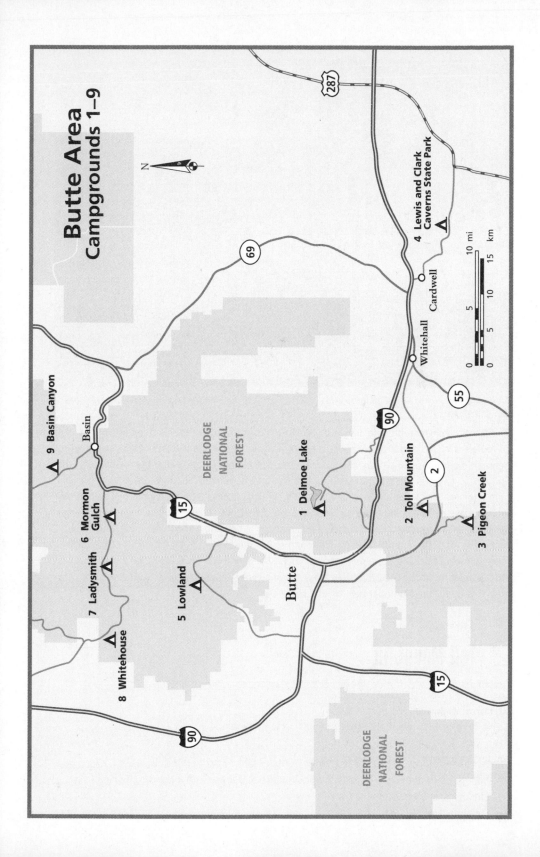

Delmoe Lake is a beautiful place to relax, fish, or try your luck at finding smoky quartz crystals.

About the campground: Large granite boulders hide in the shade of the pine forest that surrounds this lake. An attractive picnic area, complete with boat ramp, clings to the shoreline between the two camping loops. The first loop takes off to the right just after the fee station. Tents and pickup campers are more suitable for this first one. Both camping areas are equally distant from the lakeshore, though it is in sight. The long, twisting access road tests both nerves and skill for maneuvering long units, though it is quickly forgotten. Upon arrival you just might want to stay the full sixteen days allowed—especially if you manage to settle in while the campground is empty during the week. Plentiful deadfall for firewood lies just out of sight in the shadows of the thick lodgepole pine engulfing the area. If the fish aren't biting or if you are looking for a change of routine, hunt for smoky quartz crystals along the shoreline. Depending upon weather, the campground is open from Memorial Day through Labor Day.

2 Toll Mountain

Location: 17 miles southeast of Butte.
Facilities: Vault toilet, fire rings, tables.
Sites: 5 for tents or RVs/Trailer combinations up to 40 feet long.
Fee: None, 16-day limit.
Managing agency: Beaverhead-Deerlodge National Forest, (406) 683–3900.
Activities: Hiking.

Finding the campground: Travel south on Harrison Avenue in Butte to Montana State Highway 2. Turn left and travel 14 miles, over Pipestone Pass. Turn left onto gravel Forest Road 240 and follow the campground directional signs for 3 miles.

About the campground: Douglas fir trees and thick underbrush shade these camping spots found on the north side of some steep, forested ridges. A small stream bubbles through the middle, though it didn't look too hopeful for fishing during our visit. Wildlife will reward the diligent and patient alike. You can find some very fine quality smoky quartz crystals here; occasionally an amethyst has been reported. There is private land in the area, so be alert with respect to fence lines and other warnings. Firewood appeared easy to gather, but this camping area is not very popular in comparison to other nearby spots. That, of course, could change by the time this book is printed. The campground is open from Memorial Day through Labor Day.

3 Pigeon Creek

Location: 19 miles southeast of Butte on Fish Creek.
Facilities: Vault toilet, fire rings, tables, drinking water.
Sites: 6 for tents (trailers are not recommended).
Fee: None, 16-day limit.
Managing agency: Deerlodge National Forest, Butte Ranger District, (406) 494-2147.
Activities: Hiking, fishing.
Finding the campground: Travel south on Harrison Avenue in Butte to Montana State Highway 2. Turn left and travel 15 miles, over Pipestone Pass. Turn right onto gravel-becoming-dirt Forest Road 668 and travel 4 miles. The campground is to the left on the opposite shore of Fish Creek; the sign may or may not be present.

About the campground: This enchanted spot snuggles up to the rock-smashing waters of Fish Creek. The parking spaces offer the only flat area for a long distance, with steep rocky ridges all the way around. Ancient Douglas fir trees tower above sparse brush, a few aspen, and short grass. Brook trout make their home in the eddies and cut banks, and doubtless witness elk and deer drinking during the summer months. Pigeon Creek joins Fish Creek at the campground, adding its 1-foot width to the 6-foot-wide stream. The steep, one-lane road bounces over sharp rocks between long stretches of dirt, which will become mud with any amount of rain. If the weather looks wet and you don't have time to wait for sunshine, this would be an area to pass by. The campground is open from Memorial Day through September 15.

4 Lewis and Clark Caverns State Park

Location: 34 miles east of Butte.
Facilities: Vault and flush toilets, RV dump station, showers, fire rings, tables, drinking water.
Sites: 3 cabins, 1 tepee, 40 for tents or RVs/Trailer combinations up to 60 feet long.
Fee: $$, 14-day limit.
Managing agency: Montana State Parks, (406) 287-3541.

Activities: Hiking, fishing, wildlife viewing.

Finding the campground: Take I-90 east out of Butte for 29 miles to Cardwell/exit 256. Follow the directions to Montana State Highway 2 and travel east for 5 miles. Turn left at milepost 271.

About the campground: The trees in the camp are native to the area; however, the grassy field they occupy likely had none to begin with. Camping here is more of a convenience for those wanting to experience the local attractions, such as the cave tours and interpretive trails. Fishing sites are close by and add to the overall appeal. Firewood is available for purchase; otherwise be sure to bring plenty of your own. The campground is open all year long, but cave tours run only from May 1 through September 30.

5 Lowland

Location: 18 miles north of Butte.

Facilities: Vault toilets, fire rings, tables, drinking water, picnic area.

Sites: 11 for tents or RVs/Trailers up to 22 feet long.

Fee: $, 16-day limit.

Managing agency: Deerlodge National Forest, Butte Ranger District, (406) 494-2147.

Activities: Hiking, wildlife viewing.

Finding the campground: Take I-15 north out of Butte for 8 miles to Elk Park/exit 138. Turn left onto gravel Forest Road 442 and travel west for 8 miles. Turn left onto gravel Forest Road 9485 and travel 2 miles.

About the campground: This campground settles comfortably into the pine forest, which has elk and deer for year-round residents. Naturally, the wildlife seems to disappear during the hunting season. All the same they are generally still at home, just in a different "room," so to speak. Gathering firewood requires some effort, but when you do find it, there is plenty. A host is present, but reservations cannot be made. Weekends and holidays fill all the available spots, so if you have your heart set on a forest camp out, make plans to arrive here in the middle of the week. Longer trailers can fit; however, unhooking is required. All of the units are back-in sites. The toilets and the water are close to the entrance, which leaves the farthest units on the sole loop for latecomers. The picnic area offers the best water and parking, but no overnight stays. The campground is open from Memorial Day through Labor Day.

6 Mormon Gulch

Location: 33 miles north of Butte.

Facilities: Pit toilets, fire rings, tables.

Sites: 16 for tents or RVs/Trailers up to 16 feet long.

Fee: None, 14-day limit.

Managing agency: Deerlodge National Forest, Butte Ranger District, (406) 494-2147.

Activities: Hiking.

Finding the campground: Take I–15 north out of Butte for 31 miles to Bernice/exit 151. Turn left onto paved-becoming-gravel Forest Road 82 and travel 2 miles. The campground is on the left side of the road.

About the campground: This camping area sits far enough off the road that little traffic noise penetrates the thick pine forest engulfing it. A small trickle of water just out of sight in a deep cut winds its way through the area. Trailers require unhooking and backing skills for placement. However, once everything is in place, you might want to stay the full fourteen-day limit. The campground is open from May 25 through December 1.

7 Ladysmith

Location: 35 miles north of Butte.
Facilities: Pit toilet, fire rings.
Sites: 6 for tents.
Fee: None, 14-day limit.
Managing agency: Deerlodge National Forest, Butte Ranger District, (406) 494-2147.
Activities: Hiking.
Finding the campground: Take I–15 north out of Butte for 31 miles to Bernice/exit 151. Turn left onto paved-becoming-gravel Forest Road 82 and travel 4 miles. The campground is on the left side of the road.

About the campground: Trailers do manage to fit here, but not without a good amount of work unhooking and leveling. The units are scattered about within the pines on a hillside near the road. Traffic can get heavy with a major intersection just past the camping area. Of course, the heavy traffic is relative with respect to being in the country. All the same, you might want to consider one of the other nearby campgrounds if you like sitting around camp during the day with little "machinery" noise. This campground is a good spot if you like hiking. The backyard, so to speak, is a forest full of wildlife that as a rule has few visitors. Fishing could be an option, but the stream directly across the road is on private land and requires permission that may or may not be given. The campground is open from Memorial Day through Labor Day.

8 Whitehouse

Location: 39 miles north of Butte on the Boulder River.
Facilities: Pit toilets, fire rings, tables, drinking water.
Sites: 5 for tents or RVs/Trailers up to 22 feet long.
Fee: None, 16-day limit.
Managing agency: Deerlodge National Forest, Butte Ranger District, (406) 494-2147.
Activities: Hiking, fishing, wildlife viewing.
Finding the campground: Take I–15 north out of Butte for 31 miles to Bernice/exit 151. Turn left onto paved-becoming-gravel Forest Road 82 and travel 4 miles. Just past Ladysmith

Campground bear right to stay on FR 82 and travel 4 miles. The campground entrance is on the left side of the road.

About the campground: There is plenty of room here for about any size RV, if you don't mind not having a table or fire ring. The more popular sites settle in under fir trees along the river-bank, which has willow brush outlining the water's edge. Rolling grassy meadows checkerboard the forest in this mountain setting, making it one of the more popular spots on weekends and holidays. You might consider setting up camp before making a short trip for gathering firewood. Forest Road 82 has some blind spots just past Ladysmith Campground, so be alert. The flowered crosses are not there because someone wanted to improve the view. Please don't donate any more. The campground is open from Memorial Day through Labor Day.

9 Basin Canyon

Location: 38 miles north of Butte.
Facilities: Pit toilet, fire rings, tables.
Sites: 2 for tents or RVs/Trailers up to 16 feet long.
Fee: None, 14-day limit.
Managing agency: Deerlodge National Forest, Butte Ranger District, (406) 494-2147.
Activities: Hiking.
Finding the campground: Take I-15 north out of Butte for 35 miles to Basin/exit 158 and cross to the opposite side of the highway. Travel through town to gravel Forest Road 172. Take FR 172 northwest up Basin Creek for 3 miles. The campground is along the right side of the road.
About the campground: This is more of a campground in name only. Nearby Basin Creek is located on private land and requires permission to access. Traffic creates plenty of dust for campers in this spot. However, the pine forest offers shade and solitude for those willing to hike off the road and past the campground. It is open from May 25 through September 15.

10 Racetrack

Location: 40 northwest of Butte on Racetrack Creek.
Facilities: Vault toilets, fire rings, tables, drinking water, picnic area.
Sites: 13 for tents or RVs/Trailers up to 22 feet long.
Fee: None, 14-day limit.
Managing agency: Deerlodge National Forest, Pintler Ranger District, (406) 859-3211.
Activities: Hiking, fishing.
Finding the campground: Take I-90 west out of Butte for 29 miles to Racetrack/exit 195 and turn left. Continue straight across the frontage road past the few businesses for 1 mile. Turn left onto gravel County Road 34 and travel about 9 miles. The road will bear south for 0.75 mile and then turn toward the mountains. Continue straight ahead on this route; your destination lies in the pine forest in the distance. CR 34 becomes Forest Road 169, but there are no markers until very near the campground.

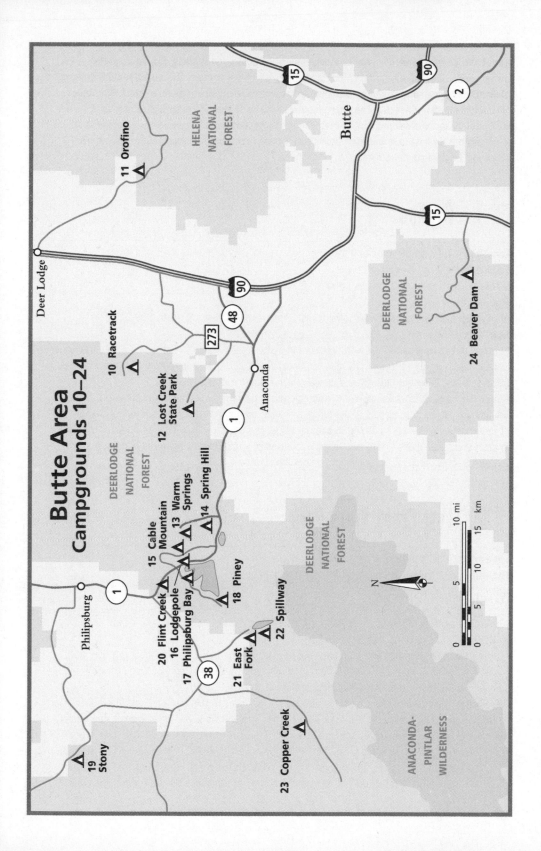

Butte Area
Campgrounds 10–24

About the campground: Tall, mature Douglas fir trees stand guard along the banks of Racetrack Creek in this camping area. During the early spring the creek is more of a raging torrent, offering pleasant background music to outdoor lovers. It seems like a very long and unappealing drive for all but the last few miles, but finally getting there makes all the difference. All-terrain vehicles are very popular in the area and can be bothersome on holidays and hot summer weekends. A space is provided for a host, but filling the position can be a problem. The campground is open from Memorial Daythrough Labor Day.

11 Orofino

Location: 44 miles northwest of Butte.
Facilities: Pit toilet, fire rings, tables.
Sites: 10 for tents or RVs/Trailers up to 22 feet long.
Fee: None, 14-day limit.
Managing agency: Deerlodge National Forest, Pintler Ranger District, (406) 859–3211.
Activities: Hiking.
Finding the campground: Take I–90 west out of Butte for 29 miles. Get off I–90 at Racetrack/exit 195. Turn right and travel 0.75 mile to County Road 193. Turn right onto this gravel road and travel 9 miles. Turn right onto gravel Forest Road 82 and travel 5 miles.
About the campground: Tall pine trees snuggle up to camping units and mountainsides alike. This area may get more visitors in the future as roads are improved. Currently, the last portion of the access road tends to discourage return visits. The relatively level parking spots consist of improved dirt with grass taking over in the less popular spots. The campground is open May 25 through September 15, weather and road conditions allowing.

12 Lost Creek State Park

Location: 26 miles west of Butte on Lost Creek.
Facilities: Vault toilets, fire rings, tables, drinking water.
Sites: 25 for tents or RVs/Trailer combinations up to 40 feet long.
Fee: $, dependent upon resident/nonresident status; 14-day limit.
Managing agency: Montana State Parks, (406) 287–3541.
Activities: Hiking, fishing, wildlife viewing.
Finding the campground: Take I–90 west out of Butte for 15 miles to Anaconda/exit 208 and travel 4 miles on Montana Highway 1. Turn right onto paved County Road 273 and travel 2 miles. Turn left at the Lost Creek State Park sign and travel 5 miles.
About the campground: There is an upper and a lower part to this campground. The newer and more popular units are located in the upper portion, which has some tight corners and relatively steep hills to traverse. An impressive waterfall crashes over 50-foot cliffs just upstream from the campground, bringing more than a few onlookers throughout the course of a summer day. Moose, mountain goats, and bighorn sheep frequent the area. Pack plenty of warm clothing. The temperature goes down with the sun, which does not reach the bottom of this canyon

until late in the day and leaves shortly after arriving. The campground is open from May 11 through November 30.

13 Warm Springs

Location: 33 miles west of Butte on Warm Springs Creek.
Facilities: Vault toilet, fire rings, tables, drinking water, picnic area.
Sites: 6 for tents.
Fee: None, 14-day limit.
Managing agency: Deerlodge National Forest, Pintler Ranger District, (406) 859-3211.
Activities: Hiking, fishing.
Finding the campground: Take I-90 west out of Butte for 15 miles to Anaconda/exit 208 and travel 15.5 miles on Montana State Highway 1, passing through Anaconda. Turn right onto gravel Forest Road 170 and travel 2.5 miles.
About the campground: Lodgepole pine trees occupy the banks of the crystal-clear creek that borders this camping area. Improvements have upgraded the area into a very nice, quiet little escape. Weekends are likely to find this one full, so if possible, arrive early. The campground is open from May 25 through September 25.

14 Spring Hill

Location: 31 miles west of Butte.
Facilities: Vault toilet, fire rings, tables, drinking water, picnic area.
Sites: 13 for tents or RVs/Trailers up to 22 feet long.
Fee: $$ per night, 16-day limit.
Managing agency: Deerlodge National Forest, Pintler Ranger District, (406) 859-3211.
Activities: Hiking, wildlife viewing.
Finding the campground: Take I-90 west out of Butte for 15 miles. Get off I-90 at Anaconda/exit 208 and travel 16 miles on Montana State Highway 1.
About the campground: Reservations can be made at this site; call (877) 444-6777. Firewood shouldn't be too hard to find in this relatively thick lodgepole pine forest, though it may take some hiking. The nearby highway produces traffic noises that tend to diminish during the night, except on holidays. The more popular camping areas are farther up the road, but that does not leave this pleasant wooded area unvisited. The campground is open from May 25 through September 5, with a locked gate between seasons.

15 Cable Mountain

Location: 36 miles west of Butte on North Fork Flint Creek.
Facilities: Vault toilets, fire rings, tables, drinking water.

Sites: 11 for tents or RVs/Trailers up to 22 feet long.

Fee: $$ per night, 14-day limit.

Managing agency: Deerlodge National Forest, Pintler Ranger District, (406) 859-3211.

Activities: Hiking, fishing.

Finding the campground: Take I-90 west out of Butte for 15 miles. Get off I-90 at Anaconda/exit 208 and travel 17 miles on Montana State Highway 1. Turn right onto paved Discovery Basin Road/Forest Road 65 and travel 3 miles. Turn right onto gravel Forest Road 242 and travel 1 mile. The campground is on the right side of the road.

About the campground: Two loops deep into this pine forest separate campers. North Fork Flint Creek, with its cold, deep clear pools, beckons anglers and waders alike. Willow brush lines the bank of this mountain stream. Firewood will take some effort to gather, but it is not far away. The hand pump for drinking water takes time to build back up after use, so if a camper passes by with a full bucket, a short waiting period is in order. This is a popular spot in the summer heat, so have an alternative place as a second choice on a hot weekend. The campground is open from May 29 through September 15.

16 Lodgepole

Location: 34 miles west of Butte near Georgetown Lake.

Facilities: Vault toilets, fire rings, tables, drinking water.

Sites: 31 for tents or RVs/Trailers up to 32 feet long.

Fee: $$ per night, 16-day limit.

Managing agency: Deerlodge National Forest, Pintler Ranger District, (406) 859-3211.

Activities: Hiking, fishing.

Finding the campground: Take I-90 west out of Butte for 15 miles. Get off I-90 at Anaconda/exit 208 and travel 19 miles on Montana State Highway 1. The campground is on the right side of the road.

About the campground: Some sites can be reserved; call (877) 444-6777. A boat ramp is located across the highway on Georgetown Lake, a short walk from the camping units. Keep your camera handy. Moose are frequently spotted feeding in the area. The campground is open from May 22 through September 30.

17 Philipsburg Bay

Location: 35 miles west of Butte on Georgetown Lake.

Facilities: Vault toilets, fire rings, tables, drinking water, boat ramp.

Sites: 69 for tents or RVs/Trailer combinations up to 60 feet long.

Fee: $$ per night, 16-day limit.

Managing agency: Deerlodge National Forest, Pintler Ranger District, (406) 859-3211.

Activities: Hiking, fishing, wildlife viewing, boating, swimming.

Finding the campground: Take I-90 west out of Butte for 15 miles. Get off I-90 at Anaconda/exit 208 and travel 19 miles on Montana Highway 1. Just after Lodgepole Campground watch carefully for a sharp left turn. Turn left onto paved Lakeshore Road and travel 1 mile.

About the campground: Some sites can be reserved; call (877) 444-6777. Three loops offer plenty of choices for campers in this healthy pine forest. Paved roads lead to roomy, level, asphalt parking units, creating a sense of separation not all that common in other campgrounds. The camping units are a short hike from Georgetown Lake. A boat ramp includes a parking area for the boat trailers, along with nearby extra parking for overflow vehicles. A host is present, generally in each individual loop.

Near the end of summer, anglers often hook 16-inch trout in the late evening light. Be sure to have plenty of film or memory cards to capitalize on the photo opportunities. The mountains loom over the waters, providing scenic shots just about any time of day. Wildlife adds a perfect touch to the menu as well. Moose frequently wander through the camping area, with plenty of deer between sightings. The campground is open from May 15 through September 30, with a locked gate between seasons.

18 Piney

Location: 37 miles west of Butte on Georgetown Lake.
Facilities: Vault toilets, fire rings, tables, drinking water, boat ramp.
Sites: 48 for tents or RVs/Trailers up to 32 feet long.
Fee: $$ per night, 16-day limit.
Managing agency: Deerlodge National Forest, Pintler Ranger District, (406) 859-3211.
Activities: Hiking, fishing, wildlife viewing, boating, swimming.
Finding the campground: Take I-90 west out of Butte for 15 miles. Get off I-90 at Anaconda/exit 208 and travel 19 miles on Montana Highway 1. Just after Lodgepole Campground watch carefully for a sharp left turn. Turn left onto paved Lakeshore Road and travel 3 miles.
About the campground: Some sites can be reserved; call (877) 444-6777. This campground settles into the lodgepole pine along the shores of Georgetown Lake. It could be thought of as an extension of other campgrounds along the lake. Fishing and boating are the primary focus of campers, but plentiful wildlife and mountain scenery add "icing to the cake." The campground is open from May 22 through September 15.

19 Stony

Location: 116 miles west of Butte on Stony Creek.
Facilities: Vault toilet, fire rings, tables, drinking water.
Sites: 10 for tents or RVs/trailers up to 32 feet long.
Fee: None, 14-day limit.
Managing agency: Deerlodge National Forest, Pintler Ranger District, (406) 859-3211.
Activities: Hiking, fishing, wildlife viewing.
Finding the campground: Take I-90 west out of Butte for 71 miles. Get off I-90 at Drummond/exit 153. Turn left onto paved Montana State Highway 1 and travel 26 miles. Turn right onto Rock Creek Road and travel 19 miles.

About the campground: Pine trees inhabit the camping area, with aspen lining the access road. Stony offers scenic views in this mountain canyon not far from Rock Creek. If fishing is not good in the adjacent Stony Creek, it is not too far to try other waters. Rock Creek is both large enough and close enough to serenade campers with its stone-crashing music. Bighorn sheep live in the area, so stay alert and keep the camera ready. If the snow is not too deep, the campground is open from May 25 through September 30.

20 Flint Creek

Location: 105 miles west of Butte on Flint Creek.
Facilities: Vault toilets, fire rings, tables.
Sites: 16 for tents or RVs/Trailers up to 22 feet long.
Fee: None, 14-day limit.
Managing agency: Deerlodge National Forest, Pintler Ranger District, (406) 859-3211.
Activities: Hiking, fishing.
Finding the campground: Take I-90 west out of Butte for 71 miles. Get off I-90 at Drummond/exit 153. Turn left onto paved Montana State Highway 1 and travel 34 miles past Philipsburg.
About the campground: Tall Douglas fir trees share the shoreline with aspen and willow brush along this creek. Upon entering the camping area, a large sign warns of the need to evacuate when sirens sound off. Should a flash flood occur, all persons in the area must leave immediately. The tables are scattered about, with some a goodly distance from the parking area. Tent campers would most likely appreciate the distance. The campground is open from May 22 through September 30.

21 East Fork

Location: 115 miles west of Butte on East Fork Rock Creek.
Facilities: Vault toilet, fire rings, tables, drinking water.
Sites: 7 for tents or RVs/Trailers up to 22 feet long.
Fee: None, 14-day limit.
Managing agency: Deerlodge National Forest, Pintler Ranger District, (406) 859-3211.
Activities: Hiking, fishing.
Finding the campground: Take I-90 west out of Butte for 71 miles. Get off I-90 at Drummond/exit 153. Turn left onto paved Montana State Highway 1 and travel 32 miles past Philipsburg. Turn right onto Montana State Highway 38 and travel 6 miles. Turn left onto Forest Road 672 and travel 5 miles. Turn right onto Forest Road 9349 and travel 1 mile.
About the campground: East Fork Rock Creek is contained in a 500-acre reservoir just above this camping area. Pine trees blanket the surrounding mountains and camping units alike. The campground is open from May 1 through September 30.

22 Spillway

Location: 116 miles west of Butte on East Fork Rock Creek.
Facilities: Vault toilets, fire rings, tables, drinking water.
Sites: 13 for tents or RVs/Trailers up to 22 feet long.
Fee: None, 16-day limit.
Managing agency: Deerlodge National Forest, Pintler Ranger District, (406) 859-3211.
Activities: Hiking, fishing, boating.
Finding the campground: Take I-90 west out of Butte for 71 miles. Get off I-90 at Drummond/ exit 153. Turn left onto paved Montana State Highway 1 and travel 32 miles past Philipsburg. Turn right onto Montana State Highway 38 and travel 6 miles. Turn left onto Forest Road 672 and travel 7 miles.
About the campground: Lodgepole pine trees have fallen victim to the pine beetles. The campground was listed on the web as closed for public safety in 2014 for this reason. As a result of the infestation, shade will be harder to find than before. Some camping units are located a short distance from the shore, while most snuggle up along the water. The 500-acre reservoir invites boaters to test the waters. The campground is open from May 1 through November 1.

23 Copper Creek

Location: 122 miles west of Butte on Middle Fork Rock Creek.
Facilities: Vault toilet, fire rings, tables, drinking water.
Sites: 7 for tents or RVs/Trailers up to 22 feet long.
Fee: None, 14-day limit.
Managing agency: Deerlodge National Forest, Pintler Ranger District, (406) 859-3211.
Activities: Hiking, fishing.
Finding the campground: Take I-90 west out of Butte for 71 miles. Get off I-90 at Drummond/ exit 153. Turn left onto paved Montana State Highway 1 and travel 32 miles past Philipsburg. Turn right onto Montana State Highway 38 and travel 9 miles. Turn left onto Forest Road 5106 and travel 10 miles.
About the campground: Middle Fork Rock Creek slides by this campground, inviting waders and anglers alike. Tall lodgepole pines and grassy banks make this a peaceful place to relax. The campground is open from June 15 through September 30.

24 Beaver Dam

Location: 25 miles southwest of Butte.
Facilities: Vault toilets, fire rings, tables, drinking water.

Sites: 15 for tents or RVs/Trailers up to 50 feet long.

Fee: $, 16-day limit.

Managing agency: Deerlodge National Forest, Butte Ranger District, (406) 494-2147.

Activities: Hiking.

Finding the campground: Take I-90 west out of Butte for 5 miles. Take I-15 south, just past the Rocker exit, for 12 miles. Get off I-15 at Feeley/exit 111, turn right onto gravel Divide Creek Road, and travel 8 miles. This gravel road may not be marked. The campground is on the left side of the road.

About the campground: Two loops meander through the lodgepole pine in this mountain draw, which hints of plentiful deadfall for firewood just out of sight. In context with its name, beavers have dammed a trickle of a stream adjacent to the pole fence that defines the campground boundary. Don't count on catching any fish here, though. The campground is open from Memorial Day through Labor Day.

West Yellowstone Area

Visitors from the Northwest will likely consider this the primary entrance for Yellowstone National Park. Snowcapped mountains, forested plateaus, and sagebrush flats mix into the whole for changing scenery all along the route. Wildlife and dramatic geologic features add to the attraction of the area. Buffalo, elk, and deer are seen frequently both within and outside the park.

Since Yellowstone National Park is so close, campers should settle in long before noon. As a rule, the camping units inside the park fill much more quickly than those outside the park.

	Group Sites	Tents	RV sites	Total sites	Hookups	Toilets	Showers	Drinking water	Dump station	Phone	Handicap Access	Recreation	Fee	Season	Stay limit (days)
1 Bakers Hole			73	73	V	*					*	HFW	$$	5/15-9/15	30
2 Rainbow Point			85	85	V	*						HFB	$$	5/5-9/27	16
3 Cabin Creek			15	15	V	*					*	HFW	$$	5/24-9/19	16
4 Beaver Creek			64	64	V	*					*	HFBW	$$	6/1-9/15	16
5 Cliff Point			6	6	V	*						HFB	$	6/1-9/15	16
6 Hilltop			18	18	V	*						HW	$	6/1-9/30	16
7 Wade Lake			30	30	V	*					*	HFBW	$	6/1-9/30	16
8 Madison River			10	10	V	*						HFW	$	6/1-9/30	16
9 West Fork Madison	7			7	V	*						HFW	$	6/1-9/15	16
10 Palisades			10	10	P	*						HFBW	$	All Year	14
11 Ruby Creek			22	22	V	*						HFW	$	5/1-12/1	14
12 Bear Creek			12	12	V	*						HW	N	6/1-11/30	16
13 Red Mountain			17	17	V	*						HF	$	4/1-12/1	14
14 Ruby Reservoir			D	D	V							HFB	N	All Year	14
15 Cottonwood			10	10	V							H	N	5/26-11/30	16
16 Mill Creek			10	10	V	*						HF	N	6/1-10/31	16
17 Branham Lakes	6			6	V							HF	N	7/1-9/15	16
18 Potosi			15	15	V	*						HFW	N	6/1-9/30	16
19 Lonesomehurst			27	27	V	*					*	HFBW	$$	5/17-9/22	16
20 Cherry Creek			7	7	V							HF	N	Memorial Day to Labor Day	16
21 Spring Creek			D	D	V							HF	N	Memorial Day to mid Oct	16
22 Upper Lake			10	10	V	*						HW	$	Summer	16
23 River Marsh			D	D	V							HW	$	Summer	16

1 Bakers Hole

Location: 3 miles north of West Yellowstone on the Madison River.

Facilities: Vault toilets, fire rings, tables, drinking water.

Sites: 73 for RVs/Trailer combinations up to 75 feet long.

Fee: $$ per night, 16-day limit.

Managing agency: Gallatin National Forest, Yellowstone Country Campgrounds, Inc., (406) 646–1012.

Activities: Hiking, fishing, wildlife viewing.

Finding the campground: Take US Highway 191 north out of West Yellowstone for 3 miles. The campground is on the right side of the road.

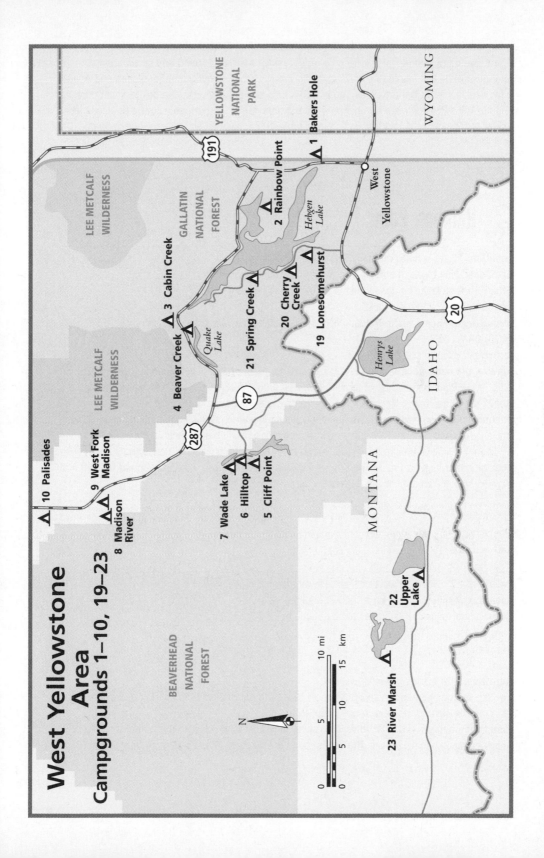

West Yellowstone Area
Campgrounds 1–10, 19–23

N

0 5 10 mi
0 5 10 15 km

BEAVERHEAD NATIONAL FOREST

LEE METCALF WILDERNESS

LEE METCALF WILDERNESS

GALLATIN NATIONAL FOREST

YELLOWSTONE NATIONAL PARK

WYOMING

MONTANA

IDAHO

191

287

87

20

△ 10 Palisades
△ 9 West Fork Madison
△ 8 Madison River
△ 7 Wade Lake
△ 6 Hilltop
△ 5 Cliff Point
△ 4 Beaver Creek
△ 3 Cabin Creek
△ 2 Rainbow Point
△ 1 Bakers Hole
△ 21 Spring Creek
△ 20 Cherry Creek
△ 19 Lonesomehurst
△ 22 Upper Lake
△ 23 River Marsh

Quake Lake

Hebgen Lake

Henrys Lake

West Yellowstone

About the campground: Thick lodgepole pines blanket the campground and surrounding countryside. Distant mountains provide scenic views, while the grassy meadows scattered about offer wildlife viewing opportunities. The gravel access and parking units can create some dust. In spite of the seemingly large number of units, the area can fill up, probably due to the closeness of Yellowstone National Park. Firewood is available to purchase on-site. Electricity is available at thirty-three of the sites for an additional fee. The campground is open from May 15 through September 30, unless the snow does not melt.

2 Rainbow Point

Location: 10 miles north of West Yellowstone on Hebgen Lake.
Facilities: Vault toilets, fire rings, tables, drinking water, boat ramp.
Sites: 85 for RVs/Trailer combinations up to 60 feet long.
Fee: $$ per night, 16-day limit.
Managing agency: Gallatin National Forest, Yellowstone Country Campgrounds, Inc., (406) 646–1012.
Activities: Hiking, fishing, boating.
Finding the campground: Take US Highway 191 north out of West Yellowstone for 5 miles. Turn left onto Forest Road 610 and travel 3 miles. Turn right onto Forest Road 6954 and travel 2 miles.
About the campground: Anyone who likes water-related activities would find Hebgen Lake quite adequate. Forested ridges and snowcapped mountains surround this large body of water. There is plenty of space between the pine trees with electricity available at some of the sites for an additional fee. The campground's close proximity to Yellowstone National Park and its ability to accommodate large RVs make it an appealing spot to set up base. The campground is open from May 15 through September 27, dependent on weather.

3 Cabin Creek

Location: 22 miles northwest of West Yellowstone on Cabin Creek.
Facilities: Vault toilets, fire rings, tables, drinking water.
Sites: 15 for tents or RVs/Trailer combinations up to 50 feet long.
Fee: $$ per night, 16-day limit.
Managing agency: Gallatin National Forest, Yellowstone Country Campgrounds, Inc., (406) 646–1012.
Activities: Hiking, fishing, wildlife viewing.
Finding the campground: Take US Highway 191 north out of West Yellowstone for 8 miles. Turn left onto US Highway 287 and travel 14 miles.
About the campground: Thick forest and steep mountainsides squeeze this camping area up against a small babbling creek. The campground is open from May 24 through September 19.

4 Beaver Creek

Location: 24 miles northwest of West Yellowstone on Earthquake Lake.
Facilities: Vault toilets, fire rings, tables, drinking water.
Sites: 64 for tents or RVs/Trailer combinations up to 50 feet long.
Fee: $$ per night, 16-day limit.
Managing agency: Gallatin National Forest, Yellowstone Country Campgrounds, Inc., (406) 646–1012.
Activities: Hiking, fishing, boating, wildlife viewing.
Finding the campground: Take US Highway 191 north out of West Yellowstone for 8 miles. Turn left onto US Highway 287 and travel 16 miles.
About the campground: Campers can settle into the rolling, forested hillsides along Earthquake Lake here. Aspen and an assortment of evergreen trees provide shade and, in places, isolation. The lake requires a bit of a hike, but with a little exploration along the loops you can find a unit at a manageable distance. The campground is open from June 1 through September 15.

5 Cliff Point

Location: 40 miles northwest of West Yellowstone on Cliff Lake.
Facilities: Vault toilets, fire rings, tables, drinking water, boat ramp.
Sites: 6 for tents or RVs/Trailers up to 16 feet long.
Fee: $ per night, 16-day limit.
Managing agency: Beaverhead National Forest, concessionaires Dave and Laurie Schmidt, (406) 682-7560.
Activities: Hiking, fishing, boating.
Finding the campground: Take US Highway 191 north out of West Yellowstone for 8 miles. Turn left onto US Highway 287 and travel 27 miles. Turn left onto gravel Forest Road 241 and travel 3 miles. Turn right onto Forest Road 572 and travel 2 miles. Bear left at the second intersection.
About the campground: After traveling across the open, dusty access road up and down the steep hillsides, this hidden oasis will leave you wishing you had an unlimited stay. Pine trees carpet the mountainsides as they slope into the shoreline of the ice-cold waters of Cliff Lake. When the weather allows, the campground is open from June 1 through September 15.

6 Hilltop

Location: 40 miles northwest of West Yellowstone.
Facilities: Vault toilets, fire rings, tables, drinking water.
Sites: 18 for tents or RVs/Trailers up to 22 feet long.
Fee: $ per night, 16-day limit.

Skeletal remains of nature's fury can be seen at Quake Lake in Gallatin National Forest.

Managing agency: Beaverhead National Forest, concessionaires Dave and Laurie Schmidt, (406) 682-7560.
Activities: Hiking, wildlife viewing.
Finding the campground: Take US Highway 191 north out of West Yellowstone for 8 miles. Turn left onto US Highway 287 and travel 27 miles. Turn left onto gravel Forest Road 241 and trav el 3 miles. Turn right onto Forest Road 572 and travel 2 miles.
About the campground: Mature pine trees stand guard over this peaceful spot. With a little travel, anglers can select either Wade or Cliff Lake to test their skills. This camping area, which opens June 1, may stay open as late as September 30, providing the cold weather arrives in normal fashion.

7 Wade Lake

Location: 40 miles northwest of West Yellowstone on Wade Lake.
Facilities: Vault toilets, fire rings, tables, drinking water.
Sites: 30 for tents or RVs/Trailers up to 30 feet long.
Fee: $ per night, 16-day limit.
Managing agency: Beaverhead National Forest, concessionaires Dave and Laurie Schmidt, (406) 682-7560.
Activities: Hiking, fishing, boating, wildlife viewing.

Finding the campground: Take US Highway 191 north out of West Yellowstone for 8 miles. Turn left onto US Highway 287 and travel 27 miles. Turn left onto gravel Forest Road 241 and travel 5 miles.

About the campground: Mountain springs feed this lake to create about 220 surface acres of scenic water. Anglers will compete with eagles and osprey in this region. Gravel parking units cling to the west side of the lake in terrace fashion, with some closer to the lakeshore. The campground is open from June 1 through September 30.

8 Madison River

Location: 47 miles northwest of West Yellowstone on the Madison River.
Facilities: Vault toilets, fire rings, tables, drinking water.
Sites: 10 for tents or RVs/Trailers up to 30 feet long.
Fee: $ per night, 16-day limit.
Managing agency: Beaverhead National Forest, Madison Ranger District, (406) 682–4253.
Activities: Hiking, fishing, wildlife viewing.
Finding the campground: Take US Highway 191 north out of West Yellowstone for 8 miles. Turn left onto US Highway 287 and travel 39 miles. Turn left at the national forest access sign and follow directional signs to the river.
About the campground: The Madison River winds its way through meadows and pine trees in the shadow of steep, forested mountains here. Sagebrush inhabits the open spaces and spices the air. The open areas provide for scenic panoramas and wildlife viewing. The campground is open from June 1 through September 30.

9 West Fork Madison

Location: 47 miles northwest of West Yellowstone on the Madison River.
Facilities: Vault toilets, fire rings, tables, drinking water.
Sites: 7 for tents.
Fee: $ per night, 16-day limit.
Managing agency: Beaverhead National Forest, concessionaires Dave and Laurie Schmidt, (406) 682-7560.
Activities: Hiking, fishing, wildlife viewing.
Finding the campground: Take US Highway 191 north out of West Yellowstone for 8 miles. Turn left onto US Highway 287 and travel 39 miles. Turn left at the national forest access sign and follow directional signs to the river.
About the campground: This campground is a continuance of the previous site, only at a different location. It is a matter of choice on which views you prefer. The campground is open from June 1 through September 15.

10 Palisades

Location: 53 miles northwest of West Yellowstone on the Madison River.
Facilities: Pit toilets, fire rings, tables, drinking water, boat ramp.
Sites: 11 for tents or RVs/Trailer combinations up to 30 feet long.
Fee: $ per night, 14-day limit.
Managing agency: Bureau of Land Management, Dillon Office, (406) 683-8000.
Activities: Hiking, fishing, boating, wildlife viewing.
Finding the campground: Take US Highway 191 north out of West Yellowstone for 8 miles. Turn left onto US Highway 287 and travel 44 miles. Turn left at the access sign onto the gravel road and travel 1 mile.
About the campground: The pine forest thins out a little as the river meanders into the more open valley. Sagebrush still perfumes the air, with mountains looming in the distance. Firewood will take a little effort to collect. The campground is open all year long.

11 Ruby Creek

Location: 63 miles northwest of West Yellowstone on the Madison River.
Facilities: Vault toilets, fire rings, tables, drinking water.
Sites: 22 for tents or RVs/Trailer combinations up to 35 feet long.
Fee: $ per night, 14-day limit.
Managing agency: Bureau of Land Management, Dillon Office, (406) 683-8000.
Activities: Hiking, fishing, wildlife viewing.
Finding the campground: Take US Highway 191 north out of West Yellowstone for 8 miles. Turn left onto US Highway 287 and travel 52 miles. Turn left at the access sign onto the gravel road and travel 3 miles.
About the campground: Willow brush takes over where the pine trees dominated farther upstream. The mountains are more distant, but you get a more complete view. Pastureland tends to be prevalent in the immediate area, with a little less sagebrush. The campground is open May 1 to December 1.

12 Bear Creek

Location: 71 miles northwest of West Yellowstone.
Facilities: Vault toilet, fire rings, tables, drinking water.
Sites: 12 for tents or RVs/Trailers up to 28 feet long.
Fee: None, 16-day limit.
Managing agency: Beaverhead National Forest, Madison Ranger District, (406) 682-4253.
Activities: Hiking, wildlife viewing.

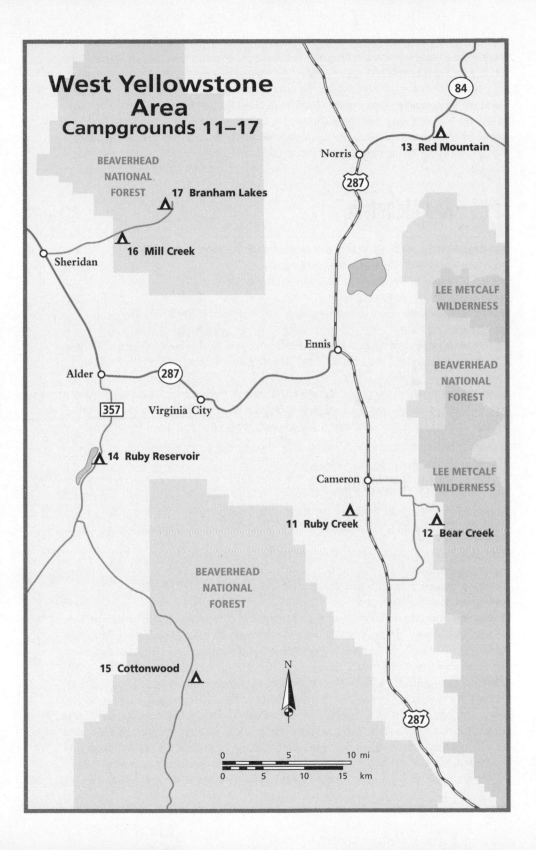

West Yellowstone Area
Campgrounds 11–17

84

13 Red Mountain

Norris

BEAVERHEAD
NATIONAL
FOREST

17 Branham Lakes

287

16 Mill Creek

Sheridan

LEE METCALF
WILDERNESS

Ennis

BEAVERHEAD
NATIONAL
FOREST

Alder

287

357

Virginia City

14 Ruby Reservoir

LEE METCALF
WILDERNESS

Cameron

11 Ruby Creek

12 Bear Creek

BEAVERHEAD
NATIONAL
FOREST

15 Cottonwood

N

287

0   5   10 mi

0   5   10   15   km

Finding the campground: Take US Highway 191 north out of West Yellowstone for 8 miles. Turn left onto US Highway 287 and travel 54 miles. In Cameron turn right at the Community Center onto Bear Creek Road and travel 9 miles. The road turns to gravel.

About the campground: This campground settles in along the Lee Metcalf Wilderness and the Bear Creek Wildlife Management Area. Consequently, wildlife viewing can be superb. Elk, deer, black bears, an occasional grizzly, and a host of other native residents are present. From June 1 through November 30, the campground typically opens and closes depending on the weather.

13 Red Mountain

Location: 99 miles northwest of West Yellowstone on the Madison River.
Facilities: Vault toilets, fire rings, tables, drinking water.
Sites: 17 for tents or RVs/Trailer combinations up to 50 feet long.
Fee: $ per night, 14-day limit.
Managing agency: Bureau of Land Management, Dillon Office, (406) 683–8000.
Activities: Hiking, fishing.
Finding the campground: Take US Highway 191 north out of West Yellowstone for 8 miles. Turn left onto US Highway 287 and travel 82 miles. Turn right onto Montana State Highway 84 and travel 9 miles.
About the campground: Mountains are definitely distant at this location. Flat, sage-filled river bottom greets visitors, making it easy to level up. Anglers are most attracted to this area, though the views are scenic in their own fashion. The campground is open April 1 to December 1.

14 Ruby Reservoir

Location: 106 miles northwest of West Yellowstone on Ruby Reservoir.
Facilities: Vault toilets.
Sites: Dispersed for tents or RVs/Trailer combinations up to 40 feet long.
Fee: None, 14-day limit.
Managing agency: Bureau of Land Management, Dillon Office, (406) 683–8000.
Activities: Hiking, fishing, boating.
Finding the campground: Take US Highway 191 north out of West Yellowstone for 8 miles. Turn left onto US Highway 287 and travel 66 miles. Turn left onto Montana State Highway 287 and travel west out of Ennis for 23 miles to Alder. Turn left at the campground directional sign onto the paved access road and travel 9 miles.
About the campground: The camping is dispersed and is limited to existing parking areas and fire rings. The mountains are here, but the forest is not. A few willows struggle to survive on the constantly fluctuating shoreline. Irrigation places changing demands upon the water stored here. Anglers and rockhounds are the most common visitors in this otherwise infrequently visited area. Ruby-red garnets, some of gem quality, can be found in the sand along the beaches. Digging is not allowed, but when the water is low, there is no need. The campground is open all year long, but it is unlikely anyone will want to experience the below-zero temperatures of a Montana winter.

15 Cottonwood

Location: 133 miles northwest of West Yellowstone.
Facilities: Vault toilet, fire rings, tables.
Sites: 10 for tents or RVs/Trailer combinations up to 28 feet long.
Fee: None, 16-day limit.
Managing agency: Beaverhead National Forest, Madison Ranger District, (406) 682–4253.
Activities: Hiking.
Finding the campground: Take US Highway 191 north out of West Yellowstone for 8 miles. Turn left onto US Highway 287 and travel 66 miles. Turn left onto Montana State Highway 287 and travel west out of Ennis for 23 miles to Alder. Turn left at the campground directional sign onto the paved access road and travel 36 miles. The road will turn to gravel after passing Ruby Reservoir.
About the campground: This is a popular area for hunters and those who like isolation. There is no drinking water or garbage service provided so be prepared. It is considered a long way to the nearest store by most. The campground is open from May 26 through November 30, when the weather allows.

16 Mill Creek

Location: 112 miles northwest of West Yellowstone on Mill Creek.
Facilities: Vault toilet, fire rings, tables, drinking water.
Sites: 10 for tents or RVs/Trailers up to 22 feet long.
Fee: None, 16-day limit.
Managing agency: Beaverhead National Forest, Madison Ranger District, (406) 682–4253.
Activities: Hiking, fishing.
Finding the campground: Take US Highway 191 north out of West Yellowstone for 8 miles. Turn left onto US Highway 287 and travel 66 miles. Turn left onto Montana State Highway 287 and travel west out of Ennis for 31 miles to Sheridan. Turn right onto Mill Creek Road and travel 7 miles.
About the campground: Tall pine trees await those who persevere on the rough, single-lane dirt road toward the end. The going is even rougher when the weather gets things wet. The campground is technically open from June 1 through October 31; however, nature reserves the right to change the dates without notice.

17 Branham Lakes

Location: 118 miles northwest of West Yellowstone on Branham Lake.
Facilities: Vault toilet, fire rings, tables.
Sites: 6 for tents only.
Fee: None, 16-day limit.

Managing agency: Beaverhead National Forest, Madison Ranger District, (406) 842-5432.
Activities: Hiking, fishing.
Finding the campground: Take US Highway 191 north out of West Yellowstone for 8 miles. Turn left onto US Highway 287 and travel 66 miles. Turn left onto Montana State Highway 287 and travel west out of Ennis for 31 miles to Sheridan. Turn right onto Mill Creek Road and travel 13 miles.
About the campground: The July 1 through September 15 season is short at this high mountain perch. At almost 9,000 feet above sea level, the days stay cool and nights get cold. Above all, winter comes early. Call the Madison Ranger District office for road conditions; otherwise, a pleasure trip could become very unpleasant.

18 Potosi

Location: 109 miles northwest of West Yellowstone on Willow Creek.
Facilities: Vault toilets, fire rings, tables, drinking water.
Sites: 15 for tents or RVs/Trailer combinations up to 22 feet long.
Fee: None, 16-day limit.
Managing agency: Beaverhead National Forest, Madison Ranger District, (406) 682-4253.
Activities: Hiking, fishing, wildlife viewing.

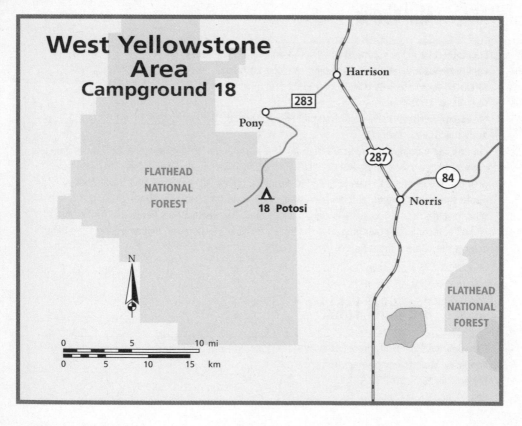

Finding the campground: Take US Highway 191 north out of West Yellowstone for 8 miles. Turn left onto US Highway 287 and travel 88 miles. At Harrison turn left onto paved County Road 283 and travel 5 miles. Just before entering Pony, turn left at the campground directional sign onto gravel County Road 1601 and travel 3 miles. Turn right onto narrow, gravel-to-improved-dirt Willow Creek Road and travel 5 miles.

About the campground: Ancient fir trees snuggle up to the creek bank and spread out at various distances into grassy meadows. Tent campers are directed to one side while RVs settle into semi-level dirt spots on the opposite side. The access routes are different and represent a longer drive for RVs; however, by the time you are situated, there is little space between the two. The surrounding countryside consists of rolling hills stretching out to snow-covered mountains, with a mixture of meadows and forest. During our visit, moose were abundant and we saw plenty of elk and deer. A popular hot spring not far from the camping area creates a great deal of traffic that can be dangerous in spots. The narrow road does not allow two vehicles to pass easily, and the speeds of some travelers make for some intense moments for those with larger units. The campground is open from June 1 through September 30.

19 Lonesomehurst

Location: 12 miles northwest of West Yellowstone on Hebgen Lake.
Facilities: Vault toilet, fire rings, tables, drinking water.
Sites: 27 for tents or RVs/Trailer combinations up to 50 feet long.
Fee: $$ per night, 16-day limit.
Managing agency: Gallatin National Forest, Hebgen Basin Campgrounds, (406) 646–1012.
Activities: Hiking, fishing, boating, wildlife viewing.
Finding the campground: Take US Highway 20 west out of West Yellowstone for 8 miles. Turn right onto Hebgen Lake Road and travel 4 miles.
About the campground: Grass occupies the spaces between pine trees in this camping area. The huge Hebgen Lake attracts wildlife and water lovers alike. The campground is open from May 17 through September 22.

20 Cherry Creek

Location: 14 miles northwest of West Yellowstone on Hebgen Lake.
Facilities: Vault toilet, fire rings, tables.
Sites: 7 tents or RVs up to 16 feet long.
Fee: None, 16-day limit.
Managing agency: Gallatin National Forest, Hebgen Lake Office, (406) 823–6961.
Activities: Hiking, fishing.
Finding the campground: Take US Highway 20 west out of West Yellowstone for 8 miles. Turn right onto Hebgen Lake Road and travel 6 miles.

About the campground: This is considered a primitive camping area, but when others are full, it can be an oasis. If it's late in the afternoon the seven units are likely to already be claimed. The campground is open from Memorial Day through Labor Day, dependent on weather and road conditions.

21 Spring Creek

Location: 18 miles northwest of West Yellowstone on Hebgen Lake.
Facilities: Vault toilet, fire rings, tables.
Sites: 6 for tents or RVs up to 16 feet long.
Fee: None, 16-day limit.
Managing agency: Gallatin National Forest, Hebgen Lake Office, (406) 823-6961.
Activities: Hiking, fishing.
Finding the campground: Take US Highway 20 west out of West Yellowstone for 8 miles. Turn right onto Hebgen Lake Road and travel 10 miles.
About the campground: This primitive area has appeal for those wanting to be away from larger crowds with noisy toys, at least relatively speaking. The campground is open from Memorial Day through mid-October.

22 Upper Lake

Location: 52 miles west of West Yellowstone on Upper Red Rock Lake.
Facilities: Vault toilets, fire rings, tables, drinking water.
Sites: 11 for tents or RVs/Trailer combinations up to 30 feet long.
Fee: $, 16-day limit.
Managing agency: Red Rock Lakes National Wildlife Refuge, (406) 276-3536.
Activities: Hiking, wildlife viewing.
Finding the campground: Take US Highway 20 west out of West Yellowstone for 12 miles. Turn right onto Montana State Highway 87 and travel 5 miles. Turn left at the Sawtell historical marker and travel 30 miles. The Red Rock Pass Road will become improved dirt after about 5 miles.
About the campground: Birds bring most visitors to this refuge, although elk, deer, and moose are no strangers. Aspen trees dominate the camp, with pine and fir trees to the south blanketing the steep mountainside that shadows the area. The dirt access road can be very difficult to travel when wet. The campground is open during the summer.

23 River Marsh

Location: 62 miles west of West Yellowstone on Lower Red Rock Lake.
Facilities: Vault toilets, fire rings.

Sites: Dispersed for tents or RVs/Trailer combinations up to 30 feet long.

Fee: $, 16-day limit.

Managing agency: Red Rock Lakes National Wildlife Refuge, (406) 276-3536.

Activities: Hiking, wildlife viewing.

Finding the campground: Take US Highway 20 west out of West Yellowstone for 12 miles. Turn right onto Montana State Highway 87 and travel 5 miles. Turn left at the Sawtell historical marker and travel 37 miles. The Red Rock Pass Road will become improved dirt after about 5 miles. Turn right at the campground directional sign and travel 3 miles.

About the campground: Wildlife, especially water birds are often seen in this open grassland camping area. If a campfire is important to you, be sure to bring enough wood. A short distance south, steep mountains with forested sides loom above. To the north, a seemingly flat plain stretches out to the forested mountains along the West Fork Madison River. The local habitat provides food and shelter for the more than 230 species of birds that are the primary, though not the only, native residents here. The campground is open during the summer.

Dillon Area

Sagebrush covers most of the ground in this countryside, and snowcapped mountains define the boundary between open flats and rolling, forested ridges. Those who wish can collect gem-quality quartz crystals in the shadow of the Pioneer Mountains at Crystal Park. Rafters frequently float on any one of the ice-cold mountain streams for adventure, wildlife viewing, and scenic panoramas that cannot be seen any other way.

Ghost towns and historic cabins of the Old West are scattered throughout, adding a sense of mystery. Sacajawea, of Lewis and Clark fame, was reunited with her family members south of Dillon, contributing even more to the legends riding on the winds. Chief Joseph of the Nez Perce also passed through, though not without casualty and sadness. Overall, this area is one in which to contemplate our nation's past in light of where we would like to go in the future. Someone has said, "A man learns from his mistakes, but a wise man learns from the mistakes of others."

	Group Sites	Tents	RV sites	Total sites	Hookups	Toilets	Showers	Drinking water	Dump station	Phone	Handicap Access	Recreation	Fee	Season	Stay limit (days)
1 Barretts Park		D	D			V		*			*	FB	N	All Year	14
2 Clark Canyon Reservoir			109	109		V		*			*	FB	N	All Year	14
3 Bannack State Park	2		22	24		V		*			*	HFW	$	Memorial Day to Labor Day	14
4 Grasshopper			24	24		V		*				HF	$	6/16-9/15	16
5 North Van Houten			3	3		V						HF	N	Memorial Day to Labor Day	16
6 South Van Houten			3	3		V						HF	N	Memorial Day to Labor Day	16
7 Miner Lake	2		16	18		V		*				HFB	$	7/5-9/1	16
8 Twin Lakes			21	21		V		*				HFB	$	7/4-9/1	16
9 Mussigbrod			10	10		V		*				HFB	$	7/5-9/1	16
10 May Creek			21	21		V		*				HF	$	6/25-9/6	16
11 Dinner Station			8	8		V		*			*	HF	N	5/15-9/15	16
12 Divide Bridge			13	13		V					*	HF	$	All Year	14
13 Pettengill			3	3		V						HFR	$	6/15-9/30	16
14 Fourth of July			5	5		V		*				HFR	$	6/15-9/30	16
15 Boulder			13	13		V		*				HFR	$	6/15-9/15	16
16 Lodgepole			10	10		V		*				HFR	$	5/25-9/15	16
17 Willow			5	5		V						HFR	$	6/15-9/30	16
18 Little Joe			5	5		V		*				HFR	$	6/15-9/30	16
19 Mono Creek	2		3	5		V		*				HFR	$	6/15-9/30	16
20 Price Creek			28	28		V		*				HR	$	5/29-9/4	16
21 Reservoir Lake			16	16		V		*				HFB	N	6/15-9/15	16
22 Steel Creek			7	7		V		*				HF	$	6/26-9/6	16
23 Seymour			17	17		V						HF	N	5/25-9/15	14

1 Barretts Park

Location: 5 miles southwest of Dillon on the Beaverhead River.

Facilities: Vault toilets, fire rings, tables, drinking water.

Sites: Dispersed for tents or RVs/Trailer combinations up to 30 feet long.

Fee: None, 14-day limit.

Managing agency: US Bureau of Reclamation, (406) 683-6472.

Activities: Fishing, boating.

Finding the campground: Take I-15 southwest out of Dillon for 5 miles.

About the campground: The river flows through a heavily used area. An active railroad, a busy interstate, two very well-traveled country roads, and a large number of private dwellings in the immediate vicinity tend to push the "country" away from the camping area. The campground is open all year long.

2 Clark Canyon Reservoir

Location: 20 miles southwest of Dillon at Clark Canyon Reservoir.
Facilities: Vault toilets, fire rings, tables, drinking water, boat ramp.
Sites: 109 for tents or RVs up to 60 feet long.
Fee: None, 14-day limit.
Managing agency: US Bureau of Reclamation, (406) 683-6472.
Activities: Fishing, boating.
Finding the campground: Take I-15 southwest out of Dillon for 20 miles.
About the campground: Lewis and Clark are historic campers at this location. A member of their group was reunited with family at the site of Camp Fortunate as well. Sacajawea, of the Lemhi Shoshone tribe, recognized her brother Cameahwait while interpreting for the expedition.

This area encompasses nearly 5,000 surface acres of water, with nine camping areas in different localities. All have the same amenities and ultimately the same drawbacks. The lack of trees and the close mountainsides give the wind priority. Water sports and water-related activities dominate here. Travelers looking for mountain forests should consider other alternatives. Firewood is nonexistent so bring plenty. The camping area is open all year long; however, winter winds can be life threatening.

3 Bannack State Park

Location: 28 miles west of Dillon on Grasshopper Creek.
Facilities: Vault toilets, fire rings, tables, drinking water.
Sites: 28 for tents or RVs/Trailer combinations up to 50 feet long.
Fee: $ per night, 14-day limit.
Managing agency: Montana Fish, Wildlife & Parks, (406) 834-3413.
Activities: Hiking, fishing, wildlife viewing.
Finding the campground: Take I-15 southwest out of Dillon for 3 miles to exit 59. Turn right onto paved Montana State Highway 278 and travel 21 miles. Turn left onto the Bannack State Park access road and travel 4 miles.
About the campground: Many campers have previously settled in along Grasshopper Creek, the most notable being the gold seekers of Old West fame. Bannack was Montana's first gold camp and its first territorial capital. The original campers have long since moved on, but not without leaving a lot of memory and material behind. Buildings and Old West features have been restored to "Old West" standards. A tepee is available for overnight use. Three loops provide adequate space between units, and tall cottonwood trees provide shade when the leaves are on. For those who enjoy going back in time, this living ghost town would be well worth staying at. There are

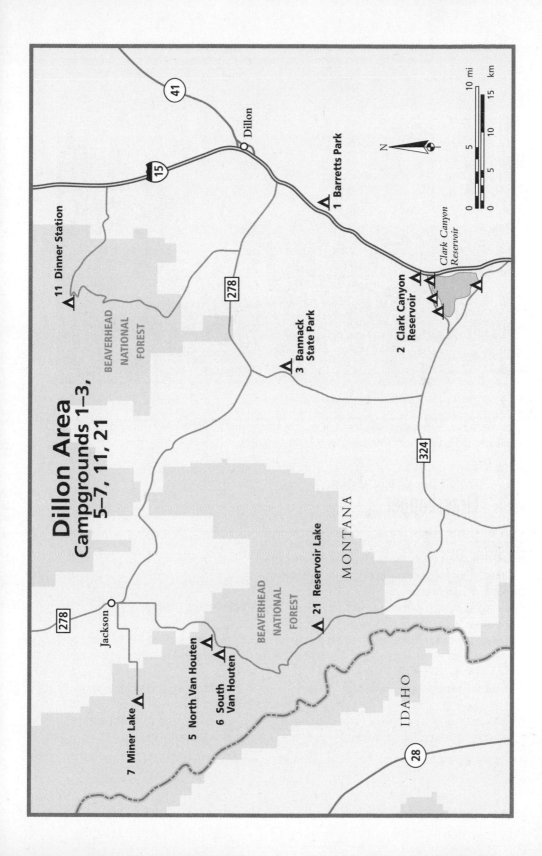

Dillon Area
Campgrounds 1–3, 5–7, 11, 21

41

Dillon

15

11 Dinner Station

278

1 Barretts Park

N

10 mi
km
15
10
5
5
0
0

Clark Canyon Reservoir

BEAVERHEAD NATIONAL FOREST

3 Bannack State Park

2 Clark Canyon Reservoir

324

278

Jackson

MONTANA

7 Miner Lake

5 North Van Houten

6 South Van Houten

BEAVERHEAD NATIONAL FOREST

21 Reservoir Lake

IDAHO

28

This tepee is for rent at Bannack State Park.

various activities throughout the year, but most are scheduled during the summer months. The campground is open from Memorial Day through Labor Day.

4 Grasshopper

Location: 42 miles northwest of Dillon on Grasshopper Creek.
Facilities: Vault toilets, fire rings, tables, drinking water.
Sites: 24 for tents or RVs/Trailers up to 30 feet long.
Fee: $, 16-day limit.
Managing agency: Beaverhead National Forest, Dillon Ranger District, (406) 683–9000.
Activities: Hiking, fishing.
Finding the campground: Take I-15 southwest out of Dillon for 3 miles to exit 59. Turn right onto paved Montana State Highway 278 and travel 22 miles. Turn right onto paved Pioneer Mountains Scenic Byway and travel 13 miles.
About the campground: Grasshopper Creek is smaller in this narrow canyon and has plenty of pine trees along its banks. The parking units, which follow the creek, are far enough apart to create a sense of isolation. The passing gravel road produces plenty of dust, so the farthest units are more appealing. The campground is open from June 16 through September 15.

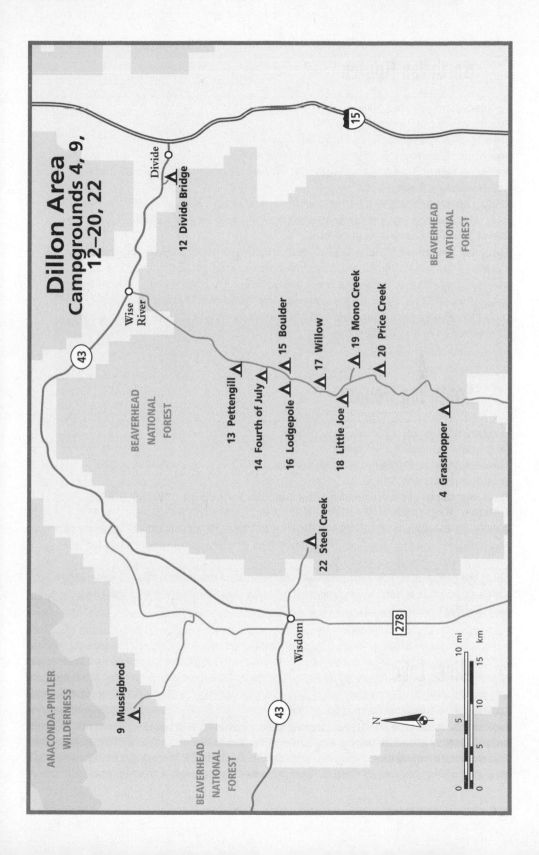

5 North Van Houten

Location: 55 miles west of Dillon.
Facilities: Vault toilet, fire rings, tables.
Sites: 3 for tents or RVs/Trailers up to 20 feet long.
Fee: None, 16-day limit.
Managing agency: Beaverhead National Forest, Wisdom Ranger District, (406) 689-3243.
Activities: Hiking, fishing.
Finding the campground: Take I-15 southwest out of Dillon for 3 miles to exit 59. Turn right onto paved Montana State Highway 278 and travel 42 miles (1 mile south of Jackson). Turn left onto Skinner Meadows Road and travel 10 miles.
About the campground: Weather and fires kept us from visiting this campsite. Consequently, it is left for those who like to explore. A boat launch is listed, though from the map, the campground appears to be some distance from Van Houten Lake. The limited number of camping units suggests the area could be one of those seldom visited hideaways. Of course, the opposite also could be true, leaving the adventurous with a certain amount of risk. The campground is open from Memorial Day through Labor Day.

6 South Van Houten

Location: 55 miles west of Dillon.
Facilities: Vault toilet, fire rings, tables.
Sites: 3 for tents or RVs/Trailers up to 30 feet long.
Fee: None, 16-day limit.
Managing agency: Beaverhead National Forest, Wisdom Ranger District, (406) 689-3243.
Activities: Hiking, fishing.
Finding the campground: Take I-15 southwest out of Dillon for 3 miles to exit 59. Turn right onto paved Montana State Highway 278 and travel 42 miles (1 mile south of Jackson). Turn left onto Skinner Meadows Road and travel 10 miles.
About the campground: This campground is a continuation of the previous listing. Private land appears closer than at North Van Houten, at least on the map. The season is also limited to Memorial Day through Labor Day.

7 Miner Lake

Location: 56 miles west of Dillon at Miner Lake.
Facilities: Vault toilet, fire rings, tables, drinking water, picnic area, boat ramp.
Sites: 2 for tents and 16 for tents or RVs/Trailers up to 20 feet long.
Fee: $ per night, 16-day limit.
Managing agency: Beaverhead National Forest, Wisdom Ranger District, (406) 689-3243.

Activities: Hiking, fishing, boating.

Finding the campground: Take I–15 southwest out of Dillon for 3 miles to exit 59. Turn right onto paved Montana State Highway 278 and travel 43 miles. At Jackson turn left onto County Road 182 and travel 7 miles. Continue on Forest Road 182 for 3 miles.

About the campground: Miner Lake holds about fifty surface acres of cold mountain water. A thick pine forest encloses the camping area. The last portion of the access turns to a single-lane road that continues through the campground. Trailers can fit here, but it could turn into a circus if traffic increases. The high elevation hangs on to the snow well into summer, resulting in a season from July 5 through September 1 that is subject to change.

8 Twin Lakes

Location: 76 miles northwest of Dillon at Twin Lakes.

Facilities: Vault toilets, fire rings, tables, drinking water, picnic area, boat ramp.

Sites: 21 for tents or RVs/Trailers up to 25 feet long.

Fee: $ per night, 16-day limit.

Managing agency: Beaverhead National Forest, Wisdom Ranger District, (406) 689-3243.

Activities: Hiking, fishing, boating.

Finding the campground: Take I–15 southwest out of Dillon for 3 miles to exit 59. Turn right onto paved Montana State Highway 278 and travel 55 miles (12 miles north of Jackson). Turn left onto County Road 1290 and travel 8 miles. Turn left onto Forest Road 945 and travel 5 miles. Turn right onto Forest Road 183 and travel 5 miles.

About the campground: Not quite eighty surface acres of water await those who brave the access road. Thick pines shelter the campground, with scenic views at selected spots. It is open from July 4 through September 1, depending upon the weather.

9 Mussigbrod

Location: 83 miles northwest of Dillon at Mussigbrod Lake.
Facilities: Vault toilet, fire rings, tables, drinking water, picnic area, boat ramp.
Sites: 10 for tents or RVs/Trailers up to 30 feet long.
Fee: $ per night, 16-day limit.
Managing agency: Beaverhead National Forest, Wisdom Ranger District, (406) 689-3243.
Activities: Hiking, fishing, boating.
Finding the campground: Take I–15 southwest out of Dillon for 3 miles to exit 59. Turn right onto paved Montana State Highway 278 and travel 62 miles to Wisdom. Turn left onto Montana State Highway 43 and travel 2 miles. Turn right onto Lower North Fork Road and travel 9 miles. Turn left onto Forest Road 1082 and travel 4 miles. Turn right onto Forest Road 8984 and travel 3 miles.
About the campground: Tall pines and about one hundred surface acres of water were here when we visited. Forest fires subsequently were reported in the area, but we didn't have time to return. The campground is open from July 5 through September 1.

10 May Creek

Location: 82 miles northwest of Dillon on May Creek.
Facilities: Vault toilets, fire rings, tables, drinking water, picnic area.
Sites: 21 for tents or RVs/Trailers up to 30 feet long.
Fee: $ per night, 16-day limit.
Managing agency: Beaverhead National Forest, Wisdom Ranger District, (406) 689-3243.
Activities: Hiking, fishing.
Finding the campground: Take I–15 southwest out of Dillon for 3 miles to exit 59. Turn right onto paved Montana State Highway 278 and travel 62 miles. Turn left onto Montana State Highway 43 and travel 17 miles.
About the campground: Chief Joseph led the Nez Perce through here and camped about 8 miles east at what is now known as the Big Hole National Battlefield. Unfortunately, their stay ended with gunfire and death. Tall lodgepole pines shelter the camp, and grassy meadows infested with willow brush line the stream bank. The units seem a little close to each other, but the area is not typically visited with the same intensity as other area campgrounds. Winter snow can stay well into the summer months, so be prepared. The campground is open from June 25 through September 6.

11 Dinner Station

Location: 24 miles northwest of Dillon on Birch Creek.
Facilities: Vault toilet, fire rings, tables.
Sites: 8 for tents or RVs/Trailers up to 16 feet long.
Fee: $, 16-day limit.
Managing agency: Beaverhead National Forest, Dillon Ranger District, (406) 683-3900.
Activities: Hiking, fishing.
Finding the campground: Take I-15 north out of Dillon for 12 miles to Apex/exit 74. Turn left onto paved-becoming-improved-dirt Birch Creek Road and travel 12 miles.
About the campground: Pine trees and scenic views await those who are patient enough to make the journey. Bring plenty of supplies; you may want to stay longer. Warm clothes are also necessary as you'll be at an elevation of around 7,500 feet above sea level. Depending upon actual weather conditions, the campground is open from May 15 through September 15.

12 Divide Bridge

Location: 42 miles north of Dillon on the Big Hole River.
Facilities: Vault toilets, fire rings, tables, drinking water.
Sites: 21 for tents or RVs/Trailer combinations up to 50 feet long.
Fee: $ per night, 14-day limit.
Managing agency: Bureau of Land Management, Butte District, (406) 494-5059.
Activities: Hiking, fishing.
Finding the campground: Take I-15 north out of Dillon for 39 miles to Divide/exit 102. Turn left onto Montana State Highway 43 and travel 3 miles. Just after crossing the Big Hole River, turn left onto the gravel access road and travel 0.5 mile.
About the campground: Three pull-through units closely hug the banks of the Big Hole River, a blue-ribbon fishery. The other back-in units accommodate RVs up to 50 feet long, with parking for unhooking if needed. An additional space is provided for a host, though the position could be vacant at different times. A grove of cottonwood trees filters out any sun that finds its way into the canyon bottom. Firewood will take some effort to gather. A day-use area complete with a boat ramp is located close by, just off the access road. The boat ramp is more popular with rafters putting in to float to points below. Between the camping area and the day-use area, the Sawmill Gulch Hiking Trail provides explorers with a route to the mountain wilds as it winds up a rocky draw engulfed in pine trees. Drinking water and other amenities are not available during colder months, but the campground is open all year long.

13 Pettengill

Location: 61 miles northwest of Dillon on the Wise River.
Facilities: Vault toilet, fire rings, tables, picnic area.

Sites: 3 for RVs/Trailers up to the 24 feet long.

Fee: $ per night, 16-day limit.

Managing agency: Beaverhead National Forest, Wise River Ranger District, (406) 832-3178.

Activities: Hiking, fishing, rockhounding.

Finding the campground: Take I-15 north out of Dillon for 39 miles to Divide/exit 102. Turn left onto Montana Highway 43 and travel west for 12 miles to Wise River. In Wise River, just after crossing the river, turn left onto paved Pioneer Mountains Scenic Byway and travel 10 miles. The byway is not well marked, so watch for the turn.

About the campground: Level, paved parking units offer easy setup for campers along the byway. Tall lodgepole pines shade the intermittent grass and brush along the river. Pettengill Creek joins the Wise River nearby, adding to the chorus created from defiant boulders in its path. Firewood gathering will take a little work, but it is nearby. Drinking water is not available, so be sure to have enough. This quiet little spot is well suited for trailers or large RVs. Tent campers would most likely find other locations more suitable. The campground is open from June 15 through September 30.

14 Fourth of July

Location: 62 miles northwest of Dillon.

Facilities: Vault toilets, fire rings, tables, drinking water, picnic area.

Sites: 5 for tents or RVs/Trailers up to 30 feet long.

Fee: $ per night, 16-day limit.

Managing agency: Beaverhead National Forest, Wise River Ranger District, (406) 832-3178.

Activities: Hiking, fishing, rockhounding.

Finding the campground: Take I-15 north out of Dillon for 39 miles to Divide/exit 102. Turn left onto Montana Highway 43 and travel west for 12 miles to Wise River. In Wise River, just after crossing the river, turn left onto paved Pioneer Mountains Scenic Byway and travel 11 miles. The byway is not well marked, so watch for the turn.

About the campground: Douglas fir and some pine trees shelter the campground and most of the surrounding area, with grassy meadows in between. The paved access road stops at the parking units, which tend to fill quickly on weekends and holidays. The campground is open from June 15 through September 30.

15 Boulder

Location: 63 miles northwest of Dillon.

Facilities: Vault toilets, fire rings, tables, drinking water.

Sites: 13 for tents or RVs/Trailers up to 30 feet long.

Fee: $ per night, 16-day limit.

Managing agency: Beaverhead National Forest, Wise River Ranger District, (406) 832-3178.

Activities: Hiking, fishing, rockhounding.

Finding the campground: Take I-15 north out of Dillon for 39 miles to Divide/exit 102. Turn left onto Montana Highway 43 and travel west for 12 miles to Wise River. In Wise River, just after crossing the river, turn left onto paved Pioneer Mountains Scenic Byway and travel 12 miles. The byway is not well marked, so watch for the turn.

About the campground: Tall, mature lodgepole pines line the paved access road and parking units. The level parking aprons make spotting trailers and longer RVs convenient; however, traffic noise could be noticeable. Firewood will take some effort to gather, so bring some along. Anglers may find camping at Lodgepole Campground on the other side of the highway along the Wise River more appealing. Services are available at the campground from June 15 through September 15, but it can be used at other times, too.

16 Lodgepole

Location: 63 miles northwest of Dillon on the Wise River.
Facilities: Vault toilet, fire rings, tables, drinking water.
Sites: 10 for tents or RVs/Trailers up to 30 feet long.
Fee: $ per night, 16-day limit.
Managing agency: Beaverhead National Forest, Wise River Ranger District, (406) 832-3178.
Activities: Hiking, fishing, rockhounding.
Finding the campground: Take I-15 north out of Dillon for 39 miles to Divide/exit 102. Turn left onto Montana Highway 43 and travel west for 12 miles to Wise River. In Wise River, just after crossing the river, turn left onto paved Pioneer Mountains Scenic Byway and travel 12 miles. The byway is not well marked, so watch for the turn.

About the campground: The Wise River glides peacefully by, with lodgepole pines standing guard along the banks. Anglers will likely find this camping area more appealing than Boulder Campground just across the road. Traffic noise will be somewhat negated by its greater distance from the highway and the river music. The campground is open from May 25 through September 15.

17 Willow

Location: 65 miles northwest of Dillon on the Wise River.
Facilities: Vault toilet, fire rings, tables.
Sites: 5 for tents or RVs/Trailers up to 26 feet long.
Fee: $, 16-day limit.
Managing agency: Beaverhead National Forest, Wise River Ranger District, (406) 832-3178.
Activities: Hiking, fishing, rockhounding.
Finding the campground: Take I-15 north out of Dillon for 39 miles to Divide/exit 102. Turn right onto Montana Highway 43 and travel west for 12 miles to Wise River. In Wise River, just after crossing the river, turn left onto paved Pioneer Mountains Scenic Byway and travel 14 miles. The byway is not well marked, so watch for the turn.

About the campground: Lodgepole pines welcome visitors but do not share drinking water. Reportedly trailers up to 16 feet long can fit here; however, it will take some forethought and unhooking. The campground is open from June 15 through September 30.

18 Little Joe

Location: 71 miles northwest of Dillon on the Wise River.
Facilities: Vault toilet, fire rings, tables, drinking water, picnic area.
Sites: 5 for tents or RVs/Trailers up to 28 feet long.
Fee: $ per night, 16-day limit.
Managing agency: Beaverhead National Forest, Wise River Ranger District, (406) 832-3178.
Activities: Hiking, fishing, rockhounding.
Finding the campground: Take I-15 north out of Dillon for 39 miles to Divide/exit 102. Turn right onto Montana Highway 43 and travel west for 12 miles to Wise River. In Wise River, just after crossing the river, turn left onto paved Pioneer Mountains Scenic Byway and travel 20 miles. The byway is not well marked, so watch for the turn.
About the campground: Tall lodgepole pines share their drinking water here via a hand pump. The available firewood requires some search and seizure. The paved access road keeps both noise and dust down. The gravel parking spots are level and with planning and unhooking can accommodate trailers up to a maximum of 28 feet long. The campground is open from June 15 through September 30, depending on the weather.

19 Mono Creek

Location: 74 miles northwest of Dillon.
Facilities: Vault toilet, fire rings, tables, drinking water.
Sites: 2 for tents and 3 for RVs/Trailers up to 16 feet long.
Fee: $ per night, 16-day limit.
Managing agency: Beaverhead National Forest, Wise River Ranger District, (406) 832-3178.
Activities: Hiking, fishing, rockhounding.
Finding the campground: Take I-15 north out of Dillon for 39 miles to Divide/exit 102. Turn left onto Montana Highway 43 and travel west for 12 miles to Wise River. In Wise River, just after crossing the river, turn left onto paved Pioneer Mountains Scenic Byway and travel 22 miles. The byway is not well marked, so watch for the turn. Turn left onto the gravel road at the campground directional sign and travel 1 mile. The campground is on the left side of the road.
About the campground: The nearby ghost town of Coolidge attracts many visitors. Consequently, dust levels near the entrance to the campground can get rather high. The gravel access road and semi-level parking spots might not be appealing to those who wish to be farther from the main highway. The campground is open from June 15 through September 30.

20 Price Creek

Location: 78 miles northwest of Dillon.
Facilities: Vault toilets, fire rings, tables, drinking water.
Sites: 28 for tents or RVs/Trailers up to 30 feet long.
Fee: $ per night, 16-day limit.
Managing agency: Beaverhead National Forest, Dillon Ranger District, (406) 683-3900.
Activities: Hiking, rockhounding.
Finding the campground: Take I-15 north out of Dillon for 39 miles to Divide/exit 102. Turn left onto Montana Highway 43 and travel west for 12 miles to Wise River. In Wise River, just after crossing the river, turn left onto paved Pioneer Mountains Scenic Byway and travel 27 miles. The byway is not well marked, so watch for the turn.
About the campground: This campground, at the end of the paved road, is easy to miss. If you leave the pavement, start looking for a safe place to turn around. Crystal Park, about 1 mile before the campground, is another landmark. Rockhounds could find this pine-shaded area very appealing. Digging for gem-quality quartz crystals is a popular activity for visitors of all ages at Crystal Park. Parking units are spaced far enough apart to allow a sense of privacy, but there is little underbrush between the tall lodgepole pines. Open, grassy meadows are nearby and offer the chance of spotting wildlife. Some year's snow hangs around a long time, which may affect the open dates of May 29 through September 4.

21 Reservoir Lake

Location: 61 miles west of Dillon on Reservoir Lake.
Facilities: Vault toilets, fire rings, tables, drinking water, picnic area, boat ramp.
Sites: 16 for tents or RVs/Trailers up to 16 feet long.
Fee: $, 16-day limit.
Managing agency: Beaverhead National Forest, Dillon Ranger District, (406) 683-3900.
Activities: Hiking, fishing, boating (electric motors).
Finding the campground: Take I-15 southwest out of Dillon for 20 miles to Clark Canyon Reservoir/exit 44. Turn right onto Montana State Highway 324 and travel 20 miles. Turn right at the campground sign onto the gravel road and travel 21 miles. The road gets rough toward the end and can test both mind and machine.
About the campground: A little over ten surface acres of ice-cold mountain water snuggle up to the hillside this campground occupies. First arrivals have a choice between pine-shaded spots and sagebrush with a view. Winter can hang on well past expected dates and affect the general season from June 15 through September 15.

22 Steel Creek

Location: 74 miles northwest of Dillon on Steel Creek.
Facilities: Vault toilets, fire rings, tables, drinking water.

Sites: 2 for tents or 7 for RVs/Trailers up to 22 feet long.
Fee: $ per night, 16-day limit.
Managing agency: Beaverhead National Forest, Wisdom Ranger District, (406) 689–3243.
Activities: Hiking, fishing.
Finding the campground: Take I–15 south out of Dillon for 3 miles to exit 59. Turn right onto paved Montana State Highway 278 and travel 62 miles to Wisdom. Turn right onto Montana State Highway 43 and travel 1 mile (1/4 mile out of town). Turn right onto gravel Steel Creek Road and travel 9 miles.
About the campground: Lodgepole pines dominate the tree population, with Douglas fir scattered about. Steel Creek makes its way in between on its ocean-bound journey. This place could easily be one of those well-kept secrets, but it does require a sacrifice of sorts with respect to the dusty, rutted access. The campground is open from June 26 through September 6.

23 Seymour

Location: 71 miles northwest of Dillon.
Facilities: Vault toilets, fire rings, tables.
Sites: 17 for tents or RVs/Trailers up to 18 feet long.

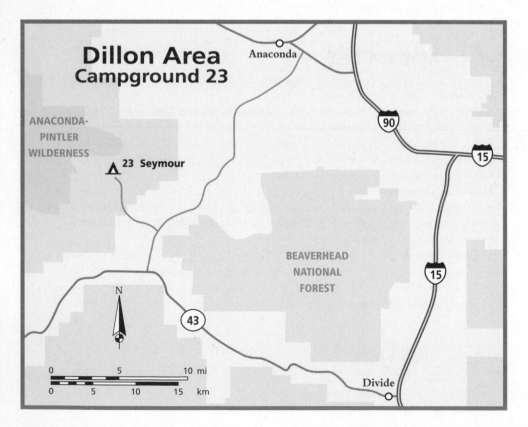

Fee: None, 14-day limit.

Managing agency: Beaverhead National Forest, Wise River Ranger District, (406) 832–3178.

Activities: Hiking, fishing nearby.

Finding the campground: Take I-15 north out of Dillon for 39 miles to Divide/exit 102. Turn left onto Montana Highway 43 and travel west for 22 miles. Turn right onto the paved road at the Anaconda directional sign and travel 4 miles. Turn left onto the gravel road at the campground directional sign and travel 8 miles.

About the campground: Anglers must journey about 1 mile to attempt catching trout. The hand pumps no longer provide drinking water, so be sure to pack some with you. Also, this is a pack-it-in/pack-it-out camping area; there is no garbage service. The campground settles snugly into thick pines, and when weather permits, is open from May 25 through September 15.

Great Falls Area

The Great Falls of the Missouri River prevented riverboats from going any farther upstream. Lewis and Clark visited the site on their historic trip and got to see it before the modern desire for electricity dammed the mighty river. There is still plenty of history and unspoiled landscape for those who seek it, albeit with some effort to find it.

The majority of the campgrounds in this area reside in mountain hideaways that could be classified as islands in a vast prairie sea. Wildlife is plentiful but tends to migrate into the lush pastures of nearby ranches.

	Group Sites	Tents	RV sites	Total sites	Hookups	Toilets	Showers	Drinking water	Dump station	Phone	Handicap Access	Recreation	Fee	Season	Stay limit (days)
1 Cave Mountain			14	14		V		*				HF	$	Summer	14
2 West Fork Teton	6			6		V		*				H	N	Summer	14
3 Lake Elwell Reservoir			D	D		V		*			*	HFB	N	All Year	14
4 Coalbanks			13	13		V						HFB	N	All Year	14
5 Fresno Reservoir			D	D		V					*	FB	N	All Year	14
6 Judith Landing			10	10		V		*				HFB	$	6/15-10/15	14
7 Thain Creek			20	20		V		*			*	HF	$	Summer	16
8 Logging Creek			25	25		V		*			*	HF	$	Summer	16
9 Aspen			6	6		V		*				H	$	Summer	16
10 Many Pines			23	23		V		*			*	HF	$	Summer	16
11 Kings Hill			18	18		V		*			*	H	$	Summer	16
12 Jumping Creek			15	15		V		*			*	HF	$	Summer	16
13 Moose Creek			6	6		V		*				HF	$	Summer	16
14 Grasshopper Creek			12	12		V		*				HF	$	Summer	16
15 Richardson Creek			3	3		V						HF	N	Summer	16
16 Spring Creek			10	10		V		*				HF	$	Summer	14
17 Dry Wolf			26	26		V		*				HF	$	Summer	16
18 Indian Hill			7	7		V		*				HF	N	Summer	16
19 Hay Canyon			7	7		V						HF	N	Summer	16
20 Ackley Lake State Park			23	23		V						FB	$	All Year	14
21 Crystal Lake			28	28		V					*	HF	$	Summer	16

1   Cave Mountain

Location: 78 miles northwest of Great Falls on the North Fork Teton River.
Facilities: Vault toilets, fire rings, tables, drinking water.
Sites: 14 for tents or RVs/Trailers up to 35 feet long.
Fee: $ per night, 14-day limit.
Managing agency: Lewis and Clark National Forest, Rocky Mountain Ranger District, (406) 466-5341.
Activities: Hiking, fishing.
Finding the campground: Take I-15 northwest out of Great Falls for 10 miles to exit 290. Turn left onto US Highway 89 and travel 45 miles to the Teton Pass Winter Sports Area. Turn left at the recreational directional sign onto Forest Road 144 and travel 23 miles. The last 5 miles turn to gravel and dirt.

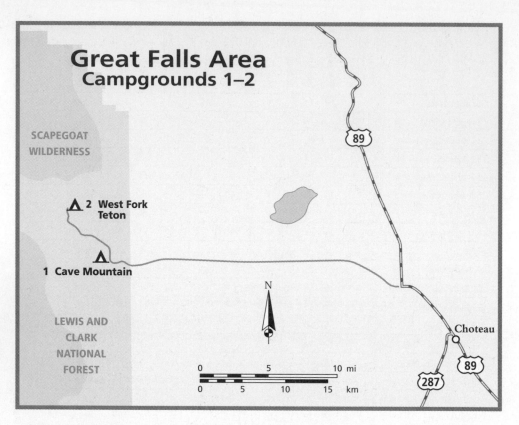

Great Falls Area
Campgrounds 1–2

SCAPEGOAT
WILDERNESS

▲ 2 West Fork
Teton

▲
1 Cave Mountain

N

LEWIS AND
CLARK
NATIONAL
FOREST

Choteau

0   5   10 mi
0   5   10   15   km

About the campground: Aspen and fir trees supply shade for most of the camping units, which have plenty of space in between. The first arrivals will have a choice of sites overlooking the river. There are no set dates; the campground is open when the weather permits.

2 West Fork Teton

Location: 88 miles northwest of Great Falls

Facilities: Vault toilet, fire rings, tables, drinking water.

Sites: 6 for tents.

Fee: None, 14-day limit.

Managing agency: Lewis and Clark National Forest, Rocky Mountain Ranger District, (406) 466–5341.

Activities: Hiking.

Finding the campground: Take I-15 northwest out of Great Falls for 10 miles to exit 290. Turn left onto US Highway 89 and travel 45 miles to the Teton Pass Winter Sports Area. Turn left at the recreational directional sign onto Forest Road 144 and travel 33 miles. The last 15 miles turn to gravel and dirt.

About the campground: This is a wilderness access with no room for RVs. This is bear country; consequently, bear-proof food storage is mandatory. Be prepared. Weather dictates exactly when and how long the campground will be open, and it can close without notice.

3 Lake Elwell Reservoir

Location: 143 miles north of Great Falls on Lake Elwell.
Facilities: Vault toilets, fire rings, tables, drinking water.
Sites: Dispersed and developed for tents and RVs.
Fee: None, 14-day limit.
Managing agency: US Bureau of Reclamation, (406) 759-5077.
Activities: Hiking, fishing, boating.
Finding the campground: Take I-15 north out of Great Falls for 82 miles to Shelby. Take US Highway 2 east out of Shelby for 42 miles to Chester. Turn right onto County Road 223 and travel 12 miles. Turn right at the campground directional sign and travel 7 miles.
About the campground: Wind-sculpted sandstone formations and approximately 50 miles of shoreline await your visit. There are six different camping areas scattered along the reservoir: Willow Creek, North Bootlegger, Island Area, Sanford Park, VFW Campground, and South Bootlegger. Visitors

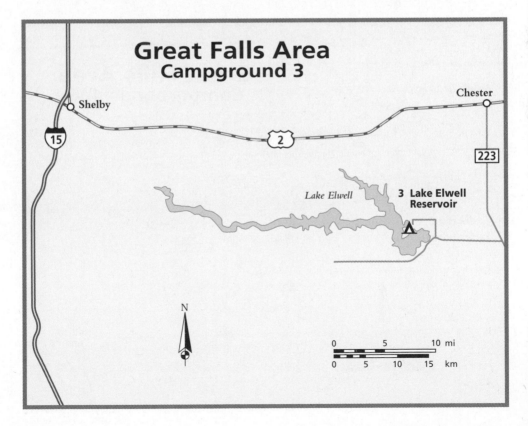

are primarily interested in water sports, enough so to support a marina. Camping is allowed year-round; however, winter can be brutal if you are not prepared.

4 Coalbanks

Location: 73 miles northeast of Great Falls on the Missouri River.
Facilities: Vault toilets, fire rings, tables.
Sites: 13 for tents or RVs/Trailer combinations up to 40 feet long.
Fee: $, 14-day limit.
Managing agency: Bureau of Land Management, Fort Benton Office, (406) 622-4000.
Activities: Hiking, fishing, boating.
Finding the campground: Take US Highway 87 northeast out of Great Falls for 68 miles. Turn right at the Upper Missouri Wild & Scenic River sign onto the gravel Gardiner Road and travel about 7 miles. Turn left onto the Virgelle Ferry Road and travel 1 mile.
About the campground: This popular place finds many following the historic steps of Lewis and Clark, among others. The Missouri River is much the way early explorers found it. Steamboats at one time dug coal from the banks near here for fuel. The campground is open all year long.

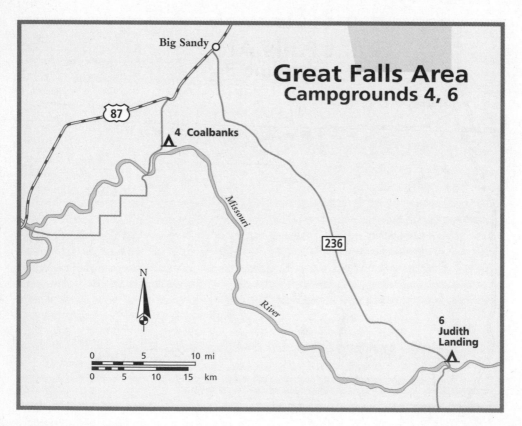

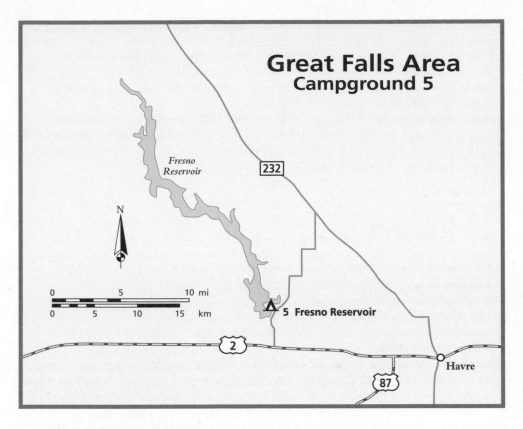

5 Fresno Reservoir

Location: 128 miles northeast of Great Falls on Fresno Reservoir.
Facilities: Vault toilet, fire rings, tables.
Sites: Dispersed for tents and RVs.
Fee: None, 14-day limit.
Managing agency: US Bureau of Reclamation, (406) 759-5077.
Activities: Fishing, boating.
Finding the campground: Take US Highway 87 northeast out of Great Falls for 114 miles to Havre. Take US Highway 2 west out of Havre for 12 miles. Turn right at the sign and travel 2 miles.
About the campground: Anglers are more attracted to this prairie setting than are touring campers. Three separate campgrounds, River Run, Kiehns, and Kremlin, are open all year long, but Kiehns is the only one well suited for trailers.

6 Judith Landing

Location: 123 miles northeast of Great Falls on the Missouri River.
Facilities: Vault toilets, fire rings, tables, drinking water, boat ramp.

Sites: 10 for tents or RVs/Trailer combinations up to 60 feet long.
Fee: $, 14-day limit.
Managing agency: Bureau of Land Management, Lewistown Field Office, (406) 538–1900.
Activities: Hiking, fishing, boating.
Finding the campground: Take US Highway 87 northeast out of Great Falls for 79 miles to Big Sandy. Turn right onto County Road 236 and travel 44 miles.
About the campground: Large cottonwood trees and the mighty Missouri await travelers here much the same as Lewis and Clark would have seen it. Of course, today's accommodations are far more modern, but the overall landscape invites you to interpret past events. The campground is open from June 15 through October 15.

7 Thain Creek

Location: 37 miles east of Great Falls on Thain Creek.
Facilities: Vault toilets, fire rings, tables, drinking water.
Sites: 20 for tents or RVs/Trailers up to 22 feet long.
Fee: $ per night, 16-day limit.
Managing agency: Lewis and Clark National Forest, Judith Ranger District, (406) 566–2292.
Activities: Hiking, fishing.
Finding the campground: Take US Highway 89 east out of Great Falls for 6 miles to County Road 228. Turn left onto paved CR 228 and travel 13 miles. Continue straight on gravel County Road 121 for about 10 miles to the Highwood intersection. Turn right to stay on CR 121 and travel 6 miles. Follow the signs to the campground for another 2 miles on the very rough Forest Road 8840.
About the campground: Tall lodgepole pine and aspen trees offer a sense of seclusion for those determined to travel the frustrating access. The last loop of three settles into more of a clear setting, though it is quite a bit farther away from the stream. If hearing water bubble over boulders is important, the first loop is best. Parking spots are grassy and for the most part unleveled. Trailers do fit; however, unhooking is required. Steep, forested mountains surround this hidden spot, so be sure to bring plenty of warm clothes. The campground is open during the summer with no dates listed. No doubt, the weather dictates the exact dates.

8 Logging Creek

Location: 48 miles southeast of Great Falls on Logging Creek.
Facilities: Vault toilets, fire rings, tables, drinking water.
Sites: 25 for tents or RVs/Trailers up to 30 feet long.
Fee: $ per night, 16-day limit.
Managing agency: Lewis and Clark National Forest, Belt Creek Ranger District, (406) 236–5511.
Activities: Hiking, fishing.
Finding the campground: Take US Highway 87/89 east out of Great Falls for 25 miles. Turn right at the campground directional sign onto US 89 and travel 11 miles. Turn right onto the paved-

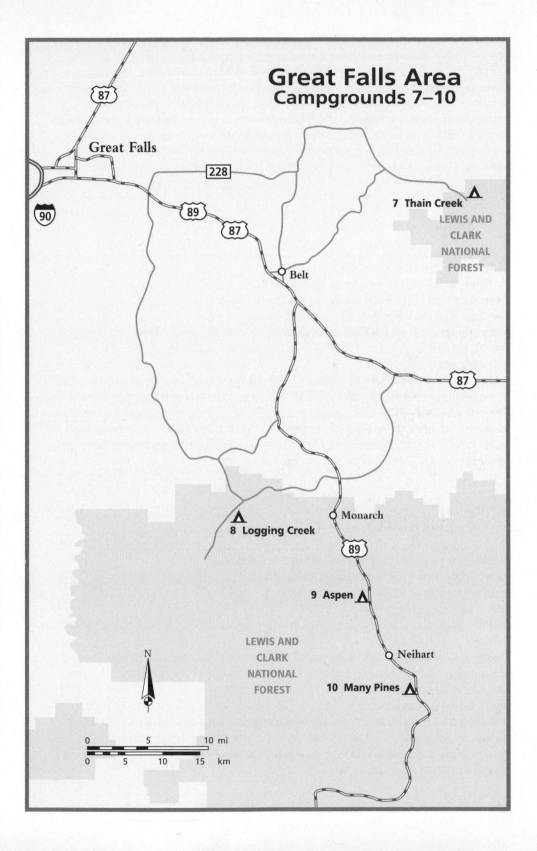

Great Falls Area
Campgrounds 7–10

87

Great Falls

228

90

89

87

7 Thain Creek

LEWIS AND
CLARK
NATIONAL
FOREST

Belt

87

8 Logging Creek

Monarch

89

9 Aspen

Neihart

10 Many Pines

LEWIS AND
CLARK
NATIONAL
FOREST

N

0   5   10 mi
0   5   10   15 km

becoming-gravel Sluice Boxes State Park access road and travel 6 miles. Bear left onto Forest Road 67 and travel 4 miles. Turn right onto Forest Road 839 and travel 2 miles.

About the campground: Campers will find lots of room between parking units in the tall pine trees here. Crystal-clear Logging Creek slides along over limestone stair steps and there are numerous handmade dams, obvious efforts of past visitors to deepen the pools. The campground occupies relatively flat terrain with cliffs defining the north stream bank and steep, rocky ridges the south. Trailers do fit well here, but the only way out is via the loop at the very end. Opening and closing dates are subject to weather conditions.

9 Aspen

Location: 55 miles southeast of Great Falls.
Facilities: Vault toilet, fire rings, tables, drinking water.
Sites: 6 for tents or RVs/Trailer combinations up to 40 feet long.
Fee: $ per night, 16-day limit.
Managing agency: Lewis and Clark National Forest, White Sulfur Springs Ranger District, (406) 547–3361.
Activities: Hiking.
Finding the campground: Take US Highway 87/89 east out of Great Falls for 25 miles. Turn right at the campground directional sign onto US 89 and travel 30 miles. The campground is on the right side of the highway.
About the campground: The gravel parking spots are level and very close to the main highway. Aspen mingles with lodgepole pine, randomly sprouting up among the more dominant tall grass. The campground is open during the summer, weather permitting.

10 Many Pines

Location: 62 miles southeast of Great Falls on Belt Creek.
Facilities: Vault toilet, fire rings, tables, drinking water.
Sites: 24 for tents or RVs/Trailers up to 30 feet long.
Fee: $ per night, 16-day limit.
Managing agency: Lewis and Clark National Forest, Belt Creek Ranger District, (406) 236–5511.
Activities: Hiking, fishing.
Finding the campground: Take US Highway 87/89 east out of Great Falls for 25 miles. Turn right at the campground directional sign onto US 89 and travel 37 miles. The campground is on the right side of the highway.
About the campground: Two loops with some pull-throughs divide near the water hand pump at the entrance. Mature lodgepole pines share the area with a few Douglas fir trees just off the highway. Anglers will have a bit of a hike to access the better fishing. Longer trailers could fit here, but unhooking is required. As with other campgrounds in this area, the weather determines when it's open and when it's closed.

11 Kings Hill

Location: 68 miles southeast of Great Falls.
Facilities: Vault toilets, fire rings, tables, drinking water.
Sites: 18 for tents or RVs/Trailers up to 20 feet long.
Fee: $ per night, 16-day limit.
Managing agency: Lewis and Clark National Forest, White Sulphur Springs Ranger District, (406) 547-3361.
Activities: Hiking.
Finding the campground: Take US Highway 87/89 east out of Great Falls for 25 miles. Turn right at the campground directional sign onto US 89 and travel 43 miles. The campground is on the right side of the highway.
About the campground: The campground was closed for the 2018 season to take care of a hazardous tree issue so there will be less shade in spots. The camping units take advantage of any level spots, creating some interesting accesses to the fire rings and tables. Leveling should not pose much of a problem on the gravel aprons. Firewood will take some effort both to find and to transport. The operational season is strictly dependent upon the weather.

12 Jumping Creek

Location: 77 miles southeast of Great Falls on Jumping Creek.
Facilities: Vault toilet, fire rings, grills, tables, drinking water.
Sites: 15 for tents or RV/Trailers combinations up to 40 feet long.
Fee: $ per night, 16-day limit.
Managing agency: Lewis and Clark National Forest, White Sulphur Springs Ranger District, (406) 547-3361.
Activities: Hiking, fishing.
Finding the campground: Take US Highway 87/89 east out of Great Falls for 25 miles. Turn right at the sign onto US 89 and travel 52 miles. The campground is on the left side of the highway.
About the campground: After winding a short distance through the thick fir trees and crossing the clear mountain waters of Jumping Creek, you will have to choose between two loops. Both are well shaded and far enough from the highway to help you feel secluded. The drinking water comes from a hand pump, providing the weather is favorable. Things can get cold early and stay that way for a long time, so the campground is open only during the summer.

13 Moose Creek

Location: 90 miles southeast of Great Falls on Moose Creek.
Facilities: Vault toilet, fire rings, tables, drinking water, picnic area.
Sites: 6 for tents or RVs/Trailer combinations up to 46 feet long.
Fee: $ per night, 16-day limit.

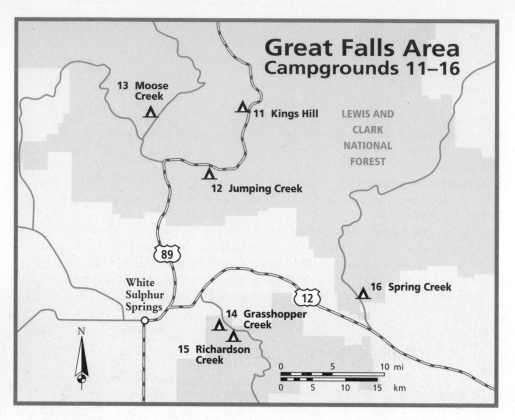

Great Falls Area
Campgrounds 11–16

13 Moose Creek

11 Kings Hill

LEWIS AND CLARK NATIONAL FOREST

12 Jumping Creek

89

White Sulphur Springs

12

16 Spring Creek

14 Grasshopper Creek

N

15 Richardson Creek

| 0 | | 5 | | 10 mi |
| 0 | 5 | 10 | 15 | km |

Managing agency: Lewis and Clark National Forest, White Sulphur Springs Ranger District, (406) 547-3361.

Activities: Hiking, fishing.

Finding the campground: Take US Highway 87/89 east out of Great Falls for 25 miles. Turn right at the sign onto US 89 and travel 56 miles. Turn right onto gravel Forest Road 119 and travel 6 miles. Turn right onto gravel Forest Road 204 and travel 3 miles.

About the campground: Fir trees shelter the campground and blanket the surrounding mountains. Moose Creek runs along the edge, though none of the units sit directly on the bank. Numerous regulation signs are posted regarding alcohol use. During our visit no violations occurred, all the same these signs were not prevalent at other nearby camping areas. Longer RVs could fit here, but it will take some creative forethought. True to the nature of this wild area, the weather dictates open dates.

14 Grasshopper Creek

Location: 104 miles southeast of Great Falls on Grasshopper Creek.

Facilities: Vault toilet, fire rings, tables, drinking water.

Sites: 12 for tents or RVs up to 22 feet long.

Drinking water is available at Grasshopper Creek once the pump handle is attached in warmer weather.

Fee: $ per night, 16-day limit.

Managing agency: Lewis and Clark National Forest, White Sulphur Springs Ranger District, (406) 547–3361.

Activities: Hiking, fishing.

Finding the campground: Take US Highway 87/89 east out of Great Falls for 25 miles. Turn right at the highway sign onto US 89 and travel 71 miles. Turn left onto US Highway 12 and travel 4 miles. Turn right at the National Forest Access/Forest Road 211 sign onto the rough gravel road and travel 4 miles. Turn right at the intersection and travel a short distance to the campground.

About the campground: Grasshopper Creek bubbles by with nature's music serenading campers and the forest alike. Grassy meadows surround pine trees and thick brush. Leveling the grassy spots will take both forethought and work. The campground is open or closed at various times, depending upon snow cover.

15 Richardson Creek

Location: 105 miles southeast of Great Falls on Richardson Creek.

Facilities: Vault toilet, fire rings, tables; no drinking water provided.

Sites: 3 for tents or RVs/Trailers up to 16 feet long.

Fee: None, 16-day limit.

Managing agency: Lewis and Clark National Forest, White Sulphur Springs Ranger District, (406) 547–3361.

Activities: Hiking, fishing.

Finding the campground: Take US Highway 87/89 east out of Great Falls for 25 miles. Turn right at the highway sign onto US 89 and travel 71 miles. Turn left onto US Highway 12 and travel 4 miles. Turn right at the National Forest Access/Forest Road 211 sign onto the rough gravel road and travel 4 miles. Turn left at the intersection and travel 1 mile.

About the campground: The campground dominates a meadow that slopes away from the ice-cold waters of Richardson Creek. Mature pines blanket the surrounding mountainsides and march along the creek bank. Richardson Creek is noticeably larger than Grasshopper Creek and has deep, clear pools that tempt anglers and waders alike. Reaching the better pools involves some hiking from the camping area, but the scenery and a chance of spotting deer, elk, or other wildlife make the exercise worth it. As with Grasshopper Creek, camping seasons depend upon snow cover.

16 Spring Creek

Location: 126 miles southeast of Great Falls on Spring Creek.

Facilities: Vault toilets, fire rings, tables, drinking water.

Sites: 10 for tents or RVs/Trailers up to 30 feet long.

Fee: $ per night, 14-day limit.

Managing agency: Lewis and Clark National Forest, Musselshell Ranger District, (406) 632–4391.

Activities: Hiking, fishing.

Finding the campground: Take US Highway 87/89 east out of Great Falls for 25 miles. Turn right at the sign onto US 89 and travel 71 miles. Turn left onto US Highway 12 and travel 26 miles. Turn left at the sign onto paved-becoming-single-lane-gravel Forest Road 274 and travel 4 miles.

About the campground: Ponderosa pine, cottonwood, and aspen trees, with wild rose bushes in between, shelter both campground and Spring Creek. For those who survive the single-lane access, it is a most pleasant place to stay. The season here depends on the weather; however, the campground is on the southern exposure of the forested mountains. Consequently, more sunlight tends to allow it to open sooner and close later.

17 Dry Wolf

Location: 88 miles southeast of Great Falls on Dry Wolf Creek.
Facilities: Vault toilets, fire rings, tables, drinking water.
Sites: 26 for tents or RVs/Trailers up to 32 feet long.
Fee: $ per night, 16-day limit.
Managing agency: Lewis and Clark National Forest, Judith Ranger District, (406) 566-2292.
Activities: Hiking, fishing.
Finding the campground: Take US Highway 87/89 southeast out of Great Falls for 25 miles. Continue straight on US 87 for 37 miles toward Stanford. At the campground sign (about 1 mile north of Stanford) turn right onto the paved, quickly-becoming-gravel road and travel 20 miles. Bear right at the Y intersection, about 5 miles from US 87. Turn left onto single-lane, gravel-dirt Forest Road 251 and travel 8 miles.

About the campground: Spruce and fir trees outline grassy meadows in this scenic canyon. Dry Wolf Creek invites anglers and waders alike. Getting to this peaceful hideaway takes patience and determination. The last stretch of the access road is not a raceway and will show no mercy to the inattentive. As with other campgrounds in this area, weather sets the season.

18 Indian Hill

Location: 95 miles southeast of Great Falls.
Facilities: Vault toilet, fire rings, tables, drinking water.
Sites: 7 for tents or RVs/Trailers up to 20 feet long.
Fee: None, 16-day limit.
Managing agency: Lewis and Clark National Forest, Judith Ranger District, (406) 566-2292.
Activities: Hiking, fishing.
Finding the campground: Take US Highway 87/89 southeast out of Great Falls for 25 miles. Continue straight on US 87 for 42 miles to Windham. Turn right onto paved Montana State Highway 541 and travel 13 miles to Utica. At Utica turn right onto the gravel county road and travel 15 miles southwest. The county road will turn into Forest Road 487 for the last 3 miles.

About the campground: Those with specific destinations not including this remote campground will do best to select other alternatives. The last 15 miles could easily seem like a whole lot

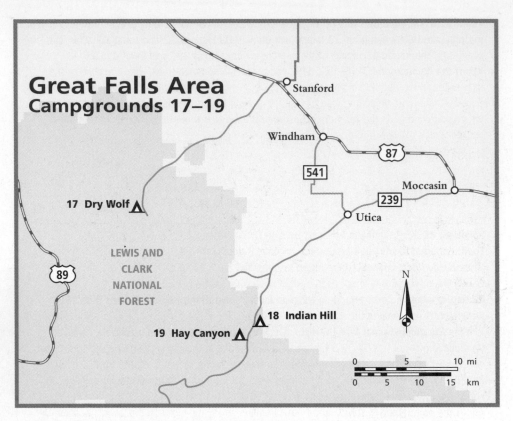

**Great Falls Area
Campgrounds 17–19**

Stanford

Windham

87

541

Moccasin

239

17 Dry Wolf

Utica

LEWIS AND
CLARK
NATIONAL
FOREST

89

N

18 Indian Hill

19 Hay Canyon

0		5		10 mi
0	5	10	15	km

more. For those with a desire to settle in and then explore the surrounding forest and related mountain country, however, it could be almost heaven. The campground is open during the summer months, but exact dates are directly controlled by the weather.

19 Hay Canyon

Location: 97 miles southeast of Great Falls.
Facilities: Vault toilet, fire rings, tables.
Sites: 7 for tents or RVs/Trailers up to 30 feet long.
Fee: None 16-day limit.
Managing agency: Lewis and Clark National Forest, Judith Ranger District, (406) 566–2292.
Activities: Hiking, fishing.
Finding the campground: Take US Highway 87/89 southeast out of Great Falls for 25 miles. Continue straight on US 87 for 42 miles to Windham. Turn right onto paved Montana State Highway 541 and travel 13 miles to Utica. At Utica turn right onto the gravel county road and travel 17 miles southwest. The county road will turn into Forest Road 487 for the last 5 miles.

About the campground: Bring plenty of drinking water as there is none available here. The recommended trailer length is 30 feet, which may require unhooking. The campground is open during the summer months, but exact dates are directly controlled by the weather.

20 Ackley Lake State Park

Location: 90 miles southeast of Great Falls at Ackley Lake.
Facilities: Vault toilets, fire rings, tables, drinking water, boat ramps.
Sites: 15 for tents or RVs/Trailer combinations up to 44 feet long.
Fee: None for MT Residents $$ for nonresidents per night, 14-day limit.
Managing agency: Ackley State Park (406) 727-1212.
Activities: Fishing, boating.
Finding the campground: Take US Highway 87/89 southeast out of Great Falls for 25 miles. Continue straight on US 87 for 58 miles to Hobson. Take Montana State Highway 400 south out of Hobson for 5 miles. Turn right onto the gravel county road and travel 2 miles.
About the campground: Water sports attract most visitors to this grassland area. Trout invite anglers to try their skill in the 160-surface-acre lake. Firewood is not very prevalent, especially with the lack of forest. The area is open all year long, but camping can be a trying experience in the winter.

21 Crystal Lake

Location: 120 miles southeast of Great Falls on Crystal Lake.
Facilities: Vault toilets, fire rings, tables, drinking water.
Sites: 28 for tents or RVs/Trailers up to 32 feet long.
Fee: $ per night, 16-day limit.
Managing agency: Lewis and Clark National Forest, Judith Ranger District, (406) 566–2292.
Activities: Hiking, fishing.
Finding the campground: Take US Highway 87/89 southeast out of Great Falls for 25 miles. Continue straight on US 87 for 73 miles. Turn right onto improved, dirt Crystal Lake Road and travel 5 miles. Stay left at the intersection and travel 4 miles to the recreation area sign. Turn left and travel 13 miles.
About the campground: Crystal Lake captures about one hundred or so surface acres of mountain water. Spruce trees populate the forest in the campground and on the surrounding mountainsides. Parking units are well spaced and offer a sense of privacy. The only catch to this beautiful area is access. Crystal Lake Road narrows to a single lane in spots with some tight corners that challenge longer units. The last few miles and the camping units are paved, but that does little to eliminate the grief of a muddy set of parallel ruts on a wet day. The campground opens around June 15 and closes around September 15, depending upon snow levels.

Billings Area

Most, if not all, of the campgrounds in this section are located in rugged mountain terrain. Camping is allowed at fishing accesses; however, not all the accesses are included in this section. The key word here is "allowed," meaning that the sites are not developed for such. Camping areas off the main route to Yellowstone National Park are typically located along streams or lakes at the base of the mountains. Some are visited more frequently than others, depending upon the wilderness access. Campgrounds along the main route to the park are at much higher elevations.

For campers en route to Yellowstone National Park, the northeastern entrance offers a less frequently used access via the spectacular Beartooth Scenic Highway. This road climbs through a series of hairpin switchbacks from the valley floor near Red Lodge to places where trees do not grow and the ice stays on the ground all year long. Be sure to have warm clothes, even during the summer months. The first significant snowfall of the year closes this highway until the next year's thaw. If you find heights and long, steep drop-offs nerve racking you'd best find another way. The drive is an unforgettable experience.

	Group Sites	Tents	RV sites	Total sites	Hookups	Toilets	Showers	Drinking water	Dump station	Phone	Handicap Access	Recreation	Fee	Season	Stay limit (days)
1 Afterbay			40	40		V		*				HFB	$$	All Year	14
2 Sage Creek			12	12		V		*				HF	$	Memorial Day to Labor Day	16
3 Horseshoe Bend (WY)			48	48		C		*	*	*	*	HFSBR	$$	All Year	14
4 Barry's Landing			10	10		V						HFBWR	$	All Year	14
5 Palisades			6	6		V					*	HFW	N	Memorial Day to Labor Day	16
6 Basin			30	30		V		*			*	HFW	$$	5/27-9/5	16
7 Cascade			30	30		V		*				HF	$$	5/27-9/5	16
8 Sheridan	2	7	9			V		*				F	$$	5/27-9/5	16
9 Rattin	3	3	6			V		*				HF	$$	5/27-9/5	16
10 Parkside			28	28		V		*			*	HF	$$	5/27-9/5	16
11 Greenough Lake			18	18		V		*			*	HF	$$	5/27-9/5	16
12 Limber Pine			13	13		V		*			*	HF	$$	5/27-9/5	16
13 M-K			10	10		V						HF	N	Memorial Day to Labor Day	16
14 Island Lake (WY)			20	20		V		*				HFB	$$	7/1-9/15	16
15 Beartooth Lake (WY)			21	21		V		*				HFBW	$$	7/1-9/15	16
16 Crazy Creek (WY)			16	16		V						HF	$	6/15-9/1	16
17 Fox Creek (WY)			33	33		V		*				HF	$$	6/15-9/1	16
18 Chief Joseph			6	6		V		*				H	$	6/1-9/30	16
19 Colter			23	23		V		*				H	$	7/1-9/7	16
20 Soda Butte			27	27		V		*				H	$	7/1-9/7	16
21 Cooney State Park			92	92		V		*				FSB	$	All Year	14
22 Itch-Kep-Pe Park			30	30		V		*				FB	N	4/1-10/31	10
23 Pine Grove			46	46		V		*			*	HFW	$	Memorial Day to Labor Day	10
24 Emerald Lake			32	32		V		*			*	HFW	$	Memorial Day to Labor Day	10
25 Jimmy Joe			12	12		V						HFW	N	Memorial Day to Labor Day	10
26 East Rosebud Lake			14	14		V		*				HFB	$	Memorial Day to Labor Day	10
27 Woodbine			44	44		V		*			*	HFW	$$	Mid-May through Mid-Sept	16

1 Afterbay

Location: 80 miles south of Billings on the Bighorn River.
Facilities: Vault toilets, fire rings, tables, drinking water, boat ramp.
Sites: 40 for tents or RVs/Trailer combinations up to 50 feet long.
Fee: $$ per night, 14-day limit.
Managing agency: National Park Service, (406) 666-2412.

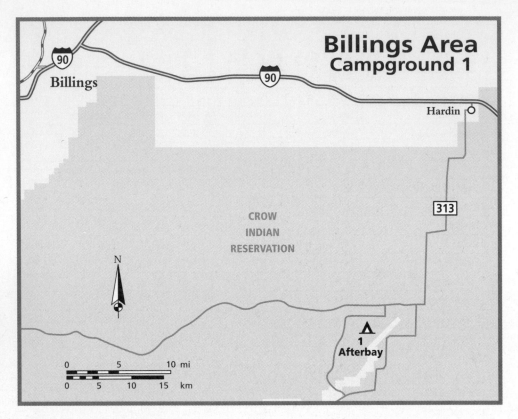

Activities: Hiking, fishing, boating.

Finding the campground: Take I-90 east out of Billings for 45 miles to Hardin/exit 495. Drive through Hardin to Montana Highway 313 and travel 44 miles. Follow the directional signs near Fort Smith to the campground.

About the campground: Camping is a means to the end here, even if the campground is open all year long. The Bighorn Canyon Recreation Area offers a variety of recreational activities. Walleye, trout, perch, ling, crappie, and catfish await anglers who attempt to reel them in. The spectacular geology and rich cultural history of the region offer a rewarding alternative when the creel is full or the fish are not biting.

2 Sage Creek

Location: 70 miles south of Billings on Sage Creek.
Facilities: Vault toilets, fire rings, tables, drinking water.
Sites: 12 for tents or RVs/Trailers up to 32 feet long.
Fee: $ per night, 16-day limit.

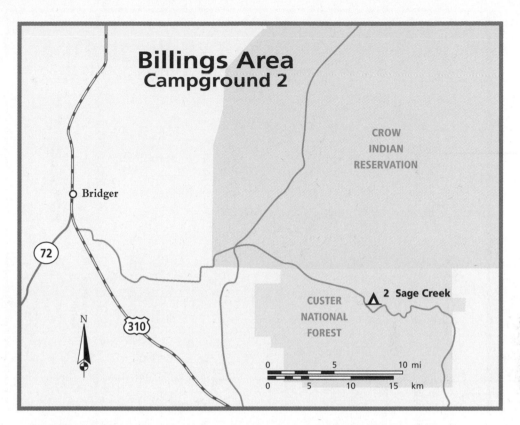

Billings Area
Campground 2

CROW
INDIAN
RESERVATION

Bridger

72

N

310

2 Sage Creek

CUSTER
NATIONAL
FOREST

0   5   10 mi

0   5   10   15   km

Managing agency: Custer National Forest, Beartooth Ranger District, (406) 446-2103.
Activities: Hiking, fishing.
Finding the campground: Take I-90 west out of Billings for 16 miles to Laurel/exit 434. Turn left onto US Highway 212 and travel 11 miles to Rockvale. Turn left onto US Highway 310 and travel 17 miles to Bridger. Continue on US 310 for 3 miles. Turn left onto paved-becoming-gravel-then-dirt Pryor Mountain Road and travel 23 miles. Pryor Mountain Road turns into Forest Road 3085 for the last mile of this trek. The campground is on the left side of the road along the creek on Forest Road 144.
About the campground: Drinking water can be problematic; if it is a must, check with the ranger office listed above before committing to the trek. Willow brush lines the creek, which has sloping ridges on both sides. The forest does not dominate the area, but it is not far away. Overall, the rough access tends to discourage most visitors. Hiking and fishing lure young and old alike. The Crow Indian Reservation boundary is very close, so be sure to obtain the correct permission and licenses before crossing that line. A point of interest quietly settles into the mountainside about 11 miles farther up Forest Road 3085. The Big Ice Cave is literally full of ice year-round. On a sweltering summer day, the dramatic change in temperature is most refreshing and almost unbelievable. The campground is typically open from Memorial Day through Labor Day.

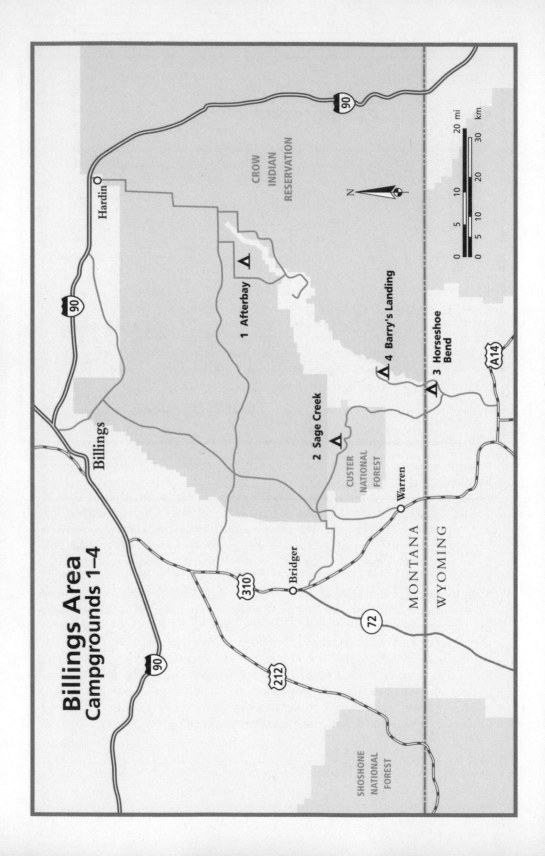

3 Horseshoe Bend (Wyoming)

Location: 105 miles south of Billings on Bighorn Lake.

Facilities: Comfort stations, fire rings, tables, drinking water, RV dump.

Sites: 48 for tents or RVs/Trailer combinations over 60 feet long.

Fee: $$ per night, 14-day limit.

Managing agency: National Park Service, (406) 666-2412.

Activities: Hiking, fishing, boating, swimming, rockhounding.

Finding the campground: Take I-90 west out of Billings for 16 miles to Laurel/exit 434. Turn left onto US Highway 212 and travel 11 miles to Rockvale. Turn left onto US Highway 310 and travel 64 miles to Lovell, Wyoming. After passing through Lovell, turn left onto US Highway 14 Alternate and travel 2 miles. Turn left at the sign onto Wyoming Highway 37 and travel 10 miles. Turn right at the Horseshoe Bend sign and travel 2 miles.

About the campground: The lack of trees—as in none—affords a full view of the night sky. Star-gazers could find that particular feature most appealing. Parking units are well spaced, providing isolation with steel shade structures scattered about. Nineteen of the units are suited for larger RVs and boats, with the best maximum fit of 60 feet long, though longer ones can be accommodated. This makes for an excellent place to park a trailer or RV in order to explore the otherwise unreachable areas in the mountains. Bright stars in a warm, unobstructed badlands sky can be extremely refreshing after the freezing mountain air. The campground is open all year long.

4 Barry's Landing

Location: 108 miles south of Billings on Bighorn Lake.

Facilities: Vault toilets, fire rings, tables, boat ramp.

Sites: 5 for tents and 10 for RVs/Trailer combinations up to 50 feet long.

Fee: $ per night, 14-day limit.

Managing agency: National Park Service, (406) 666-2412.

Activities: Hiking, fishing, boating, wildlife viewing, rockhounding.

Finding the campground: Take I-90 west out of Billings for 16 miles to Laurel/exit 434. Turn left onto US Highway 212 and travel 11 miles to Rockvale. Turn left onto US Highway 310 and travel 64 miles to Lovell, Wyoming. After passing through Lovell, turn left onto US Highway 14 Alternate and travel 2 miles. Turn left at the sign onto Wyoming Highway 37 and travel 15 miles.

About the campground: This smaller campground offers spectacular scenery and developed trails into the rugged canyons surrounding it. This remote portion of the Bighorn Canyon National Recreation Area settles into the end of the road, with the blessing of no passing traffic. The campground open all year long.

5 Palisades

Location: 62 miles southwest of Billings on Willow Creek.

Facilities: Vault toilet, fire rings.

Sites: 6 for tents or RVs/Trailers up to 20 feet long.

Fee: None, 16-day limit.

Managing agency: Custer National Forest, Beartooth Ranger District, (406) 446–2103.

Activities: Hiking, fishing, wildlife viewing.

Finding the campground: Take I–90 west out of Billings for 16 miles to Laurel/exit 434. Turn left onto US Highway 212 and travel 43 miles to Red Lodge. Follow the signs to Red Lodge Mountain Ski Area, as the road is not otherwise marked. Turn right onto the paved road and travel about 1 mile to the campground directional sign. Turn right onto the gravel-becoming-unimproved-dirt road and travel 2 miles.

About the campground: The six units reportedly available here take a stretch of the imagination and some creativity to locate. The road alone can prove to be an endurance test of both you and the mechanical strength of your vehicle. The campground has been "discovered" and is visited more frequently now than in the past; if it's late in the day, another choice may be in order, especially on weekends. Willow Creek could be a good fishing spot, but the brush cover makes it difficult. Leveling a trailer, or camper for that matter, will take forethought and sweat. If you like solitude and do not mind rough roads, this could be a haven in an otherwise crowded area. The campground is open typically from Memorial Day through Labor Day.

6 Basin

Location: 66 miles southwest of Billings on West Fork Rock Creek.

Facilities: Vault toilets, fire rings, tables, drinking water.

Sites: 30 for tents or RVs/Trailers up to 30 feet long.

Fee: $$ per night, 16-day limit.

Managing agency: Custer National Forest, Beartooth Ranger District; administering organization, Gallatin Canyon Campgrounds, (406) 587-9054.

Activities: Hiking, fishing, wildlife viewing.

Finding the campground: Take I–90 west out of Billings for 16 miles to Laurel/exit 434. Turn left onto US Highway 212 and travel 43 miles to Red Lodge. From the south end of Red Lodge, turn right onto West Fork Creek Road (Forest Road 2071) and continue on the paved road for 7 miles.

About the campground: Reservations are recommended for this very popular campground; call (877) 444-6777. Firewood is reportedly available for purchase from the campground host in this well-developed campground. The units are networked within a part of the pine forest that runs along the bank of West Fork Rock Creek, thus providing some pleasant background sound. The campground is open from mid-May through mid-September, with the exact dates dependent on the weather.

7 Cascade

Location: 69 miles southwest of Billings on West Fork Rock Creek.

Facilities: Vault toilets, fire rings, tables, drinking water.

Sites: 30 for tents or RVs/Trailers up to 30 feet long.

Fee: $$ per night, 16-day limit.

Managing agency: Custer National Forest, Beartooth Ranger District; administering organization, Gallatin Canyon Campgrounds, (406) 587-9054.

Activities: Hiking, fishing.

Finding the campground: Take I-90 west out of Billings for 16 miles to Laurel/exit 434. Turn left onto US Highway 212 and travel 43 miles to Red Lodge. From the south end of Red Lodge turn right onto West Fork Creek Road (Forest Road 2071) and travel about 10 miles. The paved road becomes gravel just past Basin Campground for the last 3 miles.

About the campground: Reservations are recommended for this very popular campground, call (877) 444-6777. Camping units are spaced a comfortable distance from each other in this rolling canyon bottom. The 2008 fire turned almost all of the trees into skeletons with a few survivors. In spite of the dust from the gravel roads and the scarred panorama this is still a popular destination. Be sure to have warm clothing. The campground is open from mid-May through mid-September, with the exact dates dependent on the weather.

8 Sheridan

Location: 70 miles southwest of Billings on Rock Creek.

Facilities: Vault toilet, fire rings, tables, drinking water.

Sites: 2 for tents and 7 for RVs up to 30 feet long.

Fee: $$ per night, 16-day limit.

Managing agency: Custer National Forest, Beartooth Ranger District; administering organization, Gallatin Canyon Campgrounds, (406) 587-9054.

Activities: Fishing.

Finding the campground: Take I-90 west out of Billings for 16 miles to Laurel/exit 434. Turn left onto US Highway 212 and travel 43 miles to Red Lodge. Continue through Red Lodge on US 212 for about 8 miles. Turn left onto gravel Forest Road 379 at the east side road campgrounds sign and travel 3 miles. Several, if not all, of the cattle guards have very obvious "No Trespassing" signs placed in a way that seems to imply the road is private. It is not!

About the campground: Reservations are recommended for this very popular campground; call (877) 444-6777. The cottonwood and Douglas fir trees shading the close units offer shade and an occasional wind-generated serenade. Firewood is available for purchase from the campground host. Though 30-foot trailers will fit, unhooking is required, with little wiggle room. Fishing seemed to be the major attraction and the reason for the full campground upon our visit during the middle of the week. It is open from mid-May through mid-September.

9 Rattin

Location: 71 miles southwest of Billings on Rock Creek.

Facilities: Vault toilet, fire rings, tables, drinking water.

Sites: 3 for tents and 3 for RVs up to 30 feet long.

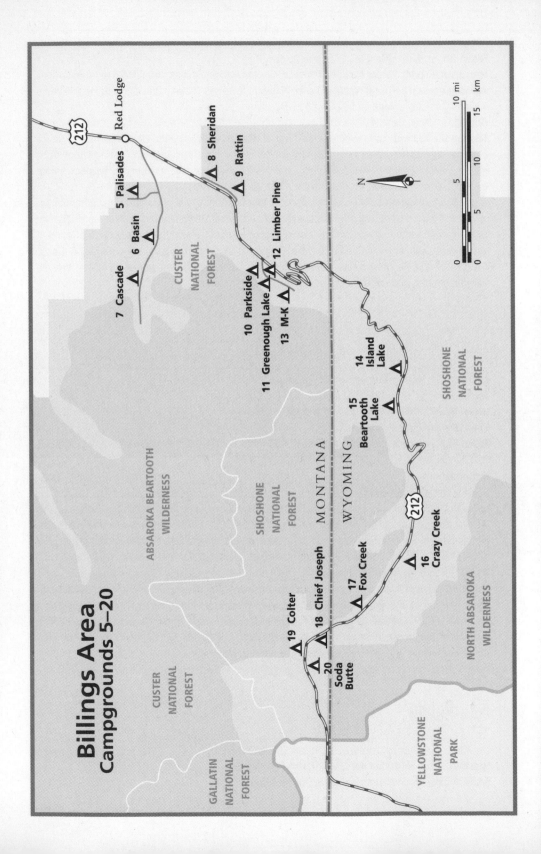

Billings Area
Campgrounds 5–20

Red Lodge

5 Palisades
6 Basin
7 Cascade
8 Sheridan
9 Rattin
10 Parkside
11 Greenough Lake
12 Limber Pine
13 M-K
14 Island Lake
15 Beartooth Lake
16 Crazy Creek
17 Fox Creek
18 Chief Joseph
19 Colter
20 Soda Butte

CUSTER NATIONAL FOREST

ABSAROKA BEARTOOTH WILDERNESS

SHOSHONE NATIONAL FOREST

MONTANA

WYOMING

SHOSHONE NATIONAL FOREST

CUSTER NATIONAL FOREST

GALLATIN NATIONAL FOREST

NORTH ABSAROKA WILDERNESS

YELLOWSTONE NATIONAL PARK

N

10 mi
km
15
10
5
5
5
0
0

Fee: $ per night, 16-day limit.
Managing agency: Custer National Forest, Beartooth Ranger District; administering organization, Gallatin Canyon Campgrounds, (406) 587-9054.
Activities: Hiking, fishing.
Finding the campground: Take I-90 west out of Billings for 16 miles to Laurel/exit 434. Turn left onto US Highway 212 and travel 43 miles to Red Lodge. Continue through Red Lodge on US 212 for about 8 miles. Turn left onto gravel Forest Road 379 at the east side road campgrounds sign and travel 4 miles. Several, if not all, of the cattle guards have very obvious "No Trespassing" signs placed in a way that seems to imply the road is private. It is not!
About the campground: Reservations are recommended for this very popular campground; call (877) 444-6777. Aspen and pine trees, with a few Douglas fir trees mingled in here and there, dominate the creek bank. Summer homes and private land do not surround this camping area like other nearby spots; all the same, you should be careful when hiking. Firewood is available for purchase from the campground host. Although the nearby highway and private homes contribute to vehicle noise at different times of the day, it does tend to get much more peaceful later at night. Rock Creek crashes by, filtering some of the noise, too. Fishing can be frustrating in the dominant rapids of this stretch. The campground is open from mid-May through mid-September, dependent on the weather.

10 Parkside

Location: 72 miles southwest of Billings on Rock Creek.
Facilities: Vault toilets, fire rings, tables, drinking water.
Sites: 28 for tents or RVs/Trailers up to 40 feet long.
Fee: $$ per night, 16-day limit.
Managing agency: Custer National Forest, Beartooth Ranger District; administering organization, Gallatin Canyon Campgrounds, (406) 587-9054.
Activities: Hiking, fishing.
Finding the campground: Take I-90 west out of Billings for 16 miles to Laurel/exit 434. Turn left onto US Highway 212 and travel 43 miles to Red Lodge. Continue through Red Lodge on US 212 for 12 miles. Turn right at the campground directional sign onto the paved access road and travel 1 mile.
About the campground: Reservations are recommended; call (877) 444-6777. Both loops are paved with level parking in the pines. A few aspen trees are sprinkled throughout. Firewood is available for purchase from the campground host. The hand pump provides plenty of water, but not without its price in exercise. Rock Creek crashes by at various distances, making site choices somewhat complicated on the weekdays. On weekends, the choices disappear quickly, and for the most part totally. The campground is open from mid-May through mid-September, dependent on the weather.

11 Greenough Lake

Location: 72 miles southwest of Billings on Rock Creek.
Facilities: Vault toilets, fire rings, tables, drinking water.

Sites: 18 for tents or RVs/Trailer combinations up to 60 feet long.

Fee: $$ per night, 16-day limit.

Managing agency: Custer National Forest, Beartooth Ranger District; administering organization, Gallatin Canyon Campgrounds, (406) 587-9054.

Activities: Hiking, fishing.

Finding the campground: Take I–90 west out of Billings for 16 miles to Laurel/exit 434. Turn left onto US Highway 212 and travel 43 miles to Red Lodge. Continue through Red Lodge on US 212 for 12 miles. Turn right at the sign onto the paved access road and travel 1 mile.

About the campground: Reservations are recommended; call (877) 444-6777. This campground is perched between Wyoming Creek and Rock Creek. It is almost a continuation of Parkside Campground, only farther away from Rock Creek. Lodgepole pine and aspen trees provide shade and an occasional wind-driven serenade. Firewood is available for purchase from the campground host. The campground is open from mid-May through mid-September, dependent on the weather.

12 Limber Pine

Location: 72 miles southwest of Billings on Rock Creek.

Facilities: Vault toilets, fire rings, tables, drinking water.

Sites: 3 for tents and 10 for RVs/Trailer combinations up to 60 feet long.

Fee: $$ per night, 16-day limit.

Managing agency: Custer National Forest, Beartooth Ranger District; administering organization, Gallatin Canyon Campgrounds, (406) 587-9054.

Activities: Hiking, fishing.

Finding the campground: Take I–90 west out of Billings for 16 miles to Laurel/exit 434. Turn left onto US Highway 212 and travel 43 miles to Red Lodge. Continue through Red Lodge on US 212 for 12 miles. Turn right at the campground directional sign onto the paved access road and travel 1 mile.

About the campground: Reservations are recommended; call (877) 444-6777. The campground is on the opposite side of Rock Creek from Greenough Lake Campground. The explosive geological features provide abrupt rock outcroppings well covered with pine trees. As a result, the camping units offer a sense of remoteness not common to the other nearby camping areas. Firewood is available for purchase from the campground host. The campground is open from mid-May through mid-September, dependent on the weather.

13 M-K

Location: 75 miles southwest of Billings on Rock Creek.

Facilities: Vault toilet, fire rings, tables; no drinking water.

Sites: 10 for tents or RVs/Trailers up to 22 feet long.

Fee: None, 16-day limit.

Managing agency: Custer National Forest, Beartooth Ranger District, (406) 446–2103.

Activities: Hiking, fishing.

Finding the campground: Take I-90 west out of Billings for 16 miles to Laurel/exit 434. Turn left onto US Highway 212 and travel 43 miles to Red Lodge. Continue through Red Lodge on US 212 for 12 miles. Turn right at the campground directional sign onto the paved access road and travel 4 miles. The last 4 miles turn from very rough gravel to improved dirt.

About the campground: There may be no fee to stay here, but there is still a price to pay. After bouncing over the bumps, dodging traffic, and eating lots of dust, you'll still have to search to find a level spot. Keep in mind there is no drinking water available and firewood will need to be obtained elsewhere. Do not forget that firewood must be from near your destination. A major amount of traffic passes the campground, all at various speeds. Along with the traffic, dust increases the desire to be somewhere else. The campground is open from Memorial Day through Labor Day, dependent on the weather.

14 Island Lake (Wyoming)

Location: 94 miles southwest of Billings at Island Lake.
Facilities: Vault toilets, fire rings, tables, drinking water.
Sites: 21 for tents or RVs/Trailers up to 32 feet long.
Fee: $$ per night, 16-day limit.
Managing agency: Shoshone National Forest, Clarks Fork Ranger District, (307) 527-6921.
Activities: Hiking, fishing, boating.

Finding the campground: Take I-90 west out of Billings for 16 miles to Laurel/exit 434. Turn left onto US Highway 212 and travel 78 miles. US 212 becomes Beartooth Scenic Highway southwest of Red Lodge, complete with switchbacks and year-round snow. Be sure to have warm clothing, even in summer!

About the campground: Alpine meadows and snowcapped mountain peaks surround the granite outcrops of these camping units. White pine and spruce defiantly cling to the rock in all three hilly loops. Loop A settles into a southern exposure just out of sight of Island Lake. Loop B offers some of the more creative hideouts. One of the units balances snugly on top of a granite knob. Loop C grants some beautiful scenery with ice-cold Island Lake in the forefront. Keep in mind that this is not only bear country, it is grizzly bear country! The campground is open from July 1 through September 15.

15 Beartooth Lake (Wyoming)

Location: 97 miles southwest of Billings on Beartooth Lake.
Facilities: Vault toilets, fire rings, tables, drinking water, picnic area, boat ramp.
Sites: 21 for tents or RVs/Trailer combinations up to 32 feet long.
Fee: $$ per night, 16-day limit.
Managing agency: Shoshone National Forest, Clarks Fork Ranger District, (307) 527-6921.
Activities: Hiking, fishing, boating, wildlife viewing.

Finding the campground: Take I-90 west out of Billings for 16 miles to Laurel/exit 434. Turn left onto US Highway 212 and travel 81 miles.

About the campground: Beartooth Lake sits peacefully under the dramatic colors of the butte that bears the same name. Hikers can exercise a little to get a closer view of the waterfall on the south side of the highway across from the camping access. Spruce and pine trees are thick, but they provide no deadfall in the immediate camping area. Firewood is not readily available. Loops A, B, and C offer different views and parking requirements. Loop B has the only pull-throughs and is the first to fill up on an active weekend or holiday. Loop C is best for tents, as the parking aprons are anything but level. Moose frequent the swamp area that borders the southern end of the campground. Bears are not shy either; as of our visit, a warning sign at the entrance reported that a grizzly bear and human encounter had recently occurred. Make sure you understand and follow the rules. The campground is open from July 1 through September 15.

16 Crazy Creek (Wyoming)

Location: 120 miles southwest of Billings on the Clarks Fork Yellowstone River.
Facilities: Vault toilets, fire rings, tables, drinking water.
Sites: 16 for tents or RVs/Trailer combinations up to 28 feet long.
Fee: $ per night, 16-day limit.
Managing agency: Shoshone National Forest, Clarks Fork Ranger District, (307) 527-6921.
Activities: Hiking, fishing.
Finding the campground: Take I-90 west out of Billings for 16 miles to Laurel/exit 434. Turn left onto US Highway 212 and travel 104 miles.
About the campground: Wilderness and a waterfall are accessible from this campground. The semi-level parking spots seem out of place among the granite outcrops. Pine and a few spruce trees provide some shade for picnic tables and parking spots alike. Sagebrush takes over where the trees stop, just above the creek. Numerous signs advise visitors that tour buses are not allowed; no doubt more than a few have wanted to examine the waterfall. Pull-throughs dominate the available parking, and there is relatively convenient access to drinking water. The campground is open from June 15 through September 1.

17 Fox Creek (Wyoming)

Location: 125 miles southwest of Billings on the Clarks Fork Yellowstone River.
Facilities: Vault toilets, fire rings, tables, drinking water.
Sites: 33 for tents or RVs/Trailer combinations up to 32 feet long.
Fee: $$ per night, 16-day limit.
Managing agency: Shoshone National Forest, Clarks Fork Ranger District, (307) 527-6921.
Activities: Hiking, fishing.
Finding the campground: Take I-90 west out of Billings for 16 miles to Laurel/exit 434. Turn left onto US Highway 212 and travel 109 miles.

About the campground: Spruce and pine trees of varying heights grow between parking areas, offering privacy. Ten units of almost-level parking spots are found in Loop A. Loop B bears left from the entrance, passing along a small meadow. A few spots accommodate RVs up to 40 feet long, but most push the limit at 30 feet. The campground is open from June 15 through September 1.

18 Chief Joseph

Location: 129 miles southwest of Billings.
Facilities: Vault toilets, fire rings, tables, drinking water.
Sites: 6 for RVs/Trailer combinations up to 42 feet long.
Fee: $ per night, 16-day limit.
Managing agency: Gallatin National Forest, Gardiner Ranger District, (406) 848-7375.
Activities: Hiking.
Finding the campground: Take I-90 west out of Billings for 16 miles to Laurel/exit 434. Turn left onto US Highway 212 and travel 113 miles.
About the campground: Hard-sided camping units are the only ones allowed here. Grizzly bears are active in the area, not to mention the difficult access road. If you have a tent or a low clearance vehicle, this is not your spot. Spruce and lodgepole pine of all sizes hide this campground from passing traffic. Drinking water comes from a hand pump near the entrance, which is a little inconvenient. If traffic is heavy, this may not be the most peaceful spot as well. The campground is open from June 1 through September 30.

19 Colter

Location: 130 miles southwest of Billings.
Facilities: Vault toilets, fire rings, tables, drinking water.
Sites: 23 for RVs/Trailer combinations up to 48 feet long.
Fee: $ per night, 16-day limit.
Managing agency: Gallatin National Forest, Gardiner Ranger District, (406) 848-7375.
Activities: Hiking.
Finding the campground: Take I-90 west out of Billings for 16 miles to Laurel/exit 434. Turn left onto US Highway 212 and travel 114 miles.
About the campground: The scars of past fires are still obvious but the forest is coming back to life almost like a breath of fresh air after a rain storm. Hard sided units are the only ones allowed here, as grizzly bears are active in the area. Units have a lot of room in the outer loop, with a small draw hiding most from the upper sites. Numerous spigots provide tasty drinking water, and if you're patient, the traffic noise typically decreases along with the sunlight. The campground is open from July 1 through September 7.

20 Soda Butte

Location: 131 miles southwest of Billings.
Facilities: Vault toilets, fire rings, tables, drinking water.
Sites: 27 for hard-sided units or RVs/Trailer combinations up to 48 feet long.
Fee: $ per night, 16-day limit.
Managing agency: Gallatin National Forest, Gardiner Ranger District, (406) 848–7375.
Activities: Hiking.
Finding the campground: Take I-90 west out of Billings for 16 miles to Laurel/exit 434. Turn left onto US Highway 212 and travel 115 miles.
About the campground: Hard-sided units are the only ones allowed here, as grizzly bears are active in the area. Permanent campers reside in the old Cooke City Cemetery next to the access road. These campers were here long before any road wound its way to this remote spot. Tall pine and spruce trees share the meadows with camping units. Most of the parking areas are not level, but a turnaround allows trailers and longer RVs to scope out available sites. The access road is not compatible with units longer than 48 feet. The distance between units varies, with most somewhat isolated. Numerous water spigots are easily accessible, unlike firewood. Rugged mountains, which can be seen peeking through open spots in the trees, overlook the campground. It is open from July 1 through September 7, dependent on the weather.

21 Cooney State Park

Location: 46 miles southwest of Billings at Cooney Reservoir.
Facilities: Vault toilets, fire rings, tables, drinking water, boat ramp.
Sites: 92 for tents or RVs/Trailer combinations up to 60 feet long; 3 group sites.
Fee: $ per night, 14-day limit.
Managing agency: Montana Fish, Wildlife & Parks, Project Office, (406) 445–2326.
Activities: Fishing, swimming, boating.
Finding the campground: Take I-90 west out of Billings for 16 miles to Laurel/exit 434. Turn left onto US Highway 212 and travel 22 miles. Turn right at the state park directional sign and travel 8 miles.
About the campground: The ninety-two camping units are spread out among different loops; twenty-one offer electricity. There are also three group sites available. Mature, though not ancient, cottonwoods line the shore, but they do not make it very far away from the water. Rolling hills have little tree cover, allowing any wind to get a good run before slamming into the camping units. If a campfire is important, be sure to bring plenty of wood. Anglers and water sports enthusiasts are the more frequent visitors here, especially since the area is open all year.

22 Itch-Kep-Pe Park

Location: 38 miles west of Billings on the Stillwater River.
Facilities: Vault toilets, fire rings, tables, drinking water, boat ramp.
Sites: 30 for tents or RVs/Trailer combinations up to 60 feet long.
Fee: Donation, 10-day limit.
Managing agency: City of Columbus, (406) 322–5313.
Activities: Fishing, boating.
Finding the campground: Take I-90 west of Billings for 38 miles to Columbus/exit 403. Turn left and proceed through Columbus, following the signs for Montana State Highway 78. The campground is on the left side of the highway.
About the campground: Tall cottonwood trees and willow brush define the dirt roads at various places in this camping area. Some units nuzzle up to the shoreline, but most reside in the thicker brush farther away. The units in the brush appear to offer greater seclusion; however, they do require a bit more hiking for anglers. Firewood could be available depending on water flow and tree health, but it would be best to bring some along. The campground is open from May 1 through October 31.

23 Pine Grove

Location: 76 miles southwest of Billings on West Rosebud Creek.
Facilities: Vault toilets, fire rings, tables, drinking water.
Sites: 46 for tents or RVs/Trailers up to 32 feet long.
Fee: $ per night, 10-day limit.
Managing agency: Custer National Forest, Beartooth Ranger District, (406) 446-2103.
Activities: Hiking, fishing, wildlife viewing.
Finding the campground: Take I-90 west out of Billings for 38 miles to Columbus/exit 403. Turn left and proceed through Columbus, following the signs for Montana State Highway 78. Take MT 78 south for 19 miles. Turn right onto County Road 419 and travel about 5 miles. Turn left onto County Road 425 and travel 6 miles. Continue on gravel Forest Road 72 for 8 miles.
About the campground: The Absaroka-Beartooth Wilderness boundary passes nearby, offering plenty of mountain scenery and amenities. Naturally, there is more to see of the rugged snow-capped peaks on the way to the campground just because of distance. It is open from Memorial Day through Labor Day.

24 Emerald Lake

Location: 80 miles southwest of Billings at Emerald Lake.
Facilities: Vault toilets, fire rings, tables, drinking water.
Sites: 32 for tents or RVs/Trailers up to 30 feet long.
Fee: $ per night, 10-day limit.

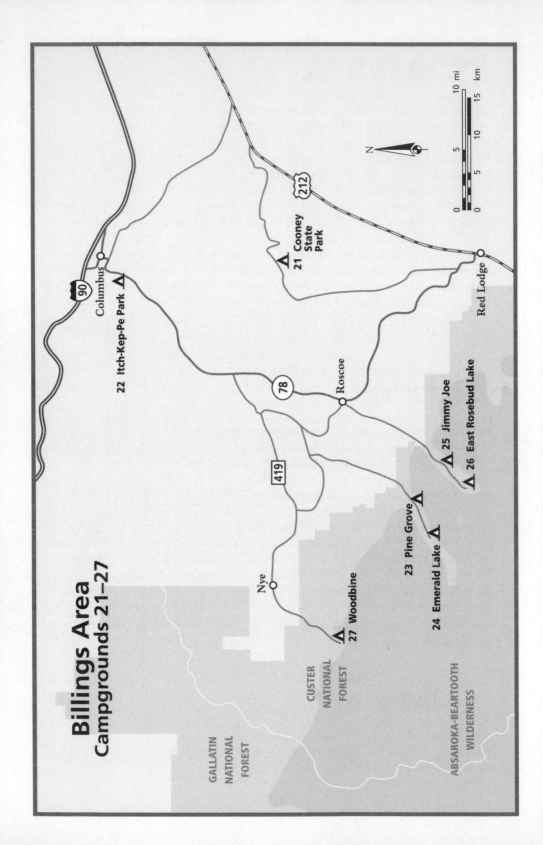

Billings Area
Campgrounds 21–27

Managing agency: Custer National Forest, Beartooth Ranger District, (406) 446-2103.

Activities: Hiking, fishing, wildlife viewing.

Finding the campground: Take I-90 west out of Billings for 38 miles to Columbus/exit 403. Turn left and proceed through Columbus, following the signs for Montana State Highway 78. Take MT 78 south for 19 miles. Turn right onto County Road 419 and travel about 5 miles. Turn left onto County Road 425 and travel 6 miles. Continue on gravel Forest Road 72 for 12 miles.

About the campground: You can see the bottom of this cold, clear lake in numerous places. Settled in at the head of the lake, the campground is far enough down the road to discourage daytime visitors from checking out the fishing or just enjoying this relatively quiet getaway. The campground is just below a hydroelectric plant that dominates a portion of the view, but there is still plenty to see. Reportedly, nearby Mystic Lake offers excellent fishing, but it will require a bit of a hike to get there. The campground is open from Memorial Day through Labor Day.

25 Jimmy Joe

Location: 76 miles southwest of Billings on East Rosebud Creek.

Facilities: Vault toilets.

Sites: 12 for tents or RVs/Trailers up to 30 feet long.

Fee: None, 10-day limit.

Managing agency: Custer National Forest, Beartooth Ranger District, (406) 446-2103.

Activities: Hiking, fishing, wildlife viewing.

Finding the campground: Take I-90 west out of Billings for 38 miles to Columbus/exit 403. Turn left and proceed through Columbus, following the signs for Montana State Highway 78. Take MT 78 south for 29 miles. At Roscoe take Forest Road 177 for 9 miles.

About the campground: This campground can see a lot of traffic going to nearby East Rosebud Lake. It is open from Memorial Day through Labor Day.

26 East Rosebud Lake

Location: 79 miles southwest of Billings on East Rosebud Lake.

Facilities: Vault toilets, fire rings, tables, drinking water, boat launch.

Sites: 14 for tents or RVs/Trailers up to 25 feet long.

Fee: $ per night, 10-day limit.

Managing agency: Custer National Forest, Beartooth Ranger District, (406) 446-2103.

Activities: Hiking, fishing, boating.

Finding the campground: Take I-90 west out of Billings for 38 miles to Columbus/exit 403. Turn left and proceed through Columbus, following the signs for Montana State Highway 78. Take MT 78 south for 29 miles. At Roscoe take Forest Road 177 for 12 miles.

About the campground: Fishing access is available, but there is plenty of private land to complicate matters. The nearby wilderness area could offer an escape for those willing to put in some legwork. The campground is open from May 27 through September 5.

27 Woodbine

Location: 88 miles southwest of Billings.

Facilities: Vault toilets, fire rings, tables, drinking water.

Sites: 44 for tents or RVs/Trailers up to 40 feet long.

Fee: $$ per night, 16-day limit.

Managing agency: Custer National Forest; administering organization, Gallatin Canyon Campgrounds, (406) 587-9054.

Activities: Hiking, fishing, wildlife viewing.

Finding the campground: Take I-90 west out of Billings for 38 miles to Columbus/exit 403. Turn left and proceed through Columbus, following the signs for Montana State Highway 78. Take MT 78 south for 19 miles. Turn right onto County Road 419 and travel 24 miles. The campground is 8 miles past Nye, very close to the end of the road.

About the campground: Reservations are recommended; call (877) 444-6777. The camping units are spread out along the mountainside, with scenic views displayed between the pines. Firewood is available for purchase from the campground host. The nearby wilderness area beckons to hikers and anglers alike, with mountain lakes providing a home for native trout. The long distance to the campground does not deter the number of visitors, especially on holidays. The campground is typically open from mid-May through mid-September, dependent on the weather.

Livingston Area

The campgrounds in the Livingston area tend to be located on forgotten or unknown territory. The gravel roads accessing these gems don't seem to be maintained very often. Such conditions tend to discourage more than a few from returning, but new adventurers are growing in number.

Black bear and deer are commonly sighted. In addition, elk and moose move into the area at certain times of the year. With few exceptions, modern conveniences are a considerable distance from any of the campgrounds, so be prepared for any kind of weather and double-check your supplies.

	Group Sites	Tents	RV sites	Total sites	Hookups	Toilets	Showers	Drinking water	Dump station	Phone	Handicap Access	Recreation	Fee	Season	Stay limit (days)
1 Grey Bear			20	20		V						FR	$	All Year	7
2 East Boulder			2	2		V						HFW	N	All Year	16
3 Falls Creek	8			8		V		*				HFW	N	All Year	16
4 Big Beaver			5	5		V						HFW	N	All Year	16
5 Aspen			8	8		V		*			*	HFW	$	Memorial Day to Labor Day	16
6 Chippy Park	2		5	7		V		*			*	HFW	$	All Year	16
7 Hells Canyon			11	11		V						HW	N	All Year	16
8 Hicks Park			16	16		V		*				HFW	$	All Year	16
9 West Boulder			10	10		V		*				HW	$	Memorial Day to Labor Day	16
10 Half Moon			12	12		V		*				HFW	$	All Year	16
11 Pine Creek	2		23	25		V		*			*	H	$$	Memorial Day to Labor Day	16
12 Loch Leven			30	30		V		*				FB	$	All Year	7
13 Mallard's Rest			13	13		V		*				FB	$	All Year	7
14 Dailey Lake			35	35		V		*				FB	$$	All Year	7
15 Snow Bank			11	11		V		*				HF	$$	Memorial Day to Labor Day	16
16 Carbella			D	D		V						FB	N	All Year	14
17 Tom Miner			16	16		V		*				HFW	$	6/1–10/31	16
18 Canyon			17	17		V						H	N	All Year	16
19 Eagle Creek			16	16		V					*	HW	$	All Year	16

1 Grey Bear (fishing access)

Location: 40 miles east of Livingston on the Yellowstone River.

Facilities: Vault toilet.

Sites: 20 for tents or RVs/Trailers up to 32 feet long.

Fee: $ per night, 7-day limit.

Managing agency: Montana Fish, Wildlife & Parks, (406) 247-2490.

Activities: Fishing.

Finding the campground: Take I-90 east out of Livingston for 34 miles to Big Timber/exit 367. Turn left onto the paved frontage road and travel 5 miles. At the fishing access sign, turn right onto the paved access road and travel 0.75 mile. The camping area is on the left.

About the campground: As of our visit, there were only a few grills and one table at the camping area. Huge cottonwood trees provide plenty of shade, but no firewood. Things get very dusty, but the river offers cool refreshment. More than twenty units could fit here if you do not mind getting close. The campground is open all year long.

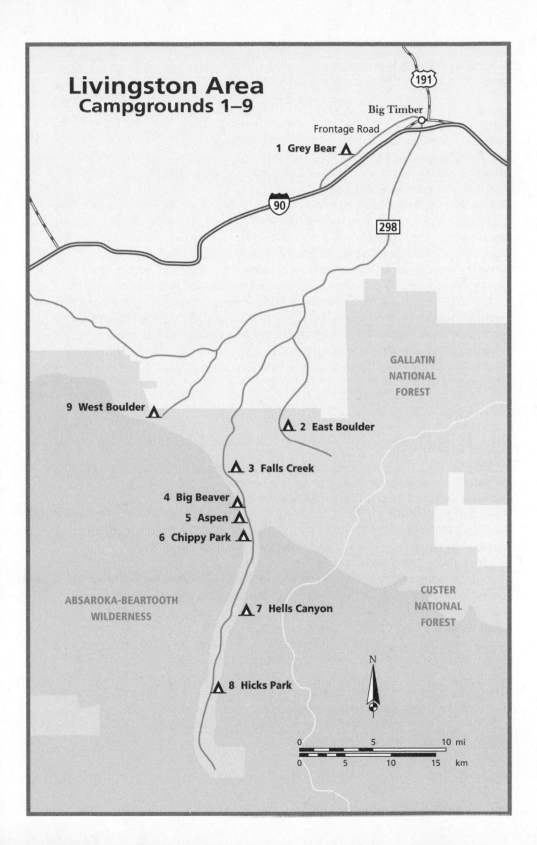

Livingston Area
Campgrounds 1–9

191

Big Timber

Frontage Road

1 Grey Bear ▲

90

298

GALLATIN
NATIONAL
FOREST

9 West Boulder ▲

▲ 2 East Boulder

▲ 3 Falls Creek

4 Big Beaver ▲

5 Aspen ▲

6 Chippy Park ▲

ABSAROKA-BEARTOOTH
WILDERNESS

CUSTER
NATIONAL
FOREST

▲ 7 Hells Canyon

▲ 8 Hicks Park

N

| 0 | | 5 | | 10 mi |

| 0 | 5 | 10 | 15 | km |

2 East Boulder

Location: 59 miles southeast of Livingston on the East Boulder River.
Facilities: Vault toilet.
Sites: 2 undesignated sites for tents or RVs up to 16 feet long.
Fee: None, 16-day limit.
Managing agency: Gallatin National Forest, Livingston Office, (406) 222-1892.
Activities: Hiking, fishing, wildlife viewing.
Finding the campground: Take I-90 east of Livingston for 34 miles to Big Timber/exit 367. Enter Big Timber, then proceed south on Montana State Highway 298 for 17 miles. Turn left onto gravel national forest access road and travel 3 miles. Turn right onto gravel East Boulder River Road and travel 5 miles. The campground is on the left side of the road.
About the campground: Large fir trees line the riverbank and blanket the surrounding mountain country. Previous use has identified the best routes and parking spots in this otherwise primitive camping area. The Stillwater Mine maintains an active underground platinum operation nearby, resulting in heavier than normal traffic. The extra activity does not seem to affect the local wildlife, as there have been plenty of deer, elk, moose, and bear sightings. All in all, this is still a very wild place. With a little planning more than two camping units could be realized, but this would result in less privacy. The campground is open all year long, but accessing it will get very tricky with wet weather.

3 Falls Creek

Location: 64 miles southeast of Livingston on Falls Creek.
Facilities: Vault toilet, fire rings, tables, drinking water.
Sites: 8 for tents. No RVs.
Fee: None, 16-day limit.
Managing agency: Gallatin National Forest, Livingston Office, (406) 222-1892.
Activities: Hiking, fishing, wildlife viewing.
Finding the campground: Take I-90 east out of Livingston for 34 miles to Big Timber/exit 367. Turn left to enter Big Timber, then proceed south on Montana State Highway 298 for 30 miles. The paved road turns to gravel in 25 miles.
About the campground: Do not pull any RVs in here. They will not fit and there is no turn-around. The walk-in units offer some isolation for those willing to carry in the needed equipment. Most of the parking areas are shared units because of the layout, and they look like they could get rather tight. They are also rather close to the dusty access road, but the actual camping spots appear to be far enough away to alleviate any major dust storms. Traffic can be heavy with the large number of private camping areas and lodges up the road. A sweat-raising hand pump typical of forest service campgrounds supplies the drinking water. The campground is open all year long; however, the water is not.

4 Big Beaver

Location: 67 miles southeast of Livingston on the Boulder River.
Facilities: Vault toilet, fire rings.
Sites: 5 for tents or RVs/Trailer combinations up to 32 feet long.
Fee: None, 16-day limit.
Managing agency: Gallatin National Forest, Livingston Office, (406) 222-1892.
Activities: Hiking, fishing, wildlife viewing.
Finding the campground: Take I-90 east out of Livingston for 34 miles to Big Timber/exit 367. Turn left to enter Big Timber, then proceed south on Montana State Highway 298 for 25 miles then travel south on County Road 212 for 8 miles. The paved road turns to gravel with an over-abundance of dust.
About the campground: The main access road splits this dusty little campground into two parts. Those with larger RVs and a dislike for rough, dusty roads should probably stop elsewhere. As with other campgrounds in the immediate area, firewood will take some effort to locate and transport. The campground is open all year long, dependent on the weather.

5 Aspen

Location: 68 miles southeast of Livingston on the Boulder River.
Facilities: Vault toilet, fire rings, tables, drinking water.
Sites: 8 for tents or RVs/Trailers up to 32 feet long.
Fee: $ per night, 16-day limit.
Managing agency: Gallatin National Forest, Livingston Office, (406) 222-1892.
Activities: Hiking, fishing, wildlife viewing.
Finding the campground: Take I-90 east out of Livingston for 34 miles to Big Timber/exit 367. Turn left to enter Big Timber, proceed south on Montana State Highway 298 for 25 miles, then travel south on County Road 212 for 8.5 miles. As mentioned in the write-up for the previous site, the gravel access road has plenty of dust potential.
About the campground: Two loops evenly divide the camping area, which has enough space between units to promote a sense of isolation. Aspen and Douglas fir trees combine with the abundant willow brush along the stream bank for additional shade in the shadows of the steep, rugged mountains confining it. This would be an area to stop and spend some time, especially if you have a larger RV. The handicap access testifies to the relatively pleasant layout. Do not be in a hurry to get here, as the road gets narrow and very rough. Occupancy at this campground varies pretty much every day of the week. It is open Memorial Day through Labor Day, dependent on the weather.

6 Chippy Park

Location: 69 miles southeast of Livingston on the Boulder River.
Facilities: Vault toilet, fire rings, tables, drinking water, picnic area.

Sites: 2 for tents and 5 for RVs/Trailers up to 32 feet long.
Fee: $ per night, 16-day limit.
Managing agency: Gallatin National Forest, Livingston Office, (406) 222–1892.
Activities: Hiking, fishing, wildlife viewing.
Finding the campground: Take I–90 east out of Livingston for 34 miles to Big Timber/exit 367. Turn left to enter Big Timber, proceed south on Montana State Highway 298 for 25 miles, then travel south on County Road 212 for 9.5 miles.
About the campground: The camping units are a bit close to the main access road. The roughness of the road tends to be a redeeming factor, since it helps to make travelers slow down. Trailers fit well for those willing to endure the access road. The campground is open from Memorial Day through Labor Day, dependent on the weather.

7 Hells Canyon

Location: 75 miles southeast of Livingston.
Facilities: Vault toilet, fire rings, tables.
Sites: 11 for tents or RVs/Trailers up to 16 feet long.
Fee: None, 16-day limit.
Managing agency: Gallatin National Forest, Livingston Office, (406) 222–1892.
Activities: Hiking, wildlife viewing.
Finding the campground: Take I–90 east out of Livingston for 34 miles to Big Timber/exit 367. Turn left to enter Big Timber, proceed south on Montana State Highway 298 for 25 miles, then travel south on County Road 212 for 15.5 miles. At the sign turn left onto the single-lane dirt road and travel 0.5 mile.
About the campground: The pine forest combines with a hidden draw to make this a well-concealed and quiet area. Nicely spaced units help to promote even more seclusion, though finding a level spot can be very difficult. The campground is open all year long, dependent on the weather.

8 Hicks Park

Location: 80 miles southeast of Livingston on the Boulder River.
Facilities: Vault toilet, fire rings, tables, drinking water.
Sites: 16 for tents or RVs/Trailer combinations up to 32 feet long.
Fee: $ per night, 16-day limit.
Managing agency: Gallatin National Forest, Livingston Office, (406) 222–1892.
Activities: Hiking, fishing, wildlife viewing.
Finding the campground: Take I–90 east out of Livingston for 34 miles to Big Timber/exit 367. Turn left to enter Big Timber, proceed south on Montana State Highway 298 for 25 miles, then travel south on County Road 212 for 21 miles.
About the campground: Douglas fir trees snuggle up to the parking units as they move away from the riverbank and carpet the surrounding mountainsides. Leveling may take some effort. The

campground is open all year long; however, water is only available from Memorial Day through Labor Day, dependent on the weather.

⑨ West Boulder

Location: 66 miles southeast of Livingston.
Facilities: Vault toilets, fire rings, tables, drinking water, trailhead.
Sites: 10 for tents or RVs/Trailers up to 20 feet long.
Fee: $ per night, 16-day limit.
Managing agency: Gallatin National Forest, Livingston Office, (406) 222–1892.
Activities: Hiking, wildlife viewing.
Finding the campground: Take I-90 east out of Livingston for 34 miles to Big Timber/exit 367. Turn left to enter Big Timber, then proceed south on paved Montana State Highway 298 for 16 miles. Turn right onto the very rough gravel West Boulder Road and travel 7 miles. Turn left onto the narrower national forest access road and travel 8 miles.
About the campground: Private property—you'll see plenty of notices—surrounds this campground. The West Boulder River is not quite in sight from the camping area. The nearby trailhead offers the only access to public land, though it still crosses a considerable amount of private property. The willow brush and aspen trees do not offer any firewood for those who choose to stay here, so bring plenty of your own. Water spigots are available for drinking water. The camping area as a whole seems to have been much larger at one time; additional units currently are neglected. No doubt the restricted access to additional public land deters many a visitor. The campground is open all year, dependent on the weather.

Thick brush offers some seclusion at West Boulder Campground.

10 Half Moon

Location: 60 miles northeast of Livingston on Big Timber Creek.
Facilities: Vault toilets, fire rings, tables, drinking water, picnic area, trailhead.
Sites: 12 for tents or RVs/Trailer combinations up to 32 feet long.
Fee: $ per night, 16-day limit.
Managing agency: Gallatin National Forest, Livingston Office, (406) 222-1892.
Activities: Hiking, fishing, wildlife viewing.
Finding the campground: Take I-90 east out of Livingston for 34 miles to Big Timber/exit 367. Turn left to enter Big Timber, then proceed north on US Highway 191 for 11 miles. Turn left onto the gravel road at the Big Timber Canyon directional sign and travel 1.5 miles. Turn right onto the gravel continuation of Big Timber Canyon Road and travel 13.5 miles. The access road divides an active cluster of cabins complete with a metal gate where the road narrows down to a single lane for the last 3 miles. Drive slowly and watch for horses and their riders.
About the campground: Douglas fir trees provide plenty of shade at this camping area, with a few pine and aspen thrown in for good measure. Steep mountains rise on each side, adding to the long shadows at both the beginning and end of the day. Leveling will take some work, though once completed, the surrounding serenity will quickly erase any discomfort. Big Timber Creek crashes through a nearby canyon complete with rapids and a waterfall above and below the

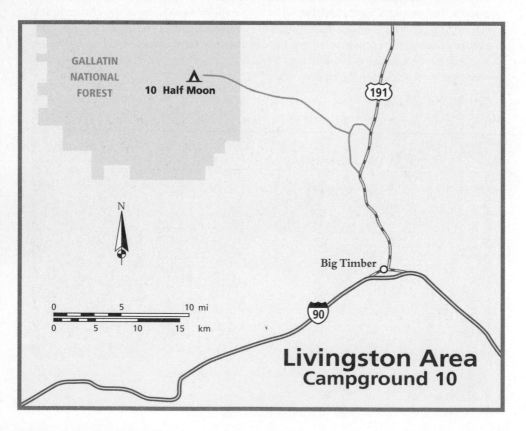

This view of the lower falls is from below Half Moon Campground.

campground. The lower falls will take a little exploring while the upper falls are just off the trail departing from the trailhead about 0.5 mile upstream. Thick brush and timber tend to conceal the high cliffs adjacent to the campground. Exercise caution around the edges, especially with small children. This popular spot fills quickly on any given weekend. For those with a strong desire to camp in a remote spot in the wilderness, it would be wise to arrive long before noon on a Friday. The campground is open all year long, with limited access dependent on the weather. Drinking water is typically available from Memorial Day through Labor Day.

11 Pine Creek

Location: 15 miles south of Livingston on Pine Creek.
Facilities: Vault toilets, fire rings, tables, drinking water.
Sites: 2 for tents and 23 for tents or RVs/Trailer combinations up to 50 feet long.
Fee: $$ per night, 16-day limit.
Managing agency: Gallatin National Forest, Livingston Ranger District, (406) 222–1892.
Activities: Hiking.
Finding the campground: Take US Highway 89 south out of Livingston for 9 miles. Turn left onto paved Pine Creek Road and travel 6 miles. Continue past the town of Pine Creek and turn onto Forest Road 202 and travel south 3 miles.
About the campground: Reservations are recommended; call (877) 444-6777. The camping units are divided into two separate areas in this stand of Douglas fir. The paved access and close proximity to Livingston combine to make this a popular place. Pine Creek did not have much, if any, water upon our visit, which of course can change with the weather. Conveniently placed water spigots, permanent benches around fire pits, and, in some places, miniature fireplaces all add to the attractiveness of this mountain setting. The campground is open from May 26 through September 15.

12 Loch Leven

Location: 15 miles south of Livingston on the Yellowstone River.
Facilities: Vault toilets, fire rings, tables, drinking water, boat ramp.
Sites: 30 for tents or RVs/Trailer combinations up to 50 feet long.
Fee: $ per night, 7-day limit.
Managing agency: Montana Fish, Wildlife & Parks, (406) 994–4042.
Activities: Fishing, boating.
Finding the campground: Take US Highway 89 south out of Livingston for 9 miles. Turn left at milepost 44 and travel 2 miles. Turn right onto paved Montana State Highway 540 and travel 4 miles. Turn right at the access sign.
About the campground: Cottonwood trees outline the riverbanks but do not provide firewood. Fishing is the major attraction, but this could be a pleasant spot on a late evening for those going on to Yellowstone National Park. The campground is open all year long, dependent on the weather.

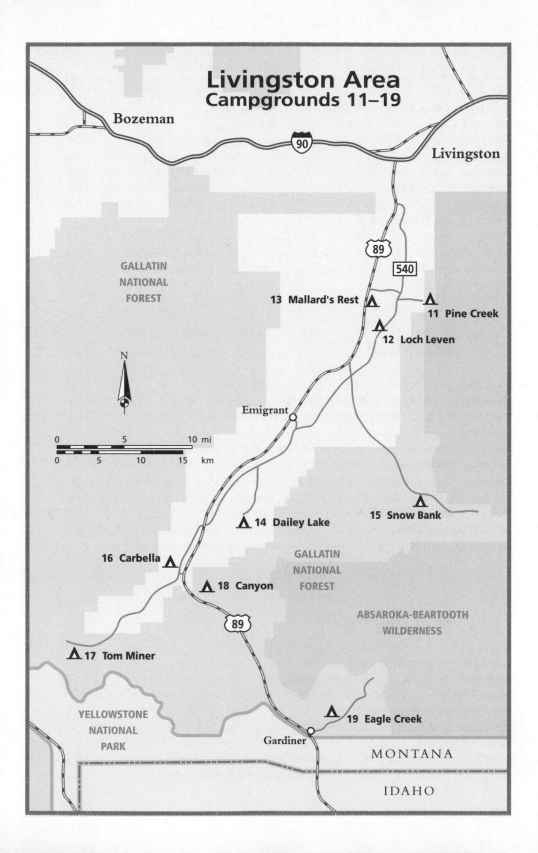

Livingston Area
Campgrounds 11–19

Bozeman

Livingston

GALLATIN
NATIONAL
FOREST

13 Mallard's Rest

11 Pine Creek

12 Loch Leven

N

0   5   10 mi

0   5   10   15 km

Emigrant

15 Snow Bank

14 Dailey Lake

16 Carbella

GALLATIN
NATIONAL
FOREST

18 Canyon

ABSAROKA-BEARTOOTH
WILDERNESS

17 Tom Miner

YELLOWSTONE
NATIONAL
PARK

19 Eagle Creek

Gardiner

MONTANA

IDAHO

13 Mallard's Rest

Location: 13 miles south of Livingston on the Yellowstone River.
Facilities: Vault toilet, fire rings, tables, drinking water, boat launch.
Sites: 13 for tents or RVs/Trailer combinations up to 50 feet long.
Fee: $$ per night, 7-day limit.
Managing agency: Montana Fish, Wildlife & Parks, (406) 994-4042.
Activities: Fishing, boating.
Finding the campground: Take US Highway 89 south out of Livingston for 13 miles. Turn left at the access sign, near milepost 42.
About the campground: The Yellowstone River beckons to anglers and floaters alike, with room for both. Noise levels can get a bit high on hot summer days when visitors seek relief in the cold mountain waters. After sundown things tend to get more peaceful. The campground is open all year long.

14 Dailey Lake

Location: 33 miles south of Livingston at Dailey Lake.
Facilities: Vault toilets, fire rings, tables, drinking water, boat ramp.
Sites: 35 for tents or RVs/Trailer combinations up to 42 feet long.
Fee: $$ per night, 7-day limit.
Managing agency: Montana Fish, Wildlife & Parks, (406) 994-4042.
Activities: Fishing, boating.
Finding the campground: Take US Highway 89 south out of Livingston for 22 miles. At Emigrant turn left onto Murphy Lane and travel 1 mile. Turn right onto Montana Highway 540 and travel 4 miles. Turn left onto Sixmile Creek Road and travel 6 miles.
About the campground: Fishing is the main attraction here and wind can be brutal, but it is not constant as a rule. Shade is absent apart from what you bring with you. The campground is open year-round.

15 Snow Bank

Location: 28 miles south of Livingston on Mill Creek.
Facilities: Vault toilets, fire rings, tables, drinking water.
Sites: 11 for tents or RVs/Trailer combinations up to 40 feet long.
Fee: $$ per night, 16-day limit.
Managing agency: Gallatin National Forest, Livingston Ranger District, (406) 222-1892.
Activities: Hiking, fishing.
Finding the campground: Take US Highway 89 south out of Livingston for 15 miles. Turn left onto paved Mill Creek Road and travel 13 miles. The last 6 miles turn to gravel.

About the campground: Reservations can be made by calling (877) 444-6777. Campers have a choice between two branches settled comfortably into the aspen trees and brush along Mill Creek. Steep mountainsides with an assortment of evergreens define the creek direction and seem to isolate the area from the rest of the world. The campground is open from Memorial Day to Labor Day, dependent on the weather. The season may be longer with reduced services. Firewood is typically available for purchase.

16 Carbella

Location: 33 miles south of Livingston on the Yellowstone River.
Facilities: Vault toilet, fire rings, tables, boat ramp.
Sites: Dispersed for tents or RVs/Trailer combinations up to 50 feet long.
Fee: None, 14-day limit.
Managing agency: Bureau of Land Management, (406) 533–7600.
Activities: Fishing, boating.
Finding the campground: Take US Highway 89 south out of Livingston for 33 miles. Turn right at the access sign and follow directions to the river.
About the campground: The access road is rough, but traveling slow is the key that opens the door to a pleasant reward at the other side. Tall cottonwood trees tower above the high-water mark of the Yellowstone River and partially shade the available tables. A large, flat, open area provides room for just about any size RV. Dust can be annoying at times, but if fishing, rafting, or mountain scenery is appealing to you, this could be a welcome spot. The openness of the camping area allows good views for the year-round season. Keep in mind that winter weather shows no mercy.

17 Tom Miner

Location: 49 miles south of Livingston on Trail Creek.
Facilities: Vault toilets, fire rings, tables, drinking water.
Sites: 16 for tents or RVs/Trailer combinations up to 42 feet long.
Fee: $ per night, 16-day limit.
Managing agency: Gallatin National Forest, Gardiner Ranger District, (406) 848–7375.
Activities: Hiking, fishing, wildlife viewing.
Finding the campground: Take US Highway 89 south out of Livingston for 33 miles. Turn right onto gravel Tom Miner Road and travel 12 miles. Follow the directional signs to Forest Road 63 and travel 4 miles.
About the campground: In this fir forest, aspen claims its territory with a defiant and brilliant display of orange in the fall. The mountains stand watch in the not-too-far distance, offering a good view and inviting the adventurous to explore. This campground is in the Gallatin Petrified Forest and collecting is allowed, provided you have a permit. Check with the forest service for details. A small bubbly creek winds past the parking units, creating a pleasant recreation option

for young and old alike. Leveling trailers will take effort in the semi-level parking spots. After grinding all the way back into this remote area, you would not likely want to go looking for another campground. It is open from June 1 through October 31, when the weather allows.

18 Canyon

Location: 35 miles south of Livingston.
Facilities: Vault toilet, fire rings.
Sites: 17 for tents or RVs/Trailer combinations up to 48 feet long.
Fee: $, 16-day limit.
Managing agency: Gallatin National Forest, Gardiner Ranger District, (406) 848-7375.
Activities: Hiking.
Finding the campground: Take US Highway 89 south out of Livingston for 35 miles. The campground is on the left side of the road.
About the campground: A unique assortment of odd shaped and sized boulders dominates this campground. Douglas fir trees struggle for any available area that will support them. This would be a good spot to consider on a late evening if you are going to Yellowstone National Park and don't have reservations. The campground is open all year long, dependent on the weather, with a somewhat rough access.

19 Eagle Creek

Location: 55 miles south of Livingston on Eagle Creek.
Facilities: Vault toilets, fire rings, tables.
Sites: 16 for tents or RVs/Trailer combinations up to 40 feet long.
Fee: $ per night, 16-day limit.
Managing agency: Gallatin National Forest, Gardiner Ranger District, (406) 848-7375.
Activities: Hiking, wildlife viewing.
Finding the campground: Take US Highway 89 south out of Livingston for 53 miles to Gardiner. Turn left onto Jardine Road and travel 2 miles. This road turns to gravel and courses along the mountainside at a steep grade.
About the campground: Yellowstone National Park is within sight from this high vantage point. Mammoth Hot Springs clearly stands out on the opposite mountainside. Short aspen trees line the creek bank with wide-open meadows offering an unobstructed view. Camping might get a bit cramped with the limited space between parking units. The dust from the nearby Jardine Road could also prove annoying. If the campgrounds are full in Yellowstone, those with larger RVs would best look elsewhere. The campground is open all year long, dependent on the weather.

Bozeman Area

This is a popular area with easier access and more modern conveniences. Campgrounds range from open-air flatlands along river bottoms to well-shaded units tucked away under a massive mountain. Rafting is a popular activity in campgrounds to the south of Bozeman.

If seclusion and less traffic noise is what you seek, choose one of the campgrounds off the main road. Spire Rock would make an excellent paradise, if you can tolerate the rough, narrow access. Generally, the harder a campground is to reach, the fewer the visitors.

	Group Sites	Tents	RV sites	Total sites	Hookups	Toilets	Showers	Drinking water	Dump station	Phone	Handicap Access	Recreation	Fee	Season	Stay limit (days)
1 Battle Ridge			13	13		V		*				HW	N	5/15–9/15	16
2 Fairy Lake			9	9		V		*			*	HW	N	7/1–9/15	16
3 Missouri Headwaters State Park			17	17		V		*				HF	$$	5/1–9/30	7
4 Langohr			19	19		V		*			*	HF	$$	5/15–9/15	16
5 Hood Creek			25	25		V		*			*	HFB	$$	5/15–9/15	16
6 Chisholm			10	10		V		*			*	HFB	$$	5/15–9/15	16
7 Spire Rock			19	19		V						HF	$$	5/15–9/15	16
8 Greek Creek			15	15		V		*			*	HF	$$	5/15–9/15	16
9 Swan Creek			13	13		V		*				HF	$$	5/15–9/15	16
10 Moose Creek Flat			13	13		V		*			*	HF	$$	5/15–9/15	16
11 Red Cliff			61	61		V		*				HF	$$	5/15–9/15	16

1 Battle Ridge

Location: 22 miles north of Bozeman.
Facilities: Vault toilets, fire rings, tables, drinking water.
Sites: 13 for tents or RVs/Trailer combinations up to 30 feet long.
Fee: None, 16-day limit.
Managing agency: Gallatin National Forest, Bozeman Ranger District, (406) 522–2520.
Activities: Hiking, wildlife viewing.
Finding the campground: Take Montana State Highway 86 north out of Bozeman for 22 miles. The campground is on the right side of the highway.
About the campground: Ancient fir trees inhabit this old and well-used campground. Longer trailers will fit, but leveling them does not come without its price. Neither does firewood. Highway traffic cannot be easily ignored, but after sundown things get a little quieter. The campground is officially open from May 15 through September 15. Access is permitted after these dates, dependent on the weather, but without services.

2 Fairy Lake

Location: 29 miles north of Bozeman at Fairy Lake.
Facilities: Vault toilet, fire rings, tables, drinking water.
Sites: 9 for tents or RVs/Trailer combinations up to 32 feet long.
Fee: None, 16-day limit.
Managing agency: Gallatin National Forest, Bozeman Ranger District, (406) 522–2520.
Activities: Hiking, wildlife viewing.

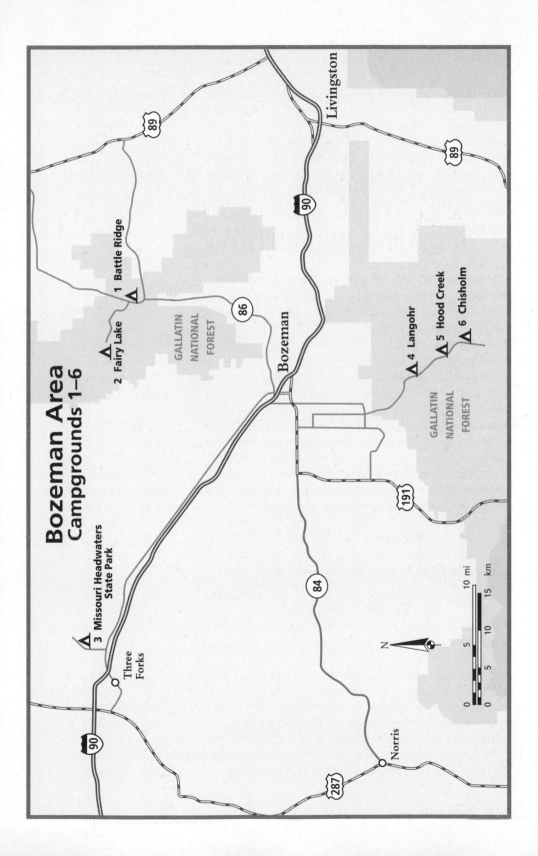

Bozeman Area
Campgrounds 1–6

Livingston

△ 1 Battle Ridge
△ 2 Fairy Lake

GALLATIN
NATIONAL
FOREST

Bozeman

△ 4 Langohr
△ 5 Hood Creek
△ 6 Chisholm

GALLATIN
NATIONAL
FOREST

△ 3 Missouri Headwaters
State Park

Three
Forks

Norris

N

89
89
90
86
191
84
287
90

10 mi
km
0   5   10
0   5   10   15

Finding the campground: Take Montana State Highway 86 north out of Bozeman for 22 miles. Turn left onto gravel Fairy Lake Road and travel 7 miles.

About the campground: The access road can be very challenging. A call to the district office for road conditions is highly advised. Trailers will fit, but be prepared for a rough road and an even rougher time of leveling. Unhooking is required to fit in the parking units. Firewood is no longer available, so be sure to bring some from an approved source. Douglas fir dominates the rocky terrain, with grassy meadows in between along the road coming in. This is a nice place to settle for a while, especially after all the work required. Depending upon the weather, the campground is open from July 1 through September 15.

3 Missouri Headwaters State Park

Location: 30 miles northwest of Bozeman on the Missouri River.
Facilities: Vault toilets, fire rings, tables, drinking water, boat ramp.
Sites: 17 for tents or RVs/Trailer combinations up to 60 feet long.
Fee: $$ per night, 7-day limit.
Managing agency: Missouri Headwaters State Park, (406) 285-3610.
Activities: Hiking, fishing.
Finding the campground: Take I-90 northwest out of Bozeman for 24 miles to Three Forks/exit 278. Turn right onto County Road 205 and travel 3 miles. Turn left onto County Road 286 and travel 3 miles.

About the campground: The Jefferson, Madison, and Gallatin Rivers all flow together at this location to become the Missouri River. Cottonwood trees and tall grass combined with the river environment support plenty of mosquitoes, so do not forget the bug spray. If you definitely want a campfire, be sure to obtain wood from an approved source. Not all the parking pads are 60 feet long; most are in the 30- to 40-foot class. If your rig is one of the longer ones, it would be wise to call ahead. The park is open all year, but the campground is only open from May 1 through September 30.

4 Langohr

Location: 13 miles south of Bozeman on Hyalite Creek.
Facilities: Vault toilets, fire rings, tables, drinking water.
Sites: 19 for tents or RVs/Trailer combinations up to 32 feet long.
Fee: $$ per night, 16-day limit.
Managing agency: Gallatin National Forest, Bozeman Ranger District, (406) 522-2520.
Activities: Hiking, fishing.
Finding the campground: Take Nineteenth Avenue south out of Bozeman for 7 miles. Turn left onto Hyalite Canyon Road/Forest Road 62 and travel 6 miles.

About the campground: Reservations can be made by calling (877) 444-6777, though there are some first come-first served units available. Paved and level parking units, along with the melodious creek water, make this area appealing. The parking aprons are wide enough to allow parking alongside after unhooking. Traffic can be heavy at times. Firewood is available for purchase. The campground is open from May 15 through September 15.

5 Hood Creek

Location: 17 miles south of Bozeman at Hyalite Reservoir.
Facilities: Vault toilets, fire rings, tables, drinking water, boat ramp.
Sites: 25 for tents or RVs/Trailer combinations up to 50 feet long.
Fee: $$ per night, 16-day limit.
Managing agency: Gallatin National Forest, Bozeman Ranger District, (406) 522-2520.
Activities: Hiking, fishing, boating.
Finding the campground: Take Nineteenth Avenue south out of Bozeman for 7 miles. Turn left onto Hyalite Canyon Road/Forest Road 62 and travel 10 miles.
About the campground: Reservations can be made by calling (877) 444-6777, though some sites may be available on a first-come, first-served basis. Firewood is available for purchase. Pine trees and camping units overlook this small reservoir. The no-wake policy for this lake keeps the noise level at more acceptable limits. Anglers can test their skill while those who find canoeing enjoyable glide by. Forested mountains fill the horizon between pine trees along the hillsides of this camping area. It is open from May 15 through September 15.

6 Chisholm

Location: 18 miles south of Bozeman at Hyalite Reservoir.
Facilities: Vault toilets, fire rings, tables, drinking water.
Sites: 10 for tents or RVs/Trailer combinations up to 60 feet long.
Fee: $$ per night, 16-day limit.
Managing agency: Gallatin National Forest, Bozeman Ranger District, (406) 522-2520.
Activities: Hiking, fishing, boating.
Finding the campground: Take Nineteenth Avenue south out of Bozeman for 7 miles. Turn left onto Hyalite Canyon Road/Forest Road 62 and travel 11 miles.
About the campground: Reservations can be made by calling (877) 444-6777, though some sites may be available on a first-come, first-served basis. The pine and fir trees stand guard around Hyalite Reservoir, with Hyalite Creek nearby. The parking aprons range from 35 to 65 feet long, but all require backing in. If mirrors and left-is-right/right-is-left increase your blood pressure, it is best to pass this campground by. Firewood is available for purchase. The campground is open from May 15 through September 15.

7 Spire Rock

Location: 20 miles south of Bozeman on Squaw Creek.
Facilities: Vault toilets, fire rings, tables.

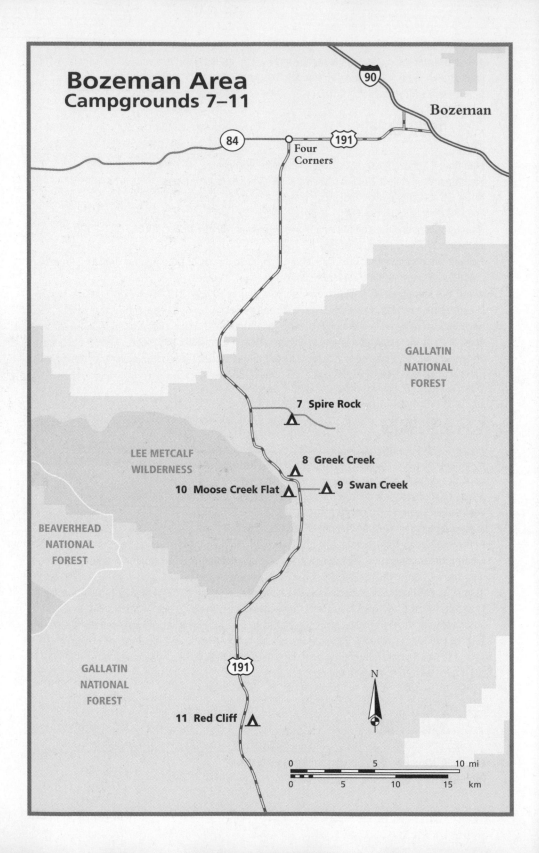

Sites: 19 for tents or RVs/Trailer combinations up to 45 feet long.
Fee: $$ per night, 16-day limit.
Managing agency: Gallatin National Forest, Bozeman Ranger District, (406) 522–2520.
Activities: Hiking, fishing.
Finding the campground: Take US Highway 191 south out of Four Corners (which may or may not be considered part of Bozeman, depending upon your point of view) for 17 miles. Turn left at the Squaw Creek Road sign to cross the Gallatin River via a concrete bridge. Continue on the rough gravel road for 3 miles.
About the campground: Reservations can be made by calling (877) 444-6777, though some sites may be available on a first-come, first-served basis. The parking aprons vary from 25 to 45 feet and length, and all require backing in. Firewood is available for purchase. Willow brush and other thick plant life share the shadows and close spaces between fir trees along the creek bank. The camping units are well enough spaced to create a sense of isolation. The sun does not reach this portion of the canyon for any great length of time, so bring plenty of warm clothes. The campground is open from May 15 through September 15.

8 Greek Creek

Location: 22 miles south of Bozeman on the Gallatin River.
Facilities: Vault toilets, fire rings, tables, drinking water.
Sites: 15 for tents or RVs/Trailer combinations up to 60 feet long.
Fee: $$ per night, 16-day limit.
Managing agency: Gallatin National Forest, Bozeman Ranger District, (406) 522–2520.
Activities: Hiking, fishing.
Finding the campground: Take US Highway 191 south out of Four Corners (which may or may not be considered part of Bozeman, depending upon your point of view) for 22 miles.
About the campground: Reservations can be made by calling (877) 444-6777, though some sites may be available on a first-come, first-served basis. Firewood is available for purchase. The parking aprons range from 25 to 60 feet long, with only one pull-through. All of the remaining units require backing in. The campground occupies both sides of the road and has paved, level access. Thick, mature pine trees shade the parking units, with one reserved as a host area. The Gallatin River rolls by rather sleepily, making a special appeal to rafters commonly seen on summer days. Traffic can be heavy and annoying on holidays and some weekends, but the noise level decreases with the waning sun. The campground is open from May 15 through September 15.

9 Swan Creek

Location: 24 miles south of Bozeman on Swan Creek.
Facilities: Vault toilets, fire rings, tables, drinking water.
Sites: 13 for tents or RVs/Trailer combinations up to 55 feet long.

Fee: $$ per night, 16-day limit.

Managing agency: Gallatin National Forest, Bozeman Ranger District, (406) 522-2520.

Activities: Hiking, fishing.

Finding the campground: Take US Highway 191 south out of Four Corners (which may or may not be considered part of Bozeman, depending upon your point of view) for 23 miles. Turn left onto narrow Swan Creek Road and travel 1 mile.

About the campground: Reservations can be made by calling (877) 444-6777, though some sites may be available on a first-come, first-served basis. Firewood is available for purchase. The campground roads are paved, but the 25- to 55-foot long aprons are gravel. All of the parking spots require backing in. Tall, mature lodgepole pines inhabit the campground and surrounding hillsides. The dusty road accessing this quiet little place is well worth the trouble for those who want to get away from the hustle and noise of the well-used highway. Swan Creek's fishing opportunities may not equal those of the nearby Gallatin River, but it is likely that there will be fewer anglers and definitely not as many rafters, if there are any at all. The campground is open from May 15 through September 15.

10 Moose Creek Flat

Location: 23 miles south of Bozeman on the Gallatin River.

Facilities: Vault toilets, fire rings, tables, drinking water.

Sites: 13 for tents or RVs/Trailer combinations up to 60 feet long.

Fee: $$ per night, 16-day limit.

Managing agency: Gallatin National Forest, Bozeman Ranger District, (406) 522-2520.

Activities: Hiking, fishing.

Finding the campground: Take US Highway 191 south out of Four Corners (which may or may not be considered part of Bozeman, depending upon your point of view) for 23 miles. The campground is on the right side of the road.

About the campground: Reservations can be made by calling (877) 444-6777, though some sites may be available on a first-come, first-served basis. Firewood is available for purchase. The parking aprons range from 25 to 60 feet long, with four pull-throughs. The remaining sites all require backing in. Lodgepole pines and grassy meadows share the riverbank almost equally just off the highway. Rafters commonly use this area for put in or take out, thus generating all the associated noises. The people noises tend to change to the more common camping types at nightfall, with the exception of passing traffic. The campground is open from May 15 through September 15.

11 Red Cliff

Location: 39 miles south of Bozeman on the Gallatin River.

Facilities: Vault toilets, fire rings, tables, drinking water.

Sites: 61 for tents or RVs/Trailer combinations up to 60 feet long.

Fee: $$ per night, 16-day limit.

Managing agency: Gallatin National Forest, Bozeman Ranger District, (406) 522–2520.

Activities: Hiking, fishing.

Finding the campground: Take US Highway 191 south out of Four Corners (which may or may not be considered part of Bozeman, depending upon your point of view) for 39 miles. The campground is on the left side of the road.

About the campground: Reservations can be made by calling (877) 444-6777, though some sites may be available on a first-come, first-served basis. The parking aprons range from 30 to 60 feet long. All of the sites require backing in. Firewood is available for purchase. The camping units relax on a flat portion of the riverbank on the Gallatin River. Twenty-seven units have electricity available for an additional fee. Lodgepole pine trees with tall grass in between drink in sunshine along the way, unless, of course, the winter months have arrived. The parking units are well spaced, allowing for a sense of isolation. However, with the lack of brush cover, neighbors will be visible. For those who are on their way to Yellowstone National Park and have no reservations, this would be a very good place to check out. The closer you get to the park, the fewer the options, especially after noon. The campground is open from May 15 through September 15.

Wolf Point Area

Fort Peck Reservoir comes to the top of the list where camping is concerned. The Missouri River is backed up for a length of 134 miles, plus or minus, based on upstream flow rates. Even the state of California doesn't have as much shoreline as the 1,520 miles that define Fort Peck Reservoir's watery domain. If the twelve camping areas were separated equally apart, which they are not, there would be 126 miles of shoreline between them. That leaves a lot of territory for leaving the crowds behind. Boats are not required to sample the pleasures of this predominately unpopulated kingdom where weather decides the outcome of those who venture here, but it is hard to imagine not having one. Be prepared for an extended stay—an unexpected storm can alter access, in as well as out.

	Group Sites	Tents	RV sites	Total sites	Hookups	Toilets	Showers	Drinking water	Dump station	Phone	Handicap Access	Recreation	Fee	Season	Stay limit (days)
1 Duck Creek			15	15								FB	N	All Year	14
2 West End			13	13	V			*			*	HFB	$$	5/1-9/6	14
3 Downstream			86	86	V			*			*	HFB	$$$	5/1-10/30	14
4 Flat Lake	D			D	P							F	N	All Year	14
5 Bear Creek			D	D	P							F	N	All Year	14
6 McGuire Creek			12	12	P							F	N	All Year	14
7 Nelson Creek			25	25	V							FB	N	All Year	14
8 Hell Creek State Park			71	71	VF			*			*	HFB	$$	All Year	14
9 Devils Creek			D	D	V							HFB	N	All Year	14
10 The Pines			30	30	V			*				FB	N	All Year	14
11 Bone Trail			10	10	V							FB	N	All Year	14
12 Nelson Reservoir			9	9	V			*				FB	N	All Year	7
13 Fourchette Bay			D	D	V							HFB	N	All Year	14
14 Camp Creek			20	20	V			*				H	$	All Year	14
15 Montana Gulch			12	12	V							H	$	All Year	14
16 James Kipp	15		19	34	V			*				HFB	$$	All Year	14

1 Duck Creek

Location: 51 miles west of Wolf Point on Fort Peck Reservoir.
Facilities: Vault toilets, fire rings, tables, boat ramp.
Sites: 15 for tents or RVs.
Fee: None, 14-day limit.
Managing agency: US Army Corps of Engineers, Fort Peck, (406) 526-3411.
Activities: Fishing, boating.
Finding the campground: Take US Highway 2 west out of Wolf Point for 35 miles. Turn left onto Montana State Highway 117 and travel 11 miles to Fort Peck. Continue on SH 117 for 2 miles west of Fort Peck. Merge onto Highway 24 and travel 1 mile. Turn left on Duck Creek Road and travel 2 miles. Turn left at the Duck Creek Recreational Access sign.
About the campground: Water sports are the major attraction here at this year-round spot.

2 West End

Location: 48 miles west of Wolf Point on Fort Peck Reservoir.
Facilities: Vault and flush toilets, showers, fire rings, tables, drinking water.

Sites: 15 for tents or RVs/Trailer combinations up to 60 feet long.
Fee: $$ per night, 14-day limit.
Managing agency: US Army Corps of Engineers, Fort Peck, (406) 526–3411.
Activities: Hiking, fishing, boating.
Finding the campground: Take US Highway 2 west out of Wolf Point for 35 miles. Turn left onto Montana State Highway 117 and travel 11 miles to Fort Peck. Continue on SH 117 for 2 miles west of Fort Peck. Merge onto Highway 24 and travel 1 mile. Turn left on Duck Creek Road and travel 1 mile. The campground will be on the left.
About the campground: A few trees offer shade at select spots, but for the most part it is open sky. This area is most known for watersports. Electricity is available, but there are no sewer or water hookups. The campground is open from May 1 through September 6.

3 Downstream

Location: 48 miles west of Wolf Point on Fort Peck Reservoir.
Facilities: Flush toilets, showers, fire rings, tables, drinking water, boat ramp.
Sites: 86 for tents or RVs/Trailer combinations up to 60 feet long.
Fee: $$ per night, 14-day limit.
Managing agency: US Army Corps of Engineers, Fort Peck, (406) 526–3411.
Activities: Hiking, fishing, boating.
Finding the campground: Take US Highway 2 west out of Wolf Point for 35 miles. Turn left onto Montana State Highway 117 and travel 11 miles to (2 miles past Park Grove)
About the campground: The camping units here can be reserved. Call (877) 444-6777 with some first-come, first-served sites available. This is a popular camping area and fills early, so don't count on snagging one of the first-come units much after 8 a.m. This campground is located along the river below the dam and does not share the reservoir shoreline. The large cottonwood trees and other vegetation offer a hint of what previous visitors could have seen before the dam. There is electricity available in seventy-one of the camping units, but no other hookups. The campground is open from May 1 through October 30.

4 Flat Lake

Location: 53 miles west of Wolf Point on Fort Peck Reservoir.
Facilities: Pit toilet, boat ramp.
Sites: Dispersed for tents or RVs/Trailer combinations up to 50 feet long.
Fee: None per night, 14-day limit.
Managing agency: US Army Corps of Engineers, Fort Peck, (406) 526–3411.
Activities: Fishing.
Finding the campground: Take US Highway 2 west out of Wolf Point for 35 miles. Turn left onto Montana State Highway 117 and travel 11 miles to Fort Peck. Turn left onto Highway 24 and travel 7 miles. The Flat Lake Recreation area will be on the right.
About the campground: This area is specifically for anglers and boaters. Wide-open spaces, rolling hills, and a huge reservoir await the traveler. The campground is open all year long. High

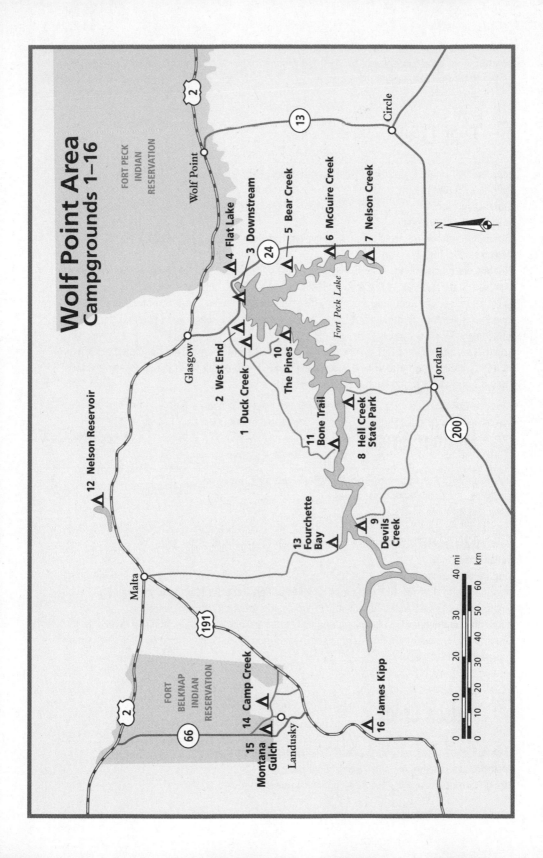

water from an overabundance of rain in 2018 prompted the closure of this campground, but it is anticipated to be open in the future.

5 Bear Creek

Location: 67 miles southwest of Wolf Point on Fort Peck Reservoir.
Facilities: Vault toilet.
Sites: Dispersed.
Fee: None, 14-day limit.
Managing agency: US Army Corps of Engineers, Fort Peck, (406) 526-3411.
Activities: Fishing.
Finding the campground: Take US Highway 2 west out of Wolf Point for 35 miles. Turn left onto Montana State Highway 117 and travel 11 miles to Fort Peck. Turn left onto Highway 24 and travel 14 miles. Turn right onto the county road and travel 7 miles. The road can become impassable in wet weather for an indefinite time. You may have to stay longer than planned, so pack accordingly.
About the campground: This is considered a primitive camping area; come prepared. Do not count on finding any firewood here. Fishing along the banks of this huge prairie reservoir is the main attraction. The campground is open all year.

6 McGuire Creek

Location: 94 miles southwest of Wolf Point on Fort Peck Reservoir.
Facilities: Vault toilet, fire rings, tables.
Sites: 12 for tents or RVs.
Fee: None, 14-day limit.
Managing agency: US Army Corps of Engineers, Fort Peck, (406) 526-3411.
Activities: Fishing.
Finding the campground: Take US Highway 2 west out of Wolf Point for 35 miles. Turn left onto Montana State Highway 117 and travel 11 miles to Fort Peck. Turn left onto Montana State Highway 24 and travel 41 miles. Turn right onto the county road and travel 7 miles.
About the campground: Long units have plenty of room, but level spots require a search-and-find effort. A few cottonwood trees offer some shade for those camped next to them. The campground is open all year long.

7 Nelson Creek

Location: 102 miles southwest of Wolf Point on Fort Peck Reservoir.
Facilities: Vault toilet, fire rings, tables, boat ramp.
Sites: 25 for tents or RVs/Trailer combinations up to 50 feet long.

Fee: None, 14-day limit.
Managing agency: US Army Corps of Engineers, Fort Peck, (406) 526–3411.
Activities: Fishing, boating.
Finding the campground: Take US Highway 2 west out of Wolf Point for 35 miles. Turn left onto Montana State Highway 117 and travel 11 miles to Fort Peck. Turn left onto Montana State Highway 24 and travel 49 miles. Turn right onto the county road and travel 7 miles.
About the campground: Sagebrush and sand settle in along the banks of Fort Peck Reservoir. If campfires are important, bring along some firewood to this year-round spot.

8 Hell Creek State Park

Location: 146 miles southwest of Wolf Point on Fort Peck Reservoir.
Facilities: Vault and flush toilets, fire rings, tables, drinking water, boat ramp.
Sites: 71 for tents or RVs/Trailer combinations up to 50 feet long.
Fee: $ per night, 14-day limit.
Managing agency: Hell Creek State Park, (406) 557–2362.
Activities: Hiking, fishing, boating.
Finding the campground: Take Montana State Highway 13 south out of Wolf Point for 53 miles. Turn right onto Montana State Highway 200 and travel 67 miles to Jordan. Turn right onto County Road 543 and travel 26 miles.
About the campground: Forty-four sites have electricity available. The rolling prairie ridges share room with sagebrush and a few pine trees. Planted trees offer a little shade in the year-round camping area, but for the most part water sports are the main attraction. When you want to cool off, jump in the water.

9 Devils Creek

Location: 168 miles southwest of Wolf Point on Fort Peck Reservoir.
Facilities: Vault toilet, fire rings, tables boat ramp.
Sites: Dispersed for tents or RVs up to 20 feet long.
Fee: None, 14-day limit.
Managing agency: US Army Corps of Engineers, Fort Peck, (406) 526–3411.
Activities: Hiking, fishing, boating.
Finding the campground: Take Montana State Highway 13 south out of Wolf Point for 53 miles. Turn right onto Montana State Highway 200 and travel 67 miles to Jordan. Turn right onto County Road 245 and travel 48 miles, following the directional signs.
About the campground: Having an extra three days of water and food is recommended in the event that wet weather makes the long access road impassable. The last portion of the access drops into some scenic river breaks with equally rough roads. This is not the best choice for just an overnight visit. After grinding along the dusty road, you will want to settle in for a while. The campground is open all year long.

10 The Pines

Location: 78 miles southwest of Wolf Point on Fort Peck Reservoir.
Facilities: Vault toilet, fire rings, tables, drinking water, boat ramp.
Sites: 30 for tents or RVs.
Fee: None, 14-day limit.
Managing agency: US Army Corps of Engineers, Fort Peck, (406) 526–3411.
Activities: Fishing, boating.
Finding the campground: Take US Highway 2 west out of Wolf Point for 35 miles. Turn left onto Montana State Highway 117 and travel 11 miles to Fort Peck. Continue on SH 117 for 2 miles west of Fort Peck. Merge onto Highway 24 and travel 4 miles. Turn left onto Maxness Road and travel 14 miles (Maxness Road will become Willow Creek Road). Turn left onto The Pines Road and travel 12 miles.
About the campground: This year-round campground offers a little more isolation with fewer visitors. The river breaks offer some pine trees and steep draws for exploration and scenic views.

11 Bone Trail

Location: 102 miles southwest of Wolf Point on Fort Peck Reservoir.
Facilities: Vault toilet, fire rings, tables, boat ramp.
Sites: 10 for tents or RVs up to 20 feet long.
Fee: None, 14-day limit.
Managing agency: US Army Corps of Engineers, Fort Peck, (406) 526–3411.
Activities: Fishing, boating.
Finding the campground: Take US Highway 2 west out of Wolf Point for 35 miles. Turn left onto Montana State Highway 117 and travel 11 miles to Fort Peck. Continue on SH 117 for 2 miles west of Fort Peck. Merge onto Highway 24 and travel 4 miles. Turn left onto Maxness Road and travel 39 miles (Maxness Road will become Willow Creek Road). Turn left onto the Burke Ranch Road/NF-213 and travel 8 miles. Turn right onto FWS-425 and travel about 3 miles.
About the campground: Having an extra three days of water and food is recommended in the event that wet weather makes the long access road impassable. A four-wheel-drive vehicle is required for boat launching. It is a long way to travel, and you may want to consider this campground for longer stays as opposed to an overnight outing. It is open all year long.

12 Nelson Reservoir

Location: 105 miles west of Wolf Point on Nelson Reservoir.
Facilities: Vault toilets, fire rings, tables, drinking water, boat ramp.
Sites: 9 for tents or RVs/Trailer combinations up to 50 feet long.
Fee: None, 7-day limit.

Managing agency: Bureau of Reclamation, (406) 759-5077.

Activities: Fishing, boating.

Finding the campground: Take US Highway 2 west out of Wolf Point for 103 miles. Turn right at milepost 148 and travel 2 miles.

About the campground: There are dispersed camping sites available as well adding to the total. Walleye fishing brings most visitors to this windswept prairie reservoir. The 4,000-acre body of water has produced a fourteen-pound, state-record walleye, with hopes of even bigger ones. The campground is open all year long.

13 Fourchette Bay

Location: 178 miles southwest of Wolf Point on Fort Peck Reservoir.

Facilities: Vault toilet, boat ramp.

Sites: Dispersed for tents or RVs.

Fee: None, 14-day limit.

Managing agency: US Army Corps of Engineers, Fort Peck, (406) 526-3411.

Activities: Hiking, fishing, boating.

Finding the campground: Take US Highway 2 west out of Wolf Point for 120 miles. Pass through Malta to County Road 364. Turn left onto CR 364 and travel 5 miles. Turn right onto Regina Road and travel 38 miles. Turn left onto Sun Prairie Road and travel 2 miles. Continue straight ahead on Fourchette Bay Road and travel 13 miles.

About the campground: The river breaks offer some pine trees and rugged terrain along the reservoir. There is plenty of wildlife, and the huge reservoir beckons to anglers. The campground is open all year long.

14 Camp Creek

Location: 176 miles southwest of Wolf Point.

Facilities: Vault toilets, fire rings, tables, drinking water.

Sites: 20 for tents or RVs/Trailer combinations up to 30 feet long.

Fee: $ per night, 14-day limit.

Managing agency: Bureau of Land Management, (406) 654-5100.

Activities: Hiking.

Finding the campground: Take US Highway 2 west out of Wolf Point for 120 miles. Take US Highway 191 south out of Malta for about 49 miles. Turn right onto Bear Gulch Road and travel 7 miles.

About the campground: The well-known Sundance Kid of the Wild Bunch once lived in this area. If you listen carefully, the wind may whisper some of the old stories as it passes through the pine branches. The Little Rockies lured miners and all the mining-related businesses long ago. Their cabins and some select relics still reside in the nearby towns of Zortman and Landusky. The campground is open all year long.

15 Montana Gulch

Location: 181 miles southwest of Wolf Point.
Facilities: Vault toilet, fire rings, tables.
Sites: 10 for tents or RVs up to 24 feet long.
Fee: $ per night, 14-day limit.
Managing agency: Bureau of Land Management, (406) 654–5100.
Activities: Hiking.
Finding the campground: Take US Highway 2 west out of Wolf Point for 120 miles. Take US Highway 191 south out of Malta for about 56 miles. Turn right onto Montana State Highway 66 and travel 5 miles. Follow the directional signs.
About the campground: Tall lodgepole pine trees offer plenty of shade, and the wind blows a pleasant music that offers tales of the past for those with imagination. The campground is open all year long.

16 James Kipp

Location: 190 miles southwest of Wolf Point on the Missouri River.
Facilities: Vault toilets, fire rings, tables, drinking water, boat ramp.
Sites: 15 for group sites and 19 for tents or RVs/Trailer combinations up to 60 feet long.
Fee: $$ per night, 14-day limit.
Managing agency: Bureau of Land Management, Lewistown Field Office, (406) 622–4000.
Activities: Hiking, fishing, boating.
Finding the campground: Take US Highway 2 west out of Wolf Point for 120 miles. Take US Highway 191 southwest out of Malta for 70 miles.
About the campground: History and cottonwood trees line the riverbank, providing a taste of what Lewis and Clark would have sampled. A host may be present during the summer months, depending upon funding and availability. Group sites make up fifteen of the thirty-four listed parking units. The campground is open all year long.

Miles City Area

Pine-forested hills and mystical badlands await the adventurous. Past fires have badly scarred a great deal of the area, but several gems still nestle in the shadows. People seem to have forgotten this area exists. The neglected camping units and broken water systems testify to much more elaborate campgrounds, once upon a time. It is both saddening and rewarding to rediscover, in a sense, some long lost friends.

	Group Sites	Tents	RV sites	Total sites	Hookups	Toilets	Showers	Drinking water	Dump station	Phone	Handicap Access	Recreation	Fee	Season	Stay limit (days)
1 Makoshika State Park			24	24		VF		*			*	H	$$	All Year	14
2 Intake			40	40		V		*				FBR	$$	All Year	7
3 Medicine Rocks State Park			12	12		V		*				H	N	All Year	14
4 Ekalaka Park			7	7		V						HW	N	5/1-11/15	14
5 Lantis Spring			5	5		V				*		HW	N	5/1-11/15	14
6 Wickham Gulch			2	2		V			*			HW	N	5/1-11/15	14
7 Holiday Springs			3	3		P			*			HW	N	5/1-11/15	10
8 Red Shale			14	14		V						W	N	5/1-11/15	10
9 Cow Creek			4	4		P						HF	N	5/1-11/15	10
10 East Rosebud			18	18		V		*				FR	$$	5/15-11/1	7

1 Makoshika State Park

Location: 75 miles northeast of Miles City.
Facilities: Vault and flush toilets, fire rings, tables, drinking water.
Sites: 24 for tents or RVs/Trailer combinations up to 60 feet long.
Fee: $$ per night, 14-day limit.
Managing agency: Makoshika State Park, (406) 377-6256.
Activities: Hiking (interpretive trails).
Finding the campground: Take I-94 northeast out of Miles City for 73 miles to Glendive/exit 210. Continue on I-94 Business Route into Glendive and follow the directional signs to Snyder Avenue. Take Snyder Avenue south out of Glendive for 2 miles.
About the campground: The paved access road divides this campground that sits on a level bench between badland ridges. The parking aprons accommodate units from 35 to 60 feet long, with one listed at 70 feet long. All but six of the units require backing in. The colorful gumbo supports some grass, a few pine trees, and juniper. Dinosaur fossils are the main attraction, though not the only one. Keep in mind that removing fossils is illegal. If you discover teeth, bones, or other fossils, do not disturb them; instead report their location to officials. More than ten species of dinosaurs, including *Tyrannosaurus rex*, have left evidence, including their fossilized skeletons. The campground is open all year long.

2 Intake

Location: 89 miles northeast of Miles City on the Yellowstone River.
Facilities: Vault toilets, fire rings, tables, drinking water, boat ramp.
Sites: 40 for tents or RVs/Trailer combinations up to 60 feet long.

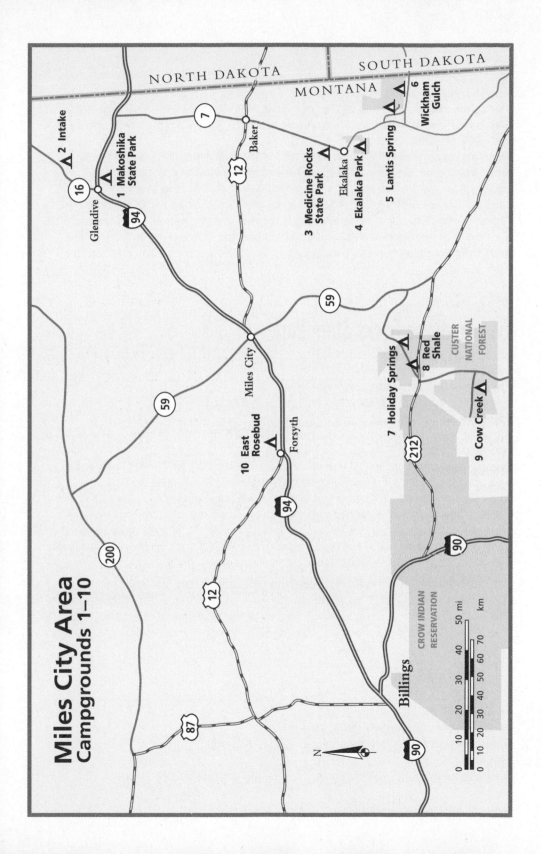

Fee: $ per night, 7-day limit.
Managing agency: Montana Fish, Wildlife & Parks, (406) 234-0900.
Activities: Fishing, boating, rockhounding.
Finding the campground: Take I-94 northeast out of Miles City for 73 miles to Glendive/exit 213. Turn left onto Montana State Highway 16 and travel 16 miles. Turn right at the access sign and follow directions.
About the campground: Cottonwoods and a rocky beach greet visitors here, and in the early spring and summer, mosquitoes make up an almost overwhelming welcoming committee. Paddlefish are the main attraction from around mid-May to the end of June, which also coincides with the annoying bugs. The famous Montana moss agates and a variety of petrified, or "agatized," wood beckons to rockhounds later in the year, when the water level is down and the majority of the bugs have died. If collecting agates is your choice of activity, be prepared to do some wading, as the better hunting tends to be on the freshly exposed gravel bars. The campground is open all year long.

3 Medicine Rocks State Park

Location: 102 miles southeast of Miles City.
Facilities: Vault toilets, fire rings, tables, drinking water.
Sites: 12 for tents or RVs/Trailer combinations up to 40 feet long.
Fee: None, 14-day limit.
Managing agency: Medicine Rocks State Park, (406) 377-6256.
Activities: Hiking.
Finding the campground: Take US Highway 12 east out of Miles City for 77 miles to Baker. Turn right onto Montana State Highway 7 and travel 25 miles.
About the campground: Leveling can be a chore, but with some creativity and planning RVs and trailers do find space here. Ponderosa and lodgepole pine share this unique geologic setting. Wind and time have sculptured an island of sandstone monuments in a sea of prairie grassland. Some of the formations include huge holes, tunneled completely through a distance greater than the total height of the rock. A hand pump at the entrance produces drinking water, no small distance from the camping and picnic areas. Do not plan to walk down to fetch a pail of it. There is no shortage of dust, especially on a holiday or during some other special event. The campground is open all year long.

4 Ekalaka Park

Location: 121 miles southeast of Miles City.
Facilities: Vault toilet, fire rings, tables, drinking water.
Sites: 7 for tents or RVs/Trailer combinations up to 30 feet long.
Fee: None, 14-day limit.
Managing agency: Custer National Forest, Sioux Ranger District, (605) 797-4432.

Activities: Hiking, wildlife viewing.

Finding the campground: Take US Highway 12 east out of Miles City for 77 miles to Baker. Turn right onto Montana State Highway 7 and travel 35 miles to Ekalaka. Turn left onto paved County Road 323 and travel 3 miles. Turn right onto Stagville Road (FR 3813) and travel 5 miles to the four-way intersection. Continue straight through this intersection 1 mile to the campground.

About the campground: Ponderosa pine, elm, and aspen trees cover the area, and chokecherry bushes fill the spaces in between. The original ten units have evolved into seven with definite improvement. A spring feeds a small trickle of water that slides through the camp, but do not plan to find any fish. For those who like solitude and primitive conditions, this could be a real gem. The campground is open from May 1 through November 15.

5 Lantis Spring

Location: 142 miles southeast of Miles City.

Facilities: Vault toilet, fire rings, tables.

Sites: 5 for tents or RVs/Trailer combinations up to 30 feet long.

Fee: None, 14-day limit.

Managing agency: Custer National Forest, Sioux Ranger District, (605) 797-4432.

Activities: Hiking, wildlife viewing.

Finding the campground: Take US Highway 12 east out of Miles City for 77 miles to Baker. Turn right onto Montana State Highway 7 and travel 35 miles to Ekalaka. Turn left onto paved County Road 323 and travel about 16 miles. Turn left onto the unmarked gravel road and travel about 3 miles to Sykes Corner. Turn left onto gravel Forest Road 818 and travel 9 miles. Turn left onto gravel Forest Road 117 and travel 1 mile. Turn left at the campground sign and travel 0.5 mile.

About the campground: Damage from past fires is less noticeable, but the forest is still significantly short of its previous number of trees. In 1902 Moses Lantis homesteaded at this location, leaving his name and some lilac bushes that came all the way from Kansas City. There are no remains of the old homestead. A strong spring flows out of the hillside a short distance below the lilacs. The campground is open from May 1 through November 15.

6 Wickham Gulch

Location: 156 miles southeast of Miles City.

Facilities: Vault toilet, fire rings, tables, drinking water.

Sites: 2 for tents or RVs/Trailers up to 16 feet long.

Fee: None, 14-day limit.

Managing agency: Custer National Forest, Sioux Ranger District, (605) 797-4432.

Activities: Hiking, wildlife viewing.

Finding the campground: Take US Highway 12 east out of Miles City for 77 miles to Baker. Turn right onto Montana State Highway 7 and travel 35 miles to Ekalaka. Turn left onto paved County Road 323 and travel about 21 miles. Turn left onto gravel Tie Creek Road and travel about 20

A magnificent view of Castle Rock can be seen near Wickham Gulch.

miles to the South Dakota border. Turn left onto the gravel road at the gravel pit and travel 2 miles. Turn right onto the single-lane dirt road at the campground sign just past the cattle guard and travel 1 mile.

About the campground: The largest parking spur is 16 feet long so a trailer will have to be unhooked. Crab apple, elm, ponderosa pine, and a multitude of bushes settle quite pleasantly in between sandstone cliffs in this remote and nearly forgotten hideaway. Spring water trickles out of a pipe a short hike up the draw, with drinking water reportedly available now. Abundant firewood from a past forest fire reminded us of the continual need to be careful with fire, even after the fact. The campground is open year-round, depending on weather. *Note:* If wet weather sets in, the access is *not* friendly.

7 Holiday Springs

Location: 114 miles southwest of Miles City.

Facilities: Pit toilet, fire rings, tables.

Sites: 3 for tents or RVs/Trailer combinations up to 30 feet long.

Fee: None, 10-day limit.

Managing agency: Custer National Forest, Ashland Ranger District, (406) 784-2344.

Activities: Hiking, wildlife viewing.

Finding the campground: Take Montana State Highway 59 south out of Miles City for 74 miles. Turn right onto US Highway 212 and travel 28 miles. Turn right at the very weathered East Fork Otter Creek Road sign and travel 12 miles.

About the campground: Old ponderosa pines randomly cling to the multiple sides of steep peninsulas along this ridge crest. The camping units typically claim whatever portion of the top can be reached by vehicle, and in some cases, it will have to be a very special vehicle. This remote little hideaway could be just the ticket for someone not wanting to be found for a very long time. Locals do use it occasionally for picnics; otherwise it tends to appear totally forgotten. It is open year round depending on weather.

8 Red Shale

Location: 112 miles southwest of Miles City.
Facilities: Vault toilets, fire rings, tables.
Sites: 14 for tents or RVs/Trailer combinations up to 30 feet long.
Fee: None, 10-day limit.
Managing agency: Custer National Forest, Ashland Ranger District, (406) 784-2344.
Activities: Wildlife viewing.
Finding the campground: Take Montana State Highway 59 south out of Miles City for 74 miles. Turn left onto US Highway 212 and travel 38 miles.
About the campground: Tall ponderosa pine trees spread out in this otherwise grassy, rolling countryside. This is an excellent spot for travelers on US Highway 212 who are looking for a campground late in the day. Passing trucks tend to get noisy with the highway so near, but the alternatives could be worse. The loop to the right at the entrance moves a little farther away from the highway. During our visit, the intermittent blasts of diesel engines were pleasantly offset by the chorus of the local coyotes. Mingled with a bright starry night, the chilling howl of the pack can make for an unforgettable experience. The campground is open from mid-April through November 30.

9 Cow Creek

Location: 139 miles southwest of Miles City on Cow Creek.
Facilities: Pit toilet, fire rings, tables.
Sites: 4 for tents or RVs/Trailer combinations up to 30 feet long.
Fee: None, 10-day limit.
Managing agency: Custer National Forest, Ashland Ranger District, (406) 784-2344.
Activities: Hiking, fishing.
Finding the campground: Take Montana State Highway 59 south out of Miles City for 74 miles. Turn left onto US Highway 212 and travel 40 miles. Turn left onto paved County Road 484 (Otter Creek Road) and travel 20 miles. Turn right onto gravel Forest Road 4095 (Cow Creek Road) and travel 5 miles.
About the campground: Pine trees emerge out of the grassy rolling terrain in various sized clusters. The road leading to the campground can be impassible if rain has had a chance to soak in so be prepared to wait for things to dry a little. The campground is open year-round dependent on weather.

10 East Rosebud

Location: At Forsyth on the Yellowstone River, 46 miles west of Miles City.

Facilities: Vault toilet, fire rings, tables, drinking water, picnic area.

Sites: 18 for tents or RVs/Trailer combinations up to 50 feet long.

Fee: $$ per night, 7-day limit.

Managing agency: Montana Fish, Wildlife & Parks, Miles City Office, (406) 234-0900.

Activities: Fishing, rockhounding.

Finding the campground: Take I-94 west out of Miles City for 46 miles to Forsyth/exit 95. Turn right and travel to Fifteenth Street in Forsyth. Turn right and travel 0.5 mile.

About the campground: Tall cottonwood trees shelter willow brush and campers alike, with lots of room between units. Spigots deliver plenty of water for drinking, while the nearby Yellowstone River beckons anglers and those who may simply want to cool off on a hot day. Some sites have electricity available for an extra fee. Firewood availability seems to be a function of river fluctuation, so bring your own. Montana moss agates and petrified wood lie in the gravel bars exposed by the river. Use a bucket to wash off suspected specimens and transport your treasure back to camp. The dirt access roads and shoreline picnic area create plenty of dust at various times of day. As of our visit, a few "younger" drivers displayed fast driving skills complete with loud engines, music, and spinning tires. A sign at the gate announced closure from 7 p.m. to 9 a.m. The campground is open from May 15 through November 1.

Yellowstone National Park

Camping in Yellowstone National Park can become a test of nerves for the unprepared. Each year the number of visitors grows, putting an even greater strain on the available camping. The increasing size of RVs also creates a very frustrating problem for campers and rangers alike. The campgrounds were originally constructed with pickup campers and tents in mind. No one at that time ever dreamed that the huge trailers and buses of today would seek a parking area for camping. Larger units and more visitors also result in more frequent road repair, among other necessary services. With a need to provide greater protection of the environment and wildlife, no small thought is being given to vehicle restriction.

Fishing Bridge RV Park is not a campground if your definition of campground means fire rings and picnic tables. This RV park was developed specifically for the larger RVs, with the hope that some of the tremendous pressure on the other campgrounds would be relieved.

Keep in mind that the days of touring the park during the day and then finding a camping spot just before dark are long gone. The more popular areas find visitors waiting for campers to leave in the morning. Reservations can be made in five out of the twelve campgrounds, but some already have been reserved as early as eighteen months in advance. If you have your heart set on camping in the park, make your plans well ahead of the time you'd like to come. If you are the sort that prefers to be in quiet, isolated places, it would be best to look to the often overlooked campgrounds in the adjacent national forest. The entrance permit to both Yellowstone and Teton National Park allows holders to exit and reenter for seven days. This opens opportunities to explore adjacent forests and enjoy some truly serene solitude at day's end.

	Group Sites	Tents	RV sites	Total sites	Hookups	Toilets	Showers	Drinking water	Dump station	Phone	Handicap Access	Recreation	Fee	Season	Stay limit (days)
1 Madison			278	278	C			*	*	*	*	HW	$$$	Varies annually	14
2 Grant Village			430	430	C			*	*		*	HFW	$$$	Varies annually	14
3 Lewis Lake			85	85	V			*				HFW	$$	Varies annually	14
4 Bridge Bay			432	432	C			*	*		*	HFW	$$$	Varies annually	14
5 Fishing Bridge RV Park			346	346	*	F	*	*	*	*	*	HFW	$$$$$	Varies annually	14
6 Canyon Village	20		253	273	C	*	*	*		*		HFW	$$$	Varies annually	14
7 Mammoth				85	85	C		*				W	$$	All year	14
8 Indian Creek			70	70	V			*				HFW	$$	Varies annually	14
9 Norris			112	112	C			*		*		HFW	$$	Varies annually	14
10 Tower Fall			31	31	V			*				HW	$$	Varies annually	14
11 Slough Creek	2		14	16	V			*				HFW	$$	Varies annually	14
12 Pebble Creek	8		19	27	V			*				HFW	$$	Varies annually	14

1 Madison

Location: 14 miles east of West Yellowstone.
Facilities: Comfort stations, fire rings, tables, drinking water, RV dump, vending machines, pay phone.
Sites: 278 for tents or RVs/Trailer combinations up to 40 feet long.
Fee: $$$ per night, 14-day limit.
Reservations: (307) 344–7311. Call for availability.
Activities: Hiking, wildlife viewing.
Finding the campground: Take West Entrance Road east of West Yellowstone for 14 miles. Turn right just before Madison Junction to access the campground.
About the campground: Pine trees shade the asphalt access and parking units, which have little room between. It is best to call for availability well in advance. The Madison River rushes by just south of the campground, inviting anglers and wildlife watchers. This campground fills during the peak season as early as 7 a.m. The opening and closing dates can vary from year to year; call to verify actual times.

2 Grant Village

Location: 50 miles southeast of West Yellowstone.
Facilities: Comfort stations, fire rings, tables, drinking water, RV dump.
Sites: 430 for tents or RVs/Trailer combinations up to 40 feet long.

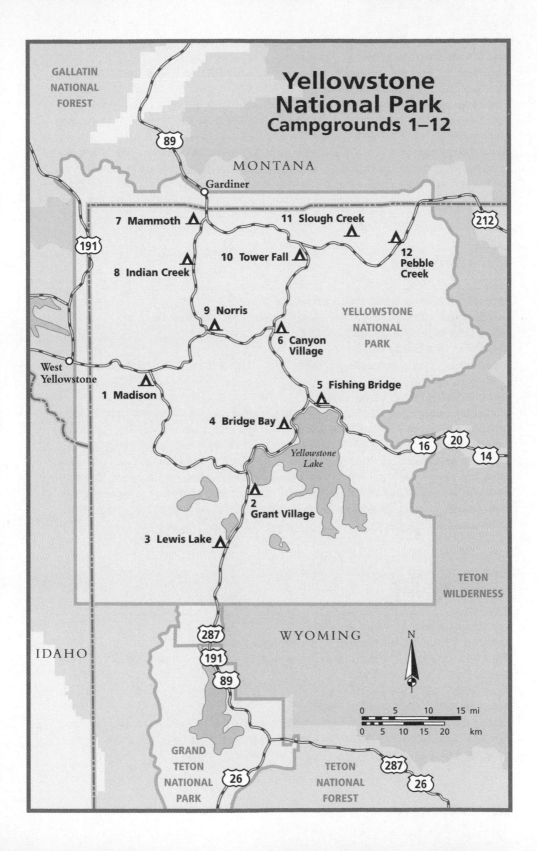

Fee: $$$ per night, 14-day limit.

Reservations: (307) 344–7311. Sites accommodating longer RV/s are limited. Call for availability.

Activities: Hiking, fishing, wildlife viewing.

Finding the campground: Take West Entrance Road east of West Yellowstone for 14 miles. Turn right onto Grand Loop Road and travel 34 miles. Turn right onto South Entrance Road and travel about 2 miles.

About the campground: These compact sites are neatly settled between pine trees. As with other campgrounds in the park, tents and pickup campers work best. Larger units do fit, but with fore-thought and extra effort. Most of the parking units are short pullouts on both sides of the access roads. The opening and closing dates can vary from year to year; call to verify actual times.

3 Lewis Lake

Location: 77 miles southeast of West Yellowstone.

Facilities: Vault toilets, fire rings, tables, drinking water, picnic area, boat ramp.

Sites: 85 for tents or RVs up to 25 feet long.

Fee: $$ per night, 14-day limit.

Reservations: First-come, first-served. For information contact Yellowstone National Park (307) 344-7381.

Activities: Hiking, fishing, wildlife viewing.

Finding the campground: Take West Entrance Road east of West Yellowstone for 14 miles. Turn right onto Grand Loop Road and travel 34 miles. Turn right onto South Entrance Road and travel 29 miles.

About the campground: Pine and spruce trees shelter the sites in three independent and unique loops. This campground is primarily for tents; though small RV's can fit they are more of an exception. The lake nestles into place a pretty fair distance away, but there is an active picnic area complete with boat ramp, which slides off to the right just after leaving the highway. The opening and closing dates can vary from year to year; call to verify actual times.

4 Bridge Bay

Location: 67 miles east of West Yellowstone.

Facilities: Comfort stations, fire rings, tables, drinking water, RV dump.

Sites: 432 for tents or RVs/Trailer combinations up to 40 feet long. Call for availability.

Fee: $$$ per night, 14-day limit.

Reservations: (307) 344–7311.

Activities: Hiking, fishing, wildlife viewing.

Finding the campground: Take West Entrance Road east of West Yellowstone for 14 miles. Turn right onto Grand Loop Road and travel 34 miles. Turn left, continuing on Grand Loop Road, and travel 19 miles.

About the campground: The more desirable units nestle into a pine forest of the upper loop while the lower loops have more open sky. Some of these sites are reserved several months in advance. Few units accommodate the longer RVs. Yellowstone Lake can be viewed from a distance at select sites; however, these fill quickly. The opening and closing dates can vary from year to year; call to verify actual times.

5 Fishing Bridge RV Park

Note: Fishing Bridge RV Park will be closed for the 2019 season to implement improvements.
Location: 69 miles east of West Yellowstone.
Facilities: Flush toilets, full hookups, shower, drinking water, dump station, phone.
Sites: 346 double sites for hard-sided RVs/Trailer combinations up to 40 feet long.
Fee: $$$$$ per night, 14-day limit.
Reservations: (307) 344–7311.
Activities: Hiking, fishing, wildlife viewing.
Finding the campground: Take West Entrance Road east of West Yellowstone for 14 miles. Turn right onto Grand Loop Road and travel 34 miles. Turn left, continuing on Grand Loop Road, and travel 21 miles. Turn right onto US Highway 16 and cross the bridge. The RV Park is on the left a short distance from the bridge.
About the campground: The double parking unit allows campers to unhook and place the towed unit beside the RV/Trailer. Keep in mind that slide-outs could minimize parking capacity. No open campfires are allowed here, though propane barbecue grills are. Campers who have discovered its conveniences make reservations up to eighteen months in advance, so don't plan on pulling in here at the last minute. Pay attention to the details when making a reservation. For example, if your RV or trailer configuration does not match the original reservation, the park will not be able to accommodate you. The opening and closing dates can vary from year to year; call to verify actual times.

6 Canyon Village

Location: 85 miles northeast of West Yellowstone.
Facilities: Comfort stations, fire rings, tables, drinking water, RV dump.
Sites: 20 for tents and 252 for tents or limited RVs/Trailer combinations up to 40 feet long. Call for availability.
Fee: $$$ per night, 14-day limit.
Reservations: (307) 344–7311.
Activities: Hiking, fishing, wildlife viewing.
Finding the campground: Take West Entrance Road east of West Yellowstone for 14 miles. Turn right onto Grand Loop Road and travel 34 miles. Turn left, continuing on Grand Loop Road, and travel 37 miles.
About the campground: Eleven separate loops wind through the lodgepole pine forest here. Most of the units are back-in spots of various lengths, with a limited number that accommodate units

40 feet long. Canyon Village offers gift shops, a cafeteria, and other amenities nearby. A laundry and showers are available in the campground. Reservations are a must if you definitely want to stay here. The opening and closing dates can vary from year to year; call to verify actual times.

7 Mammoth

Location: 61 miles south of Livingston.
Facilities: Comfort station, fire rings, tables, drinking water.
Sites: 85 for tents or RVs/Trailer combinations up to 50 feet long.
Fee: $$ per night, 14-day limit.
Reservations: First-come, first-served. For information contact Yellowstone National Park, (307) 344-7381.
Activities: Wildlife viewing.
Finding the campground: The North Entrance is 56 miles south of Livingston at Gardiner via US Highway 89. Take North Entrance Road for 5 miles. The campground is on the right side of the road.
About the campground: Junipers and Douglas firs don't offer much shade, but you can see the stars at night, along with some long-distance mountain landscape. The level pull-throughs make parking easy for larger RVs, though tent campers may not appreciate the generator noise. Sagebrush and rocky ground make up the distance between trees and parking units, some shorter than others. This campground can have all of the units claimed before eight 8 a.m. When we visited, several units appeared to be empty, but the posted receipts educated us to the fact that the vacant spots were already claimed by early campers currently touring the park. A common complaint among campers is the road noise; however, the benefits of touring the park from here seem to outweigh the dislikes. The campground is open all year long.

8 Indian Creek

Location: 74 miles south of Livingston.
Facilities: Vault toilets, fire rings, tables, drinking water.
Sites: 70 for tents or RVs/Trailer combinations up to 35 feet long.
Fee: $$ per night, 14-day limit.
Reservations: First-come, first-served. For information contact Yellowstone National Park, (307) 344-7381.
Activities: Hiking, fishing, wildlife viewing.
Finding the campground: The North Entrance is 56 miles south of Livingston at Gardiner via US Highway 89. Take North Entrance Road for 5 miles to Mammoth. Follow directions through Mammoth for Norris and travel about 12 miles. Turn right at the campground sign and travel 0.5 mile.
About the campground: Ten sites will accommodate units 35 feet long. Thirty-five sites will accommodate units 30 feet long. The remaining sites are all shorter and can be very problem-

atic, especially if unhooking is involved. The park service does not allow parking off the pavement. Tents, pickup campers, pop-up vans, and smaller RVs are best suited for this area. This campground is farther away from the main road but does have the normal camping noise when everyone wakes up. Pine trees help isolate camping spots. Indian Creek is a short hike away and offers fishing and wildlife viewing. This campground tends to be the last in the area to fill up, which might be due to the exclusion of tents here. The opening and closing dates can vary from year to year; call to verify actual times.

9 Norris

Location: 29 miles northeast of West Yellowstone.
Facilities: Comfort stations, fire rings, tables, drinking water, pay phone.
Sites: 12 for tents and 100 for RVs/Trailer combinations up to 50 feet long.
Fee: $$ per night, 14-day limit.
Reservations: First-come, first-served. For information contact Yellowstone National Park, (307) 344-7381.
Activities: Hiking, fishing, wildlife viewing.
Finding the campground: Take West Entrance Road east of West Yellowstone for 14 miles. Turn left at Madison Junction and travel 14 miles. Turn left toward Mammoth and travel 1 mile. Turn right at the Ranger Museum sign to access the campground.
About the campground: This centrally located campground is very popular, which results in newcomers arriving as early as 6:30 a.m. and getting in "line" to wait for an opening created by the previous night's occupants. Three loops snake around pine-forested knolls above the river. One loop provides walk-in sites for tents only. Short and not-too-level parking spots dominate the campground, but with a little effort, there is room to park alongside the unhooked trailers. There are two sites that accommodate units up to 50 feet long and five sites for units up to 30 feet long. Those with tents can find room without getting too close. Otherwise, things get real crowded. Meadows and clear-water streams border the lodgepole pine stand that dominates the camping area, adding to the appeal and increased demand, especially those spots with better positioning with respect to the view. The opening and closing dates can vary from year to year; call to verify actual times.

10 Tower Fall

Location: 80 miles south of Livingston.
Facilities: Vault toilet, fire rings, tables, drinking water.
Sites: 31 for tents or RVs/Trailer combinations up to 30 feet long.
Fee: $$ per night, 14-day limit.
Reservations: First-come, first-served. For information contact Yellowstone National Park, (307) 344-7381.
Activities: Hiking, wildlife viewing.

Finding the campground: The North Entrance is 56 miles south of Livingston at Gardiner via US Highway 89. Take North Entrance Road for 5 miles to Mammoth. Follow directions through Mammoth for Tower Junction and travel about 19 miles.

About the campground: This small campground fills fast so be there before 9 a.m. For the most part the available sites will be created by those departing the campground, so choices will be limited. Nearby Tower Creek drops 132 feet on its way to the Yellowstone River below. Grizzly bears and other wildlife are not too far away. The campground is open from Memorial Day through September.

11 Slough Creek

Location: 96 miles southwest of Red Lodge.
Facilities: Vault toilets, fire rings, tables, drinking water.
Sites: 2 for tents and 14 for tents or RVs/Trailer combinations up to 30 feet long.
Fee: $$ per night, 14-day limit.
Reservations: First-come, first-served. For information contact Yellowstone National Park, (307) 344-7381.
Activities: Hiking, fishing, wildlife viewing.
Finding the campground: The Northeast Entrance is 69 miles southwest of Red Lodge. Take Northeast Entrance Road for 24 miles west of the fee booth. Turn right at the sign and travel 3 miles.

About the campground: Campers easily hear Slough Creek pound corners off the boulders in its way. Most of the parking areas are only a few feet from the creek bank. Old spruce trees shade tables and fire rings alike, and there is an open meadow above. As with Pebble Creek Campground (see below), tents, tent trailers, and pickup campers fit best here. Longer RVs could fit in a few spaces, but it would require some tricky maneuvering. A host occupies one of the available spots. The rough gravel road leading back here will not keep the campground from filling up; it is best to arrive around 8 a.m. The opening and closing dates can vary from year to year; call to verify actual times.

12 Pebble Creek

Location: 77 miles southwest of Red Lodge.
Facilities: Vault toilets, fire rings, tables, drinking water.
Sites: 8 for tents or 19 for tents or RVs/Trailer combinations up to 45 feet long.
Fee: $$ per night, 14-day limit.
Reservations: First-come, first-served. For information contact Yellowstone National Park, (307) 344-7381.
Activities: Hiking, fishing, wildlife viewing.

Finding the campground: The Northeast Entrance is 69 miles southwest of Red Lodge. Take Northeast Entrance Road for 8 miles west of the fee booth. The campground is on the right side of the road.

About the campground: Pebble Creek rumbles by this campground, which is just far enough off the road to avoid hearing the majority of traffic. Smaller pine trees are scattered throughout the area, giving some sites more shade than others. Tents, tent trailers, and pickup campers fit best here. A limited number of sites will accommodate longer RVs, with some pull-throughs. Distance between units does not offer much in terms of privacy. A host occupies one of the units. The best chance of securing a site is to arrive early in the morning (6:30 a.m.) and wait for the previous night's campers to pull out. Keep in mind that the check-out time is 11 a.m., and no one is obligated to leave earlier just because others are waiting. The opening and closing dates can vary from year to year; call to verify actual times.

Appendix

Area Supervisor/District Offices

Montana Fish, Wildlife & Parks
1420 East Sixth Avenue
Helena, MT 59620
(406) 444-2535

Bureau of Land Management
Butte District Office
P.O. Box 3388
106 North Parkmont
Butte, MT 59702-3388
(406) 533-7600

Beaverhead-Deerlodge National Forest
Supervisor's Office
420 Barrett St.
Dillon, MT 59725-3572
(406) 683-3900

Butte Ranger District
1820 Meadowlark
Butte, MT 59701
(406) 494-2147

Madison Ranger District
Madison Ranger Station
5 Forest Service Road
Ennis, MT 59729
(406) 682-4253

Sheridan Work Center
Madison Ranger District
402 South Main Street
Sheridan, MT 59749
(406) 842-5432

Pintler Ranger District
88 Business Loop
Philipsburg, MT 59858
(406) 859-3211

Wisdom Ranger District
P.O. Box 238
Wisdom, MT 59761
(406) 689-3243

Wise River Ranger District
P.O. Box 100
Wise River, MT 59762
(406) 832-3178

Custer National Forest
Supervisor's Office
P.O. Box 130
10 E Babcock Ave
Bozeman, MT 59771
(406) 587-6701

Ashland Ranger District
P.O. Box 168
2378 Hwy 212
Ashland, MT 59003
(406) 784-2344

Beartooth Ranger District
6811 Hwy 212
Red Lodge, MT 59608
(406) 446-2103

Sioux Ranger District
P.O. Box 37
101 SE First Street
Camp Crook, SD 57724
(605) 797-4432

Flathead National Forest
Tally Lake Ranger District/Supervisor's Office
650 Wolf Pack Way
Kalispell, MT 59901
(406) 758-5200

Hungry Horse/Glacier View Ranger Districts
10 Hungry Horse Drive
Hungry Horse, MT 59919
(406) 387-3800

Spotted Bear Ranger District
10 Hungry Horse Drive
Hungry Horse, MT 59919
Summer: (406) 758-5376
Winter: (406) 387-3800

Swan Lake Ranger District
200 Ranger Station Road
Bigfork, MT 59911
(406) 837-7500

Gallatin National Forest
Supervisor's Office
P.O. Box 130
10 E Babcock Ave
Bozeman, MT 59771
(406) 587-6701

Billings Office
5001 Southgate Drive, Suite 2
Billings, MT 59101
(406) 587-6701

Bozeman Ranger District
3710 Fallon Street, Suite C
Bozeman, MT 59718
(406) 522-2520

Gardiner Ranger District
P.O. Box 5
805 Scott Street
Gardiner, MT 59030
(406) 848-7375

Hebgen Lake Ranger District
P.O. Box 520
West Yellowstone, MT 59758
(406) 823-6961

Yellowstone Ranger District
5242 Highway 89 South
Livingston, MT 59047
(406) 222-1892

Helena National Forest
Helena Supervisor's Office
2880 Skyway Drive
Helena, MT 59601
(406) 449-5201

Helena Ranger District
2001 Poplar Street
Helena, MT 59601
(406) 449-5490

Lincoln Ranger District
P.O. Box 219
Highway 200
Lincoln, MT 59639
(406) 362-4253

Townsend Ranger District
415 South Front, Box 29
Townsend, MT 59644
(406) 266-3425

Kootenai National Forest
Supervisor's Office
31374 US Highway 2
Libby, MT 59923-3022
(406) 293-6211

Cabinet Ranger District, Trout Creek Ranger Station
2693 Highway 200
Trout Creek, MT 59874-9503
(406) 827-3533

Libby Ranger District, Canoe Gulch Ranger Station
12557 Highway 37
Libby, MT 59923-8212
(406) 293-7773

Rexford Ranger District, Eureka Ranger Station
949 US Highway 93 North
Eureka, MT 59917-9550
(406) 296-2536

Three Rivers Ranger District, Troy Ranger Station
12858 US Highway 2
Troy, MT 59935-8750
(406) 295-4693

Lewis and Clark National Forest
Great Falls Supervisor's Office
1220 38th Street North
Great Falls, MT 59405
(406) 791-7700

Augusta Information Station
405 Manix Street
Augusta, MT 59410
(406) 562-3247

Belt Creek Information Station
4234 US Highway 89
Neihart, MT 59465
(406) 236-5100

Judith Ranger District
109 Central Avenue
Stanford, MT 59749
(406) 566-2292

White Sulphur Springs Ranger District
204 West Folsom
White Sulphur Springs, MT 59645
(406) 547-3361

Musselshell Ranger District
809 Second NW
Harlowtown, MT 59036
(406) 632-4391

Rocky Mountain Ranger District
1102 Main Avenue NW
Choteau, MT 59422
(406) 466-5341

Lolo National Forest
Supervisor's Office
24 Fort Missoula Road
Missoula, MT 59804
(406) 329-3750

Missoula Ranger District
24 Fort Missoula Road
Missoula, MT 59804
(406) 329-3814

Ninemile Ranger District
20325 Remount Road
Huson, MT 59846
(406) 626-5201

Plains/Thompson Falls Ranger District
P.O. Box 429
408 Clayton
Plains, MT 59859
(406) 826-3821

Seeley Lake Ranger District
3583 Highway 83
Seeley Lake, MT 59868
(406) 677-2233

Superior Ranger District
P.O. Box 460
209 West Riverside
Superior, MT 59872
(406) 822-4233

Shoshone National Forest
Supervisor's Office
808 Meadow Lane Avenue
Cody, WY 82414
(307) 527-6241

Clarks Fork Ranger District
203A Yellowstone Avenue
Cody, WY 82414
(307) 527-6921

About the Author

Ken and his wife, Sandy, have answered the call to explore new territory and currently live in Craig, Colorado. They still enjoy camping, watching wildlife, rockhounding, and similar outdoor activities. The adventures continue.